Towards a Jungian Theory of the Ego

Despite their prevalence and weight in many of his collected works and letters, Jung did not articulate a general theory of the ego and consciousness. *Towards a Jungian Theory of the Ego* examines the development of Jung's concept of the ego as he expanded and revised this concept, from his earliest formulations about consciousness while a student to his mature thoughts at the end of his life.

Drawing on Ego Psychology as a theoretical framework, Evers-Fahey proposes that Jung uses the concept of ego in four distinct ways and that he developed and used his ego concept based on two discrete paradigms. These distinctions explain the confusion and ambiguity found when examining the development of Jung's analytical psychology over his lifetime. This book provides an examination of ego development and ego defenses based on a unique Jungian standpoint, as well as discussion of the relationship between the ego and the Self and the ego and 'the *individuum*'. Furthermore, the inclusion of a historical framework helps to place the development of these concepts in context.

This book proposes a theory of Ego Psychology based on Jungian theory rather than traditional psychoanalytic theory, thereby filling a gap in the knowledge of Jungian theory. The book will be essential reading for academics and postgraduate students engaged in the study of Jungian psychology and psychoanalytic theory and will also be valued by those interested in Jung and Ego Psychology more generally.

Dr. Karen Evers-Fahey is a Zurich-trained Jungian analyst and is a training analyst with the international program of the CG Jung Institute Zurich. She has been a training and supervisory analyst in Zurich at the International School of Analytical Psychology as well as the Jung Institute Zurich. She is also an assistant teaching professor at the University of Victoria School of Nursing, Victoria, BC, Canada.

Research in Analytical Psychology and Jungian Studies Series

Series Advisor: Andrew Samuels, Professor of Analytical Psychology, Essex University, UK

The *Research in Analytical Psychology and Jungian Studies* series features research-focused volumes involving qualitative and quantitative research, historical/archival research, theoretical developments, heuristic research, grounded theory, narrative approaches, collaborative research, practitioner-led research, and self-study. The series also includes focused works by clinical practitioners and provides new research informed explorations of the work of C.G. Jung that will appeal to researchers, academics, and scholars alike.

Books in this series:

Time and Timelessness
Temporality in the theory of Carl Jung
Angeliki Yiassemides

Apophatic Elements in the Theory and Practice of Psychoanalysis
Pseudo-Dionysius and C.G. Jung
David Henderson

C.G. Jung and Hans Urs von Balthasar
God and evil – A critical comparison
Les Oglesby

Bridges to Consciousness
Complexes and complexity
Nancy M. Krieger

The Alchemical Mercurius
Esoteric symbol of Jung's life and works
Mathew Mather

Archetypal Psychotherapy
The clinical legacy of James Hillman
Jason A. Butler

Jung's Theory of Personality
A modern reappraisal
Clare Crellin

Psychological, Archetypal and Phenomenological Perspectives on Soccer
David Huw Burston

Music as Image
Analytical psychology and music in film
Benjamin Nagari

Laws of Inheritance
A post-Jungian study of twins and the relationship between the first and other(s)
Elizabeth Brodersen

Jung and Levinas
An ethics of mediation
Frances Gray

Symptom, Symbol, and the Other of Language
A Jungian interpretation of the linguistic turn
Bret Alderman

Post-Jungian Psychology and the Short Stories of Ray Bradbury and Kurt Vonnegut
Golden Apples of the Monkey House
Steve Gronert Ellerhoff

Eros and Economy
Jung, Deleuze, Sexual Difference
Barbara Jenkins

Towards a Jungian Theory of the Ego
Karen Evers-Fahey

Towards a Jungian Theory of the Ego

Karen Evers-Fahey

Routledge
Taylor & Francis Group
LONDON AND NEW YORK

First published 2017
by Routledge

2 Park Square, Milton Park, Abingdon, Oxfordshire OX14 4RN
711 Third Avenue, New York, NY 10017

Routledge is an imprint of the Taylor & Francis Group, an informa business

First issued in paperback 2017

British Library Cataloguing in Publication Data
A catalogue record for this book is available from the British Library

Library of Congress Cataloging-in-Publication Data
Names: Evers-Fahey, Karen, author.
Title: Towards a Jungian theory of the ego / Karen Evers-Fahey.
Description: New York, NY : Routledge, 2016.
Identifiers: LCCN 2016005692 | ISBN 9781138657489 (hardcover) | ISBN 9781315621319 (electronic)
Subjects: LCSH: Jung, C. G. (Carl Gustav), 1875–1961. | Jungian psychology.
Classification: LCC BF109.J8 E94 2016 | DDC 155.2092—dc23
LC record available at http://lccn.loc.gov/2016005692

ISBN: 978-1-138-65748-9 (hbk)
ISBN: 978-1-138-47802-2 (pbk)

Typeset in Sabon
by Apex CoVantage, LLC

To Dirk, Gioia, and Naomi
With gratitude

Contents

Figures

Acknowledgments

This book is based on research conducted at the University of Essex, Centre for Psychoanalytic Studies, and I am grateful to Andrew Samuels, Roderick Main, and Renos Popadopoulos at the Centre for their advice and guidance. I am grateful as well to my many Jungian analyst colleagues in Switzerland, Germany, and Canada and the innumerable students and training candidates over the years who have helped shape my thinking on many of the topics in this work. I would also like to thank Routledge UK and Princeton University Press for permission to quote from the Collected Works of C.G. Jung and for permission to reproduce the diagram 'The Psychic System' from Jung's 1925 seminar (Jung, 1990). Although I have changed the identifying information in the clinical examples in this book to protect the privacy of those concerned, the experiences are real, and I want to express my gratitude to all those who have allowed me to share their soul's journey.

Chapter 1

Introduction

The ego as a topic of study came to me through a dream, three dreams to be exact. Many years ago, while a diploma candidate at the CG Jung Institute in Zürich, I started my practice day by seeing a shy university student who opened his session by relating the following dream: "I was walking down a dark street at night and realized I was being followed by a brutish man. I was terrified and ran as fast as I could but he still followed me". The second client of the day, a middle-aged teacher in the middle of a divorce, began the session with her dream: "I was walking down a dark street at night and realized I was being followed by a man with a knife. Rather than run, I turn and confront him. He then silently hands his knife to me". The third client of the morning, a young shop clerk, also had the stranger dream: "I am walking down a dark street at night and realize a shapeless thing, possibly a man, possible an animal, is following me. I am terrified and begin to attack it, kicking and punching until I am sure it is dead. I am covered in blood". The tremendous coincidence – some would call it synchronicity – of these three dreams in one day was striking: all had the same opening scenario but each with very different conclusions based on the actions of the dream ego, that is, the dreamer in one's own dream. I responded to this striking experience with a new fascination for the ego concept, and I wanted to understand more about this aspect of Jung's theory. During my education in Zürich, we students had a tendency to focus on Jung's pioneering ideas about archetypes; my clients' nearly identical dream scenarios led me to reread Jung in a new light. Yet as I explored his works for an organized theory of ego, I found instead confusion and contradictions.

The ego in Jung's works

Jung clearly needs and values the ego in his theory of depth psychology. Regarding the development of consciousness, for example, in a 1943 letter to Aniela Jaffé, he states: "The Self in its divinity (i.e., the archetype) is unconscious of itself. It can become conscious only within our consciousness. And it can do that only if the ego stands firm" (Jung, 1976, vol. 1, p. 336).

In his autobiography Jung also made the observation that mankind's consciousness is "indispensable for the completion of creation" (Jung, 1983a, p. 284). These statements are made with Jung's often academic certainty, and yet they remain problematic once one begins to unpack them. They both clearly imply that the ego and the Self stand in opposition in the respective fields of consciousness and unconsciousness and that the ego factor has the decisive role in the transformation of the archetype from unconsciousness to consciousness. So important is this factor that apparently even God's work is completed by our consciousness.

Unfortunately there is a wide gulf between the evocative Jung, the Jung of metaphor and vibrant imagery, and the precise Jung, one who structures and describes a consistent theoretical framework. In the earlier quote, for example, he refers to the Self becoming conscious in the consciousness of the individual, which leads to questions about the nature of consciousness for the individual as opposed to an 'archetypal', or collective, universal consciousness.

Left unexplored in this example is the relationship between the ego and consciousness. To which form of consciousness does he refer, personal or collective? Because Jung at other times refers to ego-consciousness as one entity, is he implying the ego and consciousness are equivalent, or are they separate? If separate, then are ego and consciousness separate entities in a unified concept of the psyche or rather functionally different concepts? Is the ego a function in the psyche, part of a structure and dynamic, according to Jung, or is it describing the experience of the subjective self in an interpersonal psychology? Where do issues such as identity, self-experience, adaptation, and ego defenses fit into Jung's model of the ego and consciousness?

This is the core of the problem. Despite its presence and weight in much of what he wanted to say about the psyche in his collected works and letters, Jung did not articulate a general theory of the ego and consciousness. Lacking in Jung's writings is a metapsychology of the ego. In other words, what is lacking is a complete abstract conceptualization of the experienced, experiencing, structuring, and transforming psychological factor in mankind that is beyond the individual and the unconscious: the ego factor.

Reasons for lack of clarity

There are a number of reasons why there is a lack of clarity about the ego concept in Jung's works. First, Jung gave diverse descriptions of the ego and consciousness in his collected works and letters. For example, Jung defined the ego in his first venture at precision, as "a complex of ideas which constitutes the center of my consciousness and appears to possess a high degree of continuity and identity" (CW 6/706). At a much later point he defines ego less operationally and more imaginally: "[the] relatively constant personification of the unconscious itself, or as the Schopenhauerian mirror in which the unconscious becomes aware of its own face" (CW 14/129). At other times his ideas about the ego are ambivalent opinions: it is "the indispensable condition of all consciousness" (CW 14/129) but also "[a] petty, oversensitive personal world" (CW 7/275).

Second, Jung uses the terms 'ego', 'ego-consciousness', and 'ego-complex' in his writings in order to reflect a selected emphasis of meaning rather to describe a structured system. For example, he described the ego at another point as

> a reflection, not of one, but of very many processes and their interplay – in fact, of all those processes and contents that make up ego-consciousness. Their diversity does indeed form a unity, because their relation to consciousness acts as a sort of gravitational force drawing the various parts together, towards what might be called a virtual center. For this reason, I do not speak simply of the ego but of an ego complex, on the proven assumption that the ego, having a fluctuating composition, is changeable and therefore, cannot be simply the ego.
>
> (CW 8/611)

In this quote Jung emphasizes the dynamic qualities of the ego (a gravitational force). However, in the quotes cited previously he emphasizes instead the static qualities (continuity and identity), suggesting that ego definitions arise in order to clarify a separate theoretical issue rather than to present a unified model of the psyche.

A third factor that accounts for the contradictions in Jung's writings about the ego is that his ideas about this concept evolved over his professional life. What he had to say regarding consciousness in the period of his collaboration with Freud, for example, differs from his later ideas. In 1912, at a time when Jung disagreed with Freud about the exclusively sexual nature of the libido but still numbered himself among Freud's followers, he implied consciousness was a state of awareness or personal knowledge, a "constellation of our thoughts from the material in our memory [through] a predominantly unconscious process" (CW 4/317). Later, after his break with Freud and after a period of intense development of his own ideas, Jung would describe consciousness as a relational process rather than a state: "By consciousness I understand the relation of psychic contents to the ego, in so far as this relation is perceived as such by the ego" (CW 9/700). In the original German text, Jung used the term '*Bezogenheit*', which is translated in the English edition of the Collected Works as 'relation', to describe the connection of ego and psychic contents. *Bezogenheit* has the connotation in German however of connection with one's complete being to the complete being of the other. It is not simply a temporal connection, but rather, *Bezogenheit* implies a mutual reception and awareness of the other and the field he or she occupies. In this formulation, Jung emphasizes the ego as an interpersonal element rather than a dynamic function in the psyche. This concept of consciousness is quite different from the earlier formulation of consciousness as perception or knowledge and goes to the heart of a relational concept in Jung's Ego Psychology.

In addition, as he developed his theory of the psyche, earlier formulations were altered through re-editions of his writings. Chief among these revisions was the major reworking of what became CW 5, *Symbols of Transformation*. Originally written in 1912, this book was completely revised, whole sections removed and rewritten, in 1952. Also, the theoretical work 'The Structure of the Unconscious', first published in 1916, was revised in 1928, and later after Jung's death in 1961 based on revisions and additions discovered among his papers. The original work 'New Paths in Psychology', first published in 1912, was revised and expanded threefold in 1917 and republished as 'The Psychology of the Unconscious Processes'. This work was again revised and expanded for its final form published in 1943. Works such as these that contain detailed descriptions of Jung's theories have the unfortunate and confusing drawback, however, of carrying over old terminology that was then used in a new way.

Not only did Jung's ideas about the ego and consciousness evolve over time, there was also an expansion of his theory of the psyche beyond the drive psychology of Freud (intrapersonal) to include interpersonal (two-person) psychology as well as collective psychology. All of these views of the psyche amount to differing visions or paradigms of the role and place of ego and consciousness in the individual and mankind.

Finally, another reason Jung did not articulate a metapsychology of the ego was that ultimately his research interests lay elsewhere. After writing Volume 6 of his Collected Works, *Psychological Types*, which included some of his most differentiated ideas about the ego, and except for his 'Modern Psychology' (known as the ETH lectures, 1933–1941) and 'Analytical Psychology' (1925) seminars, Jung left this line of inquiry and pursued his lifelong research into the archetypes and the Self. In this later work, Jung dropped a promising concept in terms of Ego Psychology, the ego vs. the *individuum*, and instead pursued research into the nature of the Self.

Resolution of this problem

Psychology as hermeneutic inquiry has always striven to take multiple levels of complexity and what is uniquely human into account, but it faces a great obstacle in the process. Analysis has been called "a border science" (Edelson, 1977). In other words, it is a study of the mind at the edges of empirical inquiry and scientific rigor but also leaning hard against philosophical theorizing and the personal equation of the theorist.

Jung the hermeneutic theorist and Jung the rigorous scientist walked this divide as a way to honor the complexity of the psyche and at the same time to structure what he perceived in essence as "inaccessible" (Jung, 1983a, p. 153). He was aware of this dilemma and moved back and forth between these perspectives in his work as it evolved over time and as it deepened in his understanding.

Therefore, to understand Jung's concept of ego, one has to see it in the context of both science and philosophy. Jung was working from both traditions, and in his concept of ego in particular, one sees him drawing on his interest in philosophy and religion as well as his desire to work within scientific convention. Jung's conception of the ego as a function and a dynamic process, for example, comes from his scientific side, while his sense of the ego as a subjective experience, an interpersonal and relational factor in the psyche, comes from his philosophical and religious background.

The energic paradigm and the symbolic paradigm

I have chosen to call these two influences in Jung's work the energic paradigm and the symbolic paradigm. Paradigms describe not just a difference of interpretation of agreed upon phenomena, but rather a complete, separate manner of seeing the world (Kuhn, 1962, p. 94). The scientific view of the world in which the laws of science prevail, as others have noted (for example, Edelson, 1977; Gould, 2001; Nagy, 1991), is fundamentally at odds with the religious/philosophical view of the world, in which phenomena exist beyond physical reality and physical laws. In his works, however, Jung tries to bridge this divide by stressing physical reality is only one reality. He said in 1935, for example,

> The psyche is an extremely complex factor, so fundamental to all premises that no judgment can be regarded as 'purely empirical' but must first indicate the premises by which it judges. Modern psychology can no longer disguise the fact that the object of its investigation is its own essence, so that in certain respects there can be no 'principles' or valid judgments at all, but only phenomenology – in other words, sheer experience.
>
> (CW 18/1738)

Jung uses the scientific view in his description of the psyche as a dynamic process. In this view energic concepts borrowed from 19th century scientific psychology are used to describe the actions of psychic energy. Others refer to this as scientific materialism (the principle reviewed extensively in Sulloway, 1979). The ego in this paradigm is a part of the psychic structure involved in this dynamic process. It is for this reason I have chosen to refer to this view of psychical mechanisms as the energic paradigm.

The energic paradigm characteristic of the field of psychology of the 19th century was based on scientific assumptions borrowed from the physical sciences of the time. The psyche itself was 'observed' and investigated 'objectively': the point of reference outside the subject. Jung turned this around and instead placed the point of reference inside the subject; the images and emotional experiences of the subject became the objects of investigation. These inner experiences were facts just as tangible as reaction times. This shift in thinking on Jung's part, away from the scientific and medical developments of the 19th century and the energic paradigm and toward a paradigm based on psychical phenomenology and inner experience, characterizes the paradigm that was to dominate his mature psychological theory.

I have chosen to call this later paradigm the symbolic paradigm, a label not used by Jung himself, for a number of reasons. First, the term 'symbol' described a specific experience in Jung's psychological theory. A symbol, according to Jung, was best defined as the combination of inner experience and mental image that "states or signifies more than itself" (CW 6/817). In Jung's approach to psychical phenomenology and inner experience, there is the underlying assumption that these psychological 'facts' are filled with ineffable meaning and not quantitatively measurable. The symbolic approach thus takes into account the qualitative measure of psychical phenomena.

Second, the term 'symbolic' has grown over the years to describe Jung's basic approach to the psyche. For example, the last volume of his Collected Works published in 1977, comprised of miscellaneous writings from all areas of his life's work, is called *The Symbolic Life*. Edward Whitmont, in summing up Jung's 'working model' of the psyche in a text of Jung's basic concepts, said, "The most basic hypothesis about the human psyche with which we deal . . . is that of a pattern of wholeness that can only be described symbolically" (Whitmont, 1991, p. 15). The symbolic paradigm is a sensibility, then, an attitude toward psychical phenomena associated with Jung.

Third, the symbolic paradigm captures the aspect of *Bezogenheit* and purpose in the interaction of ego and other parts of the psyche. While the energic paradigm focuses on mechanistic dynamics, the symbolic paradigm is more mytho-poetic and views the operations and experiences in the psyche as having a teleological intention beyond psychical balance or compromise. The integrative functions of the ego, for example, would have an underlying purpose beyond personal growth and development and lead to greater consciousness and relatedness in the world in general.

Lastly, the symbolic paradigm is an approach to psychical phenomenology and inner experience, but also it is a way of understanding and working with the psyche. As a consequence, the clinical extension of Jung's symbolic approach was the development of methods and techniques for working with patients that focus on the inner experience and spontaneous image for growth and development. These innovations of Jung in the symbolic paradigm are relevant to clinical understanding in work with the ego and consciousness.

Energic and symbolic paradigms also refer to the assumptions surrounding the processes by which psychic contents contained in the unconscious become conscious. Not surprisingly, this question of how the individual becomes conscious has occupied great minds for millennia. In historical context, the concepts of energic and symbolic transformation of unconscious contents and the assumptions about the nature of the psyche implied in them, evolved from essentially three sources for Jung: medical/scientific, religious, and philosophical.

Sources from philosophy that influenced Jung's thinking in regard to these issues are primarily Immanuel Kant, Arthur Schopenhauer, and the 19th century philosophical movement known as *Naturphilosophie*. It would be difficult, however, to explore the philosophical roots of the symbolic paradigm without noting major personal influences for Jung: William James, Théodore Flournoy, and Frederick Nietzsche (in the case of Nietzsche, not through personal contact but rather through intense engagement in his ideas and philosophy, c.f. Jung's *Nietzsche Seminars*, 1984).

Important religious sources that influenced Jung in the symbolic paradigm, in addition to the Christian background in which he was raised, include religious mystics such as Meister Eckhart and Gnostic writers. Jung's encounters, through certain close friendships in his life, with Eastern religion and philosophy would also have a profound effect on his thinking about the process of becoming conscious. Later in his life, he was to embrace alchemy as a philosophical system and base his later work extensively on its principles.

Jung's choice of profession was based on the fact that psychiatry was the "empirical field common to biological and spiritual facts" (Jung, 1983a, p. 130). Just as he sought to understand and interpret the symbolism behind psychiatric disorders, so too did Jung endeavor to understand religious phenomena scientifically. Medical/scientific sources which shaped Jung's energic and symbolic paradigms for understanding ego transformation were scientists and psychologists such as Wilhelm Wundt and, again, William James and Arthur Flournoy. Of course, the influence of Freud and his own commitment to the scientific investigation of the psyche was seminal. The medicalization of psychiatry in the 19th century did not leave Jung behind. During his psychiatry training he was especially influenced directly by his supervisor, Eugen Bleuler, and professionally by the innovative pioneer in psychiatry, Emil Kraepelin.

The energic and symbolic approaches to understanding the mechanisms of the psyche were paradigms Jung struggled with and attempted to reconcile his whole life. In a wider sense, however, his personal theorizing was part of a greater struggle in the 19th and 20th centuries to reconcile the scientific and the philosophical/religious traditions he inherited. Jung's ideas evolved in and out of an atmosphere of tremendous development in science and scientific method, but also in a period in history of great cultural upheaval. It was as if Jung's ideas and theorizing not only grew out of his own great intellectual curiosity and drive, but also arose out of a climate of personal and historical turmoil for him in which, as Lifton (1979) would say, the previous psychical forms were broken and new ones were not yet available. In this examination of Jung's concept of the ego, therefore, the personal as well as the historical context anchor the chronological examination of Jung's works.

Historical and conceptual perspectives

In order to construct a Jungian Ego Psychology based on Jung's writings, then, two separate developmental processes in his work need to be taken into account. The first is the historical perspective. Jung's work – his thinking about and understanding of the psyche – evolved over time. Statements made about the ego early in his career cannot be equated with statements made later. His involvement with late 19th/early 20th century psychiatric and psychoanalytic leaders, for example, led to an emphasis on structure and the economic, dynamic aspects of the ego, whereas later, as Jung focused on philosophical and religious issues, his ego concept became more experiential and relational. Ultimately, Jung found his own integration of these two aspects that assigns the ego a functional/dynamic as well as relational nature. Therefore, the question to which the historical perspective responds is: when did Jung make this statement about the ego?

The historical perspective

I propose that there are three phases to Jung's work regarding the ego. The first phase covers the period from the 1890s, when he began his career as a physician and psychiatrist and encountered Freud, to 1912, when he published the second part of his work *Symbols of Transformation* and broke with Freud. This period, the time in his life of his encounter with Freud, "the first man of real importance" (Jung, 1983a, p. 172), saw the emergence of Jung's first ideas about consciousness and ego. In this period Jung had a materialist frame of reference regarding the psyche and its transformation influenced very much by Freud; medical psychologists such as Emil Kraepelin, William Wundt, and his chief at the Burghölzliklinik in Zürich, Eugen Bleuler; and work being done in Geneva by Théodore Flournoy. Jung's student work in this period, however, contains intimations of his later emphasis on the transformational processes whereby unconscious material becomes conscious through the participation of the ego, which reaches the full symbolic frame of reference in his final works.

The second historical phase of Jung's work is the period from 1912 after his break with Freud to about 1945 when a severe illness left Jung himself transformed by the visions he had as he lay near death. This period of intense outer research and inner transformation began with the ideas expressed in *Symbols of Transformation* regarding consciousness and the ego and covers a period of intense research and lecturing about his theory of the psyche. Jung's interests and researches into other cultures and religious philosophies as well as personal relationships he had with individuals deeply involved in studies of Eastern philosophy and religion all contributed to his further understanding of the ego. In this period Jung wrote major works dealing with the ego, including *Psychological Types* (1921), 'The Relations Between the Ego and the Unconscious' (1923) and 'The Structure of the Psyche' (1927/31). During this time Jung began to develop a new frame of reference for understanding the psyche, one that began to include the creative, integrative concept of a symbolic paradigm. It was in this spirit he wrote 'The Transcendent Function' (1916) and 'Adaptation, Individuation, and Collectivity '(1916).

The last historical phase of Jung's work, which he characterized as reaching "the unknown wing in the house" (Jung, 1983a, p. 228), began in spirit before his 1945 illness and intensified afterward until his death in 1961. Although it appears Jung began his formal study of alchemy as early as 1934, it took on a new depth for him after his 1945 illness. The turning point in Jung's paradigm for thinking about the ego and the psyche that characterizes this last phase of his life came with his essay 'Commentary on the Secret of the Golden Flower' published in 1929. Jung's alchemical research, his exploration of Eastern religion and philosophy, and his 1945 illness culminated in his magnum opus *Mysterium Coniunctionis* (1955–1956). With this work the symbolic paradigm regarding the ego and the unconscious reached its apogee.

Conceptual perspective

The historical evolution of new dimensions to Jung's conception of the ego represents a linear progression, but there is also a vertical expansion, a deepening of his vision of the role of the ego in the psyche. This second line of development in Jung's work represents the conceptual perspective, which responds to the question: which dimension of the ego is Jung referring to in his writing? In this perspective, there are four main concepts of the ego.

The first is a concept of the perceiving, experiencing, or *subjective ego* aspect of the individual, the sense of the individual that captures the essence of the experience of self-ness. This is the sense of ego Jung meant when he said, "By the ego I understand a complex of representations which constitutes the center of my consciousness and appears to possess a high degree of continuity and identity" (CW 6/706). Jung used the term 'ego' here to refer to the intra-subjective experience associated today with Self Psychology.

A further component of this subjective ego is the concept of "objective cognition" which Jung describes in his autobiography, *Memories, Dreams, Reflections* (1983a, p. 328). For Jung, this perspective of being able to look at oneself as if outside oneself, similar to the concept of the observing ego, was a developmental achievement.

A discussion of the subjective ego, therefore, would include concepts of identity, objective cognition, sense perception, ego as cognitive and physical phenomena, Self Psychology, will, judgment, and memory as Jung understood them.

Jung described mechanisms regarding adaptation and ego defense in his writings but left unclear a general theory of adaptation and ego defense. The properties of *the structural ego* in Jung's theory of the psyche would include the executive functions of the ego that operate beyond conscious awareness: defense mechanisms, adaptation, and mechanisms of individuation such as the Transcendent Function and enantiodromia. The structural ego is also responsible for the individual variations in the more general process of individuation. As the individual experiences or is affected by the individuation drive from the psyche, the structural components of ego defense, adaptation mechanisms, and mechanisms of individuation regulate the rate and degree of movement toward consciousness. The characteristics such as defense, adaptation, and integration are usually associated with modern Ego Psychology.

Beyond the subjective aspects of the ego and that unconscious aspect that regulates movement toward consciousness, there is another aspect that engages in a mutual encounter with the Self in order to achieve consciousness. *The developmental ego* is the aspect of the ego that, through its relationship with the Self, expands and matures individual consciousness. This is the aspect of the ego that is engaged in a mutual process that is more than subjective awareness of such engagement. The engagement of the developmental ego with the Self is the fundamental instrument of the symbolic process. Development of personality is another component of Ego Psychology today.

Lastly, there is also a movement toward consciousness that Jung described in his later writing that is less concerned with the individual and more concerned with the growth of collective consciousness. The engagement of the ego with the Self, according to Jung, is also an instrument for increasing the consciousness of mankind. Through this greater collective consciousness the unconscious as Self is incarnated in the world. Jung said in his autobiography,

> In the experience of the [S]elf it is no longer the opposites 'God' and 'man' that are reconciled . . . but rather the opposites within the God-image itself. That is the meaning of divine service, or the service which man can render to God, that light may emerge from the darkness, that the Creator may become conscious of His creation, and man conscious of himself.
>
> (Jung, 1983a, p. 370–371)

The role of the ego in this process is then one of *the cosmogonic ego*, so-called because of the importance Jung placed on the world-creating nature of the ego in this capacity. This view of the ego is a unique contribution of Jung's and is seen nowhere else in modern Ego Psychology.

Ego psychology: an overview

The broad range of theoretical issues ego psychology has come to include can best be understood through its historical development. From a focused study of mental functioning to the study of the growth of a subjective sense of self, Ego Psychology has shown considerable theoretical development over time but also considerable theoretical splintering.

Contemporary Ego Psychology can trace its roots to Sigmund Freud. In his 1923 book *The Ego and the Id*, Freud changed the meaning of ego, hitherto associated with selfhood and unity of person, to a function of the mind: "We have formed the idea that in each individual there is a coherent organization of mental processes; and we call this his ego" (p. 17). The term 'ego' was used then to denote all those mental functions that regulate and mediate the experience between reality and the individual, including defensive action (repression and sublimation) and synthesizing and integrating conflicting inner and outer agencies ('Agencies' refers to the id, the superego, and external reality).

This shift away from focusing primarily on the nature of the repressed id-impulse toward the way the ego dealt with it was also anticipated by Freud's theoretical adjustments in his 1914 paper 'On Narcissism'. Freud needed a way to move away from a descriptive picture of the mind that described qualities of the psyche (the topographical model) to a more dynamic model that described functions of mental states (the structural model).

Freud did at times use the term 'ego' (*das Ich* in German) to denote self, and in *Civilization and Its Discontents* (1930) he plainly equates self (*Selbst*) and ego (p. 253, "Normally, there is nothing of which we are more certain than the feeling of our self, of our own ego"). However, in another work from 1925 ('Some Additional Notes Upon Dream-Interpretation as a Whole', SE 19, p. 133), Freud explicitly distinguishes between the two uses of ego as self and ego as mental function. Overall, though, throughout his work, Freud used the term 'ego' to denote its actions as a mental function and not as a subjective sense of self (Padel, 1985, p. 273). The theoretical focus of Freud regarding the ego remained structural and conflict based.

Anna Freud took up her father's ideas about defense and expanded them into a descriptive study of the ego defenses and their mechanisms (Freud, 1936). She added the analysis of defense to the technique of analysis of conflict in clinical work. Her work fit defense analysis into Freud's structural theory and did not deviate from the basic model of the mind he constructed.

At the same time another analyst, Robert Waelder, took the elder Freud's idea of over-determined symptoms and used it to focus on the multi-determined nature of symptoms as well (Waelder, 1936, p. 45–62). His followers Arlow and Brenner applied Waelder's ideas to Freud's concept of 'compromise formation' (Arlow and Brenner, 1964; Brenner, 1982). By focusing on the actions of all agencies – id, ego, superego, as well as external reality – compromise formation led psychoanalytic theory away from the uni-focal dynamics of drive theory. (Compromise formation describes the mechanism whereby the ego mediates an intra-psychic conflict between the id and external reality, for example, to establish a kind of psychical 'truce'.)

There was thus a split in Ego Psychology between the Anna Freudians, who followed a strict interpretation of Freud's theory and focused analytical technique on analysis of defenses, and those who followed Waelder and focused their technique on a theory of multi-determined symptoms. The concept of compromise formation was appealing to many analysts because it was readily translatable into clinical practice. The concept of compromise formation has even been called "American Ego Psychology" (Marcus, 1999, p. 845); such was the power of its influence there. Compromise formation remained a theory in the structural tradition, however.

At about the same time as Anna Freud and Waelder were developing their theories, Heinz Hartmann in 1938 focused on another aspect of the ego (Hartmann, 1958). He thought there was a part of the ego that functioned outside conflict, which he characterized as a primary autonomous structure. These conflict-free areas of ego functioning include perception, intuition, comprehension, thinking, language, learning, and intelligence. This was a realm of mental organization formed independent of instinctual development. The ego had a separate path of development from the drives and this development of the autonomous apparatus led to ego functions of adaptation and synthesis. Hartmann made a distinction between the 'ego' as agency and 'self' as interpersonal object (Padel, 1985, p. 273). The ego's adaptation to reality and real relationships, not just intra-psychic ones, was emphasized in Hartmann's theory, but his mechanistic and excessively theoretical approach was, some say, inaccessible (Marcus, 1999, p. 846). His main contributions were the concepts of ego adaptation and autonomous ego development and integrative functions. Hartmann, a follower of Anna Freud, remained in the paradigm of the structural model.

Harold Blum, a former editor of the *Journal of the American Psychoanalytical Association*, has said Ego Psychology was mainly a North American phenomenon, elaborated by Hartmann and his colleagues at the New York Psychoanalytic Institute in the 1950s and '60s, and that interest in it has waned considerably since Hartmann's death in 1970 (Blum, 1998). He lists the areas, however, of lasting influence the ego psychologists have had in mainstream contemporary structural theory:

> They contributed to the elucidation and recognition of the aggressive drive on a par with the sexual drive, as well as studies of the development and function of the ego and superego. Ego Psychology emphasized structural theory, the centrality of ego activity as elaborated by Freud, defense analysis systematized by Anna Freud, the ego's controlling structures, and adaptation to external reality.
>
> (Blum, 1998)

While Hartmann and his collaborators had their heyday in North America, British analysts were more interested in issues of defense and development than in issues of ego functions and transformations. Blum believes Ego Psychology's emphasis on ego development stimulated the child observational studies of Winnicott, Spitz, and Mahler as well as explorations of ego development in the context of object relations.

Otto Kernberg (1982) in particular tried to integrate Ego Psychology and object relations theory. In his formulation, unconscious intra-psychic conflicts were not between wishful urges and defense, but between internalized object relations (self- and object-representations) and the opposing representations, as well as the associated affects. However, many felt the structural theory, the theoretical basis of Ego Psychology, and object relations theory to be "two separate, friendly but irreconcilable, paradigms" (Ornstein, 1999). These two theories reflect two fundamentally different ways of viewing people (Kennedy, 1999): Ego Psychology emphasizes conflict between psychic agencies, while object relations is in fact not about conflict between inner and outer self- and object-representations, but rather about the relationship with the other. Thus there was an ongoing debate in subsequent years in the psychoanalytic literature about whether psychoanalysis was a one-person (i.e. focused entirely on the intra-psychical world of the one patient) or a two-person (i.e. analysis as an inter-subjective process) psychology. This approach to analysis as an inter-subjective process challenged the theoretical basis of clinical work in Ego Psychology (analyst as objective observer; Blum, 1998).

The final phase of theoretical development emphasizes this intra-subjective process with concomitant implications for Ego Psychology. Ego psychology needed some correctives in the areas of empathic meaning and subjectivity because of its emphasis on "external reality as developmental catalyst, traumatizer, and organizer" (Marcus, 1999, p. 850). These concerns were addressed by the theories of Sullivan (1953), which were elaborated by Greenberg and Mitchell (1983), as well as in the object relations theory of Donald Winnicott and Ronald Fairbairn.

The culmination of this trend was a breaking away from structural theory by Heinz Kohut (1971). He emphasized the concept of deficit, not in the ego as a psychical function, but in the self as the whole person. More fundamental than conflict, deficits in self-organization, self-feeling, and self-regard were responsible for patients suffering. He proposed a theory of development that emphasized the interpersonal experiences of a grandiose self, an idealized 'Other', and identification with others. His theory has been criticized by ego psychologists as lacking the elaborated structure of the tripartite model, as well as having 'jettisoned' the concepts of internal conflict due to drive intensity, inborn ego capacities of defense and integration, as well as the role of aggression in development (Marcus, 1999, p. 853). Ego psychologists thus consider Self Psychology a splinter theory of structural theory.

Therefore, there are a number of basic theoretical principles that most ego psychologists would agree on as integral to a theory of the ego (Marcus, 1999, p. 855). These are:

1 *A Developmental Concept*: There is a mind that grows and as it does there is a corresponding growth and development in its functions, its content, and in relations between the elements of the mind.
2 *A Structural Concept*: Ego psychology has an elaborated concept of structure in which elements and dynamic processes are delineated. The dynamic organization of this structure includes affects, drives, and object relations. Conflict remains the heart of motivation in the structural theory.
3 *A Deficit Concept*: Deficits such as trauma, inborn ego problems (diminished mental capacity to organize for example), and illness (physical and mental) all contribute to ego function.
4 *An Adaptation Concept*: The ego is considered to have an innate capacity to adapt to reality and emotional experience as part of its mediating role.
5 *An Integration Concept*: Ego integrative processes operate at different levels of consciousness and at different levels of organization according to ego development. "It is the ego especially that organizes and mediates compromises, integrating each individual's unique psychic reality. Hence the name ego psychology" (Marcus, 1999, p. 855).
6 *A Defense Concept*: Defense as an ego function is a concept that influences clinical technique as well as theoretical understanding.
7 *A Self Concept*: Ego psychologists accept the concept of self in discussing clinical work despite the feeling that Self Psychology is a splinter theory. It is used in the sense of describing personality types rather than implying an interpersonal psychology. Ego psychology does not have a well-articulated metapsychology of personality (Marcus, 1999, p. 855).

As I work through the different phases of Jung's theory development, I will highlight the emerging ego theory according to this conceptual framework. Some of these concepts have been taken up by post-Jungians in various ways as well, and I will include these extensions of Jung's theory where appropriate.

Ego psychology: a Jungian overview

Critical assessments of Jung's works (Papadopoulos, 1992; Samuels, 1985) have examined his ego concept in a number of ways. First, there has been discussion about the terminology Jung used: self versus ego. Redfearn (1983) attempts to differentiate these terms as used by Freud and Freudians as opposed to the use by Jung himself as well as post-Jungians such as Michael Fordham. He points out the difficulty of communicating with other analytic schools when terms are confusing but also the real problems of formulating basic theory in a common language.

Redfearn describes two uses of the term 'self' by Jung. The first use is as a description of the whole personality, and the second use is as the psychical organizing principle. While the former use is experienced as part of one's own personality, the latter is not. This can give rise to confusion when parts of the personality that are not this latter self nevertheless are experienced as 'not-I', such as complexes or what Redfearn called "part selves" such as the persona, anima, and the shadow. He also points out confusion that arose from Fordham's description of the self in his seminal paper 'Defenses of the Self" (1974). Redfearn (1983) states, "[T]he word self is . . . being used [by Fordham] to mean an early ego or self-representation and not the total personality or primary integrate" (p. 101). Redfearn later reports a personal communication from Fordham that the use of the term 'self' in this paper was not meant to imply 'self' in the usual Jungian organizing principle sense but rather, that the individual is reacting as though his whole being is threatened. This illustrates how misunderstandings about key terms can occur.

As well, the development of Jung's theories seems to have diverged in two overall directions within the post-Jungian community. Fordham in London was very impressed by the Kleinian school of analysis (Fordham, 1993) and was able to understand his work with children in a way that led to his revisions of Jung's theories regarding, among other topics, ego development. Fordham came to represent a more developmental perspective in analytical psychology (Samuels, 1985), which in part focuses on traditional concerns of psychoanalysis such as transference/countertransference and ego development.

Fordham made significant contributions to Jung's theories either by filling in gaps left by Jung (for example, in the area of analytic technique), or by modifying Jung's theories outright. Regarding ego development, it must be noted that Fordham developed a theory of ego and ego development out of his direct work and research with children beginning in 1934 and spanning a career of almost 50 years. While Jung and other pioneering depth psychologists had speculated on development or extrapolated a theory of normal childhood from the pathology of adults, Fordham based his conclusions on empirical evidence and child observation studies.

In Fordham's theory of ego and ego development, there are two main assumptions. He first assumes there is a self present in infancy and childhood. Second, he assumes there is a dynamic sequence, a process of 'deintegration/reintegration' of this childhood self, out of which an individual ego evolves. For psychoanalysts the term 'self' refers generally to the sense of individual personhood, to the experience of one's own being. For Jungians at the structural level (Fordham, 1985, p. 20–25) the self represents a sense of primary 'cosmic' unity beyond the individual encompassing all mankind as well as the physical and psychical world. Jung also uses the word 'self' to describe the totality of the individual, as well as the experience of totality and wholeness (the baby's experience of the mother as self, for example). It also represents the transpersonal or collective unconscious. At a dynamic level (Fordham, 1985, p. 31–33), the self represents the primary organizing agency outside the conscious 'I' as well as the organizing center of the unconscious. In this sense it is essentially integrative in nature. This term 'self' as primary organizing agency and transpersonal factor is sometimes capitalized by Jungians as 'Self'.

Fordham considered defenses from two perspectives: the ego defenses as traditionally understood, but also, in a new theoretical development, what he called 'self-defenses'. As opposed to the ego defenses that address the attempt by the ego to ward off unpleasant or undesirable unconscious contents, Fordham saw a different dynamic at work with self-defenses. In this case, the defense is not against an unconscious element but rather against a split off bad object. In this view, self-defenses are defenses mobilized not by the ego but rather, by the untransformed, split off destructive deintegrates of the self. These split-off deintegrates are then expressed and experienced in projective identification. The Self, in other words, is behind this process and not the ego.

A number of problems arise with this formulation. First, it is not clear that these split-off parts represent 'pure' deintegrates of the Self. Despite their primitive and archetypal-like quality, they are nevertheless related to the personal experience and history of the individual involved. Clinically, the bad object is associated with the personal parent or equivalent but with an archetypal underlay.

Second, splitting is an effective, albeit primitive, ego defense (and as I will argue later, a natural function in the psyche). Because the deintegrate must interact with the ego at some level (otherwise it is 'off the radar screen' and not an issue) the splitting off of destructive deintegrates must involve ego participation, if not direction. The ego defends itself against the destructive object by maintaining separateness and rejecting reintegration. This failure of the ego to integrate destructive or otherwise extraordinary psychic content is also seen, for example, in the repetitive dreams of patients with post-traumatic stress syndrome.

Lastly, Fordham's formulation contains the assumption that the ego can only function defensively at an unconscious level ("In the case of part objects there is no unconsciousness . . ."; Fordham, 1985, p. 153) and therefore something else is in operation. I would argue that these total reactions to destructive inner objects are a form of ego defense consistent with an early stage of ego development. Modern infant research shows the surprising ability of infants and young children to regulate their 'threshold' of interaction tolerance. When an interaction is 'too much' the child will look away, for example. Children early on (Stern, 1985) have the capacity to differentiate and reject unpleasant social interaction at ages as young as two months. Stern makes the point that the child is regulating affect and not a cognitive event. The child has an inner, not wholly conscious, sense of what is right for him or not. This indicates an ego capacity to differentiate even at a conscious and unconscious level and engage in defensive maneuvers. So the ability exists for the child to 'look away' from malignant deintegrates, that is, exclude the psychic deintegrate from conscious integration as a 'not-me' element. Because the maneuver is primitive does not exclude it being ego driven.

The second direction in post-Jungian theory beyond this Developmental School has been called the Archetypal School (Samuels, 1985, p. 15). Here the emphasis is the archetype and the image; indeed in this school a focus on ego development is considered reductionism (Hillman, 1972). Transformation is through the encounter with the symbol, as it is experienced in its inner imaginal forms or in its outer concretized forms in projection.

Ego and consciousness are first of all understood as part of the myth of psychology: the heroic struggle of the individual out of the depths of unconscious fantasy, disorder, weakness, and immaturity toward reason, control, structure, and unity. Hillman says, for example,

> The Hero-myth tells the tale of conquest and destruction, the tale of psychology's 'strong ego', its fire and sword, as well as the career of its civilization, but it tells little of the culture of consciousness. Strange that we could still, in a psychology as subtle as Jung's, believe that this King-Hero, and his ego, is the equivalent of consciousness.
>
> (Hillman, 1985a, p. 93)

Psychology and society as a whole place a value on 'reality' at the expense of the imaginal. Yet Hillman sees the tendency of the psyche to mythologize as itself healing when there is an awareness of this drama (Hillman, 1983, p. 40).

Also, Hillman emphasizes the need to avoid the narrow perspective of consciousness as a singular entity. Consciousness resides in multiple centers in the psyche, and he rejects the psychology that sees this 'polytheism' as a pathology (Hillman, 1975a, p. 26–27). He quotes Jung to describe this sad state of affairs:

> We lack all knowledge of the unconscious psyche and pursue the cult of consciousness to the exclusion of all else. Our true religion is a monotheism of consciousness, a possession by it, coupled with a fanatical denial of the fragmentary autonomous systems.
>
> (CW 13/51)

Hillman rejects Jung's placement of the ego at the center of consciousness. He saw Jung adhering to 19th century notions of the psyche in this regard and instead places the anima at the center of the conscious-making process (1985a, p. 89). Hillman highlights a discrepancy/paradox in Jung's theory here: that Jung was contradictory regarding the central role and importance of the ego in the development of consciousness. He differentiates between the Jung who saw the psyche as an energic system with a strong central point of consciousness (ego) versus the Jung who disparaged the ego and emphasized the role of archetypes as healing forces (1985a, p. 89). Hillman saw Jung's work overall as moving away from the former to the latter, with equivocation remaining nevertheless when he still in later works equates consciousness with ego.

For Hillman, however, there was no equivocation. The ego was more like a mirage than a point of illumination, "where what today is called ego-consciousness would be the consciousness of the Platonic cave, a consciousness buried in the least-aware perspectives" (1985a, p. 93). The ego is from Hillman's perspective "an instrument for day-to-day coping, nothing more grandiose than a trusty janitor of the planetary houses" (1985a, p. 93). It is ultimately subordinate to his main topic, soul-making. In this position it is useful, however, because this lesser role is 'therapeutic', presumably meaning caring rather than transformative.

These two schools, then, the Developmental School of Fordham and the Archetypal School of Hillman, can be seen as representing the ambiguity inherent in Jung's own works, between the energic and the symbolic paradigms. Jung's concept of ego was based on an energic paradigm that understood and conceived of the psyche according to a structural model. At the same time, however, Jung had a vision of the psyche as a mutual dynamic, interactive field and the process of encounter with the symbol, the symbolic paradigm, was also based on a deficit model reminiscent of the interpersonal psychology of the Self-psychologists. In Jung's case, however, the deficit was less about lapses in development than about fulfilling a process of wholeness of personality.

Towards a Jungian theory of the ego

In this work, I examine Jung's writings and show that Jung did have a metapsychology of the ego that can be constructed from his theory of the psyche. Key points that structure this examination are:

1 There are three historical phases to Jung's use and understanding of the ego/consciousness concept. These phases, described earlier, though with much overlap are chronological and reflect his growing and deepening engagement with the psyche's purpose and functioning. There was an overall progression from an energic to a symbolic paradigm in his conception of the psyche. The metapsychology of the ego evolved accordingly.
2 That in Jung's engagement with the psyche, he expressed four discrete visions (subjective ego, structural ego, developmental ego, cosmogonic

ego) of the role and place of the ego and consciousness in the psychic life of mankind. By viewing Jung's writing on the ego through this framework, much confusion and contradiction can be clarified.

Comments on organization and scope of this work

Because the philosophical underpinnings of his theories determine the character of these theories, I will examine the two major yet contradictory influences on Jung's metapsychology. Chapter 2 will consider the scientific/materialist and medical background that comprises the energic paradigm and the philosophical and religious background that comprises the symbolic paradigm.

As I stated before, a chronological analysis of Jung's major works structures this book. In Chapter 3 I examine the works of Jung prior to and during his collaboration with Freud. Chapter 4 will examine the middle period in Jung's career after he broke from Freud and developed his own theories. Chapter 5 will then examine the late period in Jung's career, which was dominated by new formulations of his theories that coalesced in response to a life-threatening illness. Finally, Chapter 6 will present an overview of the theory of ego from a Jungian perspective.

Jung was a great thinker but he was also a clinician and his writings were ultimately meant to help people in their lives. Therefore, each phase of his work and as he developed his vision of the ego's role in the psyche has implications for clinical practice. In order to illustrate the very real benefit of Jung's theories, I will use case examples and discuss implications for clinical technique as appropriate.

In a topic as broad as the ego concept, it is inevitable that more questions will be raised than can possibly be addressed in this work. One issue in particular eminently worthy of detailed examination is the concept of ego in non-Western culture. Indeed one Jungian analyst colleague of mine, Ursula Ulmer, who has worked intensively in traditional cultures in Africa, has observed firsthand how the Western concept of ego and the individual represents only a small minority of the cultural experience on that continent. This is a fact in much of the world where traditional cultures dominate. I have also had discussions with a number of Japanese Jungian colleagues, and I understand that the ego concepts as articulated by Jung in his writings do not fully represent their experience (see, for example, Yama, 2013).

Group consciousness does not necessarily mean, however, an absence of development or structures for the individual member of the group. Jung's concept of the collective unfortunately can imply a kind of 'mob mentality' that fails to acknowledge the actual refined differentiation in the collective present in traditional groups and cultures. I do believe in any case that the framework I propose for understanding the ego can help to structure understanding its manifestation in diverse cultures.

My focus is the ego in a Western context in general and in Jung's writings in particular because Jung's ideas are, in many ways, unique. His theories on this subject challenge us to re-examine the conventional Western view in psychology today about what is the ego, what are its properties, and what is its place in the world. In other words, precisely because Jung's theories are out of the mainstream in general and because his ideas about ego in particular have not enjoyed broad recognition or acceptance, his theories can offer fresh and provocative perspectives on mainstream ego theory. In addition, because Jung worked in the Western tradition (despite his claims of universality), it is appropriate to examine his concepts in that context.

The ego, that central structure in our conscious world, touches not just issues of human growth and development, identity, and agency and will, but also, in Jung's psychology, the deepest sense of how we experience ourselves, our world, and others, and how we transform. I have had to make choices on which topics to pursue in depth and which only to highlight. This work cannot cover, for example, all the numerous currents in the literature on ego and consciousness over the past century. I have tried, however, to address and include all I felt were major and significant themes as they related to Jung's work.

Any critique of Jung's theory (as opposed to criticism of Jung the man) will inevitably involve two related themes that I have repeatedly encountered in my review of the literature: first, that he is not scientific/empirical, and second, that he is 'mystical'. These are, in Jung's philosophical and theoretical viewpoint, impossible to refute precisely because in the context of his system, he believes he is scientific and empirical. Jung wrote, for example,

> Because I am an empiricist first and foremost, and my views are grounded in experience, I have to deny myself the pleasure of reducing them to a well-ordered system and of placing them in their historical and ideological context. From the philosophical standpoint, of whose requirements I am very well aware, this is indeed a painful omission.
>
> (CW 18/1731)

To grasp Jung's intentions one has to accept or at least grant him the validity of his assumptions. There is, like opposing political parties, a philosophical gulf between his views and others that cannot be reasoned away – his philosophy is what it is, and it hangs together in this context. Accusations of mysticism, it seems to me, are a kind of shorthand to attack Jung's emphasis on spiritual or religious experience in a psychological framework. Numinosity, that sense of the presence of spirit, was to Jung an authentic human experience and an empirical fact, which he sought to understand. Jung's psychology has been called a psychology of religion and was an attempt to examine and understand a deeply personal yet 'unscientific' experience. I wonder if accusations of 'mysticism' are a rejection of this experience by Jung's critics.

From my own work as a Jungian analyst in private practice, I know the symbolic paradigm 'from the inside', as it were. A distinctly numinous experience of synchronicity sparked interest in this topic, for example. However, I also teach traditional psychiatric assessment in a university setting, and I value the precision and structure of the energic paradigm and the common vocabulary it brings to a range of human experiences and research efforts. I hope in this work to convey my equanimity toward both approaches to the psyche, because only by taking this bridging position, I believe, can one begin to appreciate the complex entity we call the ego.

A note on terminology

There is one problem I would like to address as I look at Jung's use of the terms 'ego', 'self', 'Self', 'individual', and '*individuum*'. The terms are used in two confusing ways: first as technical terms to describe specific entities and in this usage are meant to provide clarity. Unfortunately, these terms are also used colloquially – as general descriptions or as used in common everyday usage. (The problem is not one of translation; the original German is just as confusing.) With this second way and alongside the first more precise way, the terms begin to lose meaning or lead to confusion. This confusion was amplified when Jung revised earlier works and included new formulations of terms alongside old formulations.

Jung's intention, despite his assertions to the contrary, was not always toward scientific structure and clarity, but phenomenological understanding. Regarding the terms 'self' versus 'Self': Jung in his original German text capitalized the term 'Self', with the definitive article, when it was used as a proper noun (*das Selbst*) and left the term 'self' un-capitalized when it was used as a reflexive pronoun (*ich selbst*). This usage made the use of these terms clear. When the Collected Works were translated into English, this convention was dropped, leading to confusion around this term in particular. As well the term 'self' is used in psychology in a specific way in depth psychology and in Self Psychology in particular.

In addition, there is a term that Jung used in his works that has received less attention but which is nevertheless a key term when examining his ego concept. That term is 'individual'. As I will illustrate in Chapter 4, the term 'individual' is actually a description of a particular state that differs from the colloquial use of the term. This more colloquial form, which refers to the person separate from the group, will be written un-capitalized as 'individual'. 'Individual', however, is also a term used by Jung to refer to the personal entity that is the result of individuation and that has its own meaning and consequences for Jung's theoretical framework. This concept has significant implications when constructing a Jungian theory of the ego. To distinguish this more specific usage from the more colloquial version, it will be italicized as *individual.*

Chapter 2

The energic paradigm and the symbolic paradigm

'Valentina', a pretty, dark-haired Italian living in Canada, came to see me for analysis some years ago to help her with relationships that always seemed to end badly. As a graduate student with her 30th birthday fast approaching, she wanted to finally get to the bottom of her problems. After a number of hours of work together we fell into a routine in which she would read from her journal, and we would then discuss her thoughts and feelings in a superficial conversation as if over a cup of coffee. This was all she would tolerate but one day this routine changed. 'Valentina' entered and sat as usual and began to read from her journal. As she spoke, I began this time to have idle fantasies about her. "She has such lovely hair", I thought. "Why doesn't she do more with it?" and "Her cheeks look so pale. She needs more color". Just after I had these thoughts however, she read from her journal: "I saw my mother this weekend; she said my hair looked too plain and that I should wear more blush".

How does an analyst or psychotherapist begin to understand the dynamics of such an incident? What are the ways to structure the facts of what happened for therapeutic effect but also, at a more basic level, to know what happened? The energic paradigm and the symbolic paradigm, both derived from long historical antecedents and broad philosophical landscapes, are two principle roadmaps for us to follow as we explore the possibilities.

The energic paradigm

Basis in 19th century science

Energic concepts in Jung's works have their source in the medical and scientific theories of the 19th century. As Jung began his professional career as a psychiatrist in 1900, the field of psychology as a science had been making strides in retrieving the investigation and explanation of the mind from the philosophers and claiming it as a subject of scientific investigation. Furthering this trend, the scientific community had begun to articulate real methodological differences between science and philosophy. For example, Hermann von Helmholtz, one of the leading architects of this progression, said in justifying the distinction made between natural and what he called 'moral' science:

> As empirical investigation of facts has again come to the fore in the other sciences [philosophy], the opposition between them and the natural sciences has become less marked. Nonetheless, even though this opposition was expressed in an excessively stark form through the influence of the previously named philosophy [Hegel's], it is grounded in the nature of things and must be acknowledged. It depends partly upon the kinds of intellectual processes characteristic of the previously named disciplines and partly, as the names *Natur- and Geisteswissenschaften* [literally 'nature-' and 'spirit-science' but more usually translated as natural science and the humanities] indicate, on the subjects of which they treat.
>
> (Cahan, 1993, p. 544)

This effort in the 19th century to examine the nature of the mind using empirical investigation was part of the academic and professional background in which Jung studied medicine and psychiatry and began his own scientific career. Jung even said that he was attracted to the study of science precisely because of its quality of "truth based on facts" (Jung, 1983a, p. 91).

Leading theorists in the fields of experimental psychology and psychiatry were not only indirectly influential to Jung through the 19th century scientific Zeitgeist, but also professionally in more direct and personal ways. Jung began his psychiatry training at the Burghölzliklinik in Zürich, an asylum famous at the time as a center for innovative and relatively enlightened work with the mentally ill. The director of the Klinik, Eugen Bleuler, embraced the latest medical thinking of Emil Kraepelin and insisted that each patient have a thorough case history and diagnostic evaluation performed. The work being done at the time by Wilhelm Wundt with the galvanometer became an important part of this evaluation. Bleuler sought to offer the best and most promising treatments available and therefore introduced his student psychiatrists to the then newly emerging theories of Sigmund Freud.

Bleuler's influence on Jung is often underestimated in the light of Jung's subsequent alignment with Freud. It is worth noting, therefore, that although Jung became personally acquainted with Freud in 1907 and ended their relationship in early 1913 (a period of not quite five years), he spent nine years at the Burghölzliklinik in near daily contact with Bleuler. For a time at the beginning of his work at the Burghölzliklinik, Jung even gave up smoking to emulate the strait-laced Bleuler. Bleuler's disapproval of an extramarital affair may also have contributed to Jung resigning his post there as *Assistenzarzt* (Wottreng, 1999, p. 126).

Science versus philosophy

The developments in psychology in the 19th century arose out of a longer trend in science and culture begun in the early 17th century. With René Descartes, the investigation of nature and matter became structured in a way that came to be called empirical. Up to that point in history, philosophy and science were closely linked. Descartes, however, separated speculation from science and introduced the concept of physical laws (Scruton, 1995, p. 39), paving the way for Isaac Newton and others. Science became a procedure in which knowledge of the world was acquired, not by intellectual reasoning, but by making a hypothesis and testing it to establish its validity. The focus, therefore, and the object of evaluation became the external world and the concrete object.

The process of making a hypothesis and testing it became known as the scientific method. Experimentation in science was systematized to ensure replicability and therefore reliability of the results. In this context, then, scientists of the 19th century began to approach investigations of human psychology. Phenomena that leant themselves to scientific investigation were pursued first, such as perception and sensation.

The field of experimental psychology evolved from these physiological experiments. Two leading theorists and experimentalists of the 19th century who made the investigation of human psychology possible were Hermann von Helmholtz, from Potsdam, and Wilhelm Wundt, from Baden-Württemberg. Both were influential to Jung as he worked under the energic paradigm, albeit Helmholtz less directly than Wundt. Wundt was especially influential to Jung's early writings because Jung's work with Wundt's galvanometer at the Burghölzliklinik as well as Jung's attraction to his theories led to his theory of complexes. Wundt's influence can also be seen, for example, in Jung's early formulations of psychic energy. Helmholtz, meanwhile, was a greater influence on the general 19th century scientific Zeitgeist, although he had a profound influence on Jung indirectly through Freud's embrace of Helmholtzian theory, and through Freud's role as Wilhelm Wundt's physiology teacher.

Wundt made the argument in his 1902 work *Principles of Physiological Psychology* that there is a correspondence between the processes in the physical world and the psychical world; this unitary perspective justified the scientific approach to psychology:

> This division of vital processes into physical and psychical is useful and even necessary for the solution of scientific problems; however, the life of an organism is really a complex unity of processes. The processes of bodily life and the conscious processes can no more be separated than we can mark off an outer experience, mediated by sense perceptions, and oppose it, as something wholly separate and apart, to what we call 'inner' experience, the events of our own consciousness.
>
> (Wundt, 1902, p. 1)

Wundt felt strongly that a scientific approach was necessary and went on to say, "We take issue with every treatment of psychology that is based on simple self-observation or on philosophical presuppositions. We shall employ, whenever it is indicated, physiology in the service of psychology" (Wundt, 1902, p. 2).

A further break from philosophy in the study of the mind came about in the field of medicine and psychiatry. The 19th century was the era of the mental asylum, a movement that emerged from a confluence of cultural and societal trends to bring about the institutionalization of the mentally ill. Germany especially became a leader in the field of psychiatry because of its large number of universities and medical academies (France by contrast had basically only one), each competing for academic glory through scientific advancement (Shorter, 1997, p. 35). Because almost every leading academic psychiatrist was also involved in asylum administration, the asylum became a place for one to distinguish oneself in the scientific world. The mind, then, became the subject of medical investigation.

Psychiatry would have nothing to offer the mentally ill in the way of biological treatment until the 20th century. Treatment and even cure was a hope and a goal of the 19th century psychiatrist, nevertheless, if only because the condition of the typical patient was so desperate. In the context of the medical model and the scientific method, therefore, medical practitioners began to observe, describe, and categorize the symptoms they found into discrete illness groups. A pioneer in this method was Emil Kraepelin, working in Heidelberg. Kraepelin has even been called "the central figure in the history of psychiatry" (Shorter, 1997, p. 100), and his influence lives on to this day in the systems of diagnostic categories used in psychiatry worldwide.

Bleuler in Zürich embraced Kraepelin and his methods and Jung would have been occupied in his daily work with this method of observing, describing and classifying his patients. At another level, however, the principle of observation to which Kraepelin's method prescribed was to be of much greater importance and influence to Jung than the classifying method itself (Jung's theory of neurosis rejects categories, for example). For Jung, explanation of clinical material was in order to "express what I believe I have seen" (letter to Norbert Drewitt, 25 September 1937). Jung always saw his working method of careful observation as empirical science:

> The 'reality of the psyche' is my working hypothesis, and my principle activity consists in collecting factual material to describe and explain it. I have set up neither a system nor a general theory, but have merely formulated auxiliary concepts to serve me as tools, as is customary in every branch of science.
>
> (CW 18/1507)

By the end of the 19th century then when Jung began his psychiatric career, models such as the scientific method and the medical model, at least in academic medical circles, influenced investigation into the nature of the mind much more than philosophy. The energic paradigm captures the basic tenets of this way of thinking about scientific research and scientific explanation. It is based on the scientific tenets of the 19th century and is, therefore, looking back from our 21st century vantage point, easy to criticize as simplistic or even untrue based on later, more sophisticated science. Nevertheless, these tenets were what Jung had as his scientific background, and it would be unfair to evaluate the historical development of Jung's theories out of the context in which he developed them. The energic paradigm of the 19th century was, simply put, the best science of its time.

Characteristics of the energic paradigm

In this chapter I would like to review the basic concepts of the energic paradigm through an examination of their historical roots. Because this paradigm, and the symbolic paradigm discussed later, are in fact part of the entire history of ideas and touch on a multitude of ideas and currents in the world, I have chosen to focus only on those aspects that were most directly influential to Jung either from being major scientific trends in the Zeitgeist or from being a part of the influence of his most important teachers or of him personally.

The energic paradigm takes its basic tenets from the attitude of academic science of the 19th century. This means that there was a rejection of the methodology of philosophy and religion when speculating on the nature of mind and psyche. Instead, the scientific method was the respected and preferred practice. Further, the conclusions of physiology and physics and chemistry about the nature of matter and energy were extrapolated to the functioning of the mind and psychic energy. The assumption was that the mind was like matter, and its energy obeyed the same laws as energy in other natural sciences such as physics, biology, and chemistry. In the second half of the 19th century, for example, there was a decided tendency, especially in Germany, to explain mental events in terms of physiology and natural science (Macmillan, 1991, p. 170).

As one example of this tendency, I turn to Helmholtz and his scientific achievements. Hermann von Helmholz is known for co-discovering the first law of thermodynamics, the law of conservation of energy. For him this law, as well as other forces of nature that were declared 'laws' by physicists in the 19th century, was universal and allowed the scientist "to understand something of the economy of the universe with respect to the supply of effective force" (Cahan, 1993, p. 568). Forces were all of the same nature, and even the human body itself was viewed in this light as an energy-consuming, work-producing machine subject to natural forces. There are general laws regarding forces in human physiology analogous to physics. Helmholz said the task of science would be fulfilled, "if at some time, the reduction of all phenomena to elementary forces were completed, and if, at the same time, this reduction were shown to be the only possible one that the phenomena permit" (Cahan, 1993, p. 471). In other words, all natural phenomena should be, perhaps are, ultimately understandable in terms of physical laws. Others working in psychology in the 19th century of course challenged this attitude. Nevertheless, the Helmholtzian attitude was a prominent force in the atmosphere in which Jung worked and trained at the end of the 19th century and the beginning of the 20th century. Those familiar with Freud will recognize as well the pivotal influence the energic paradigm had as he constructed his metapsychology.

The view one takes toward psychic phenomena establishes the fundamental premises of one's psychological theory but also serves as the theoretical foundation for the corresponding psychological treatment. Ideas about what are mutative factors in psychology flows out of the explanatory theories. If one believes, as Freud did in 1893, for example, that symptoms appear as a result of repressed traumatic memories (Freud & Breuer, SE 2, p. 10), then the treatment would involve some mechanism to release those repressed memories and affect. This Freud and Breuer attempted with the 'cathartic' method. Whether Freud and Breuer arrived at this treatment out of the theory or they developed their theory after success with hypnosis is not as important here as the fact they saw a causal connection and causal mechanism in theory and mutative effect. In this same way, the assumptions underlying the energic paradigm regarding the psychic processes led to ideas about treatment.

The energic paradigm emphasized careful observation and objective description, but it also in a sense decreed what was worthy of observation and description. When a phenomenon is reduced to its physiochemical mechanisms, then subjective phenomena cannot be accounted for. The energic paradigm had no place for religious experience, for example, or the experience with my client described earlier, because these were interior phenomena inaccessible to experimentation. These sorts of phenomena were deemed unscientific and left to philosophy and religion to explain. William James, for example, wearing his philosopher's hat, wrote in *The Varieties of Religious Experience* in 1902 that "[s]cience . . . has ended by utterly repudiating the personal point of view. She catalogues her elements and records her laws indifferent as to what purpose may be shown forth by them, and constructs her theories quite careless of their bearing on human anxieties and fates" (James, 1982, p. 491).

The following list constitutes, then, the main characteristic of the energic paradigm of the 19th century. I will examine the works of the experimental psychologists and medical theorists associated with this paradigm who were most influential to Jung according to these characteristics:

Knowledge through scientific observation

A key tenet in the energic paradigm is the acquisition of knowledge through scientific observation. The scientific foundation of this paradigm is a rejection of rational speculation and dogmatic assertions more characteristic of philosophy and religion. Facts are what can be observed and described and are, most importantly, external rather than internal experience.

Observation in an artificial experimental situation was the preferred method because it allowed the psychologist to manipulate the experimental subject's immediate experience. Wilhelm Wundt said, for example,

> Since psychology has for its object, not specific contents of experience, but general experience in its immediate character, it can make use of no methods except such as the empirical sciences in general employ for the determination, analysis, and causal interpretation of facts.
>
> (Wundt, 1896, p. 24)

By "general experience in its immediate character" (*allgemeine Erfahrung in ihrer unmittelbaren subjektiven Beschaffenheit*), Wundt meant the processes observed in an experimental situation rather than inner subjective experience. An example of such a situation would be the physical reactions observed and recorded by the galvanometer in response to stimulus words in the word association test.

Conservation of energy and the principle of constancy

A concept co-discovered by Hermann von Helmholtz in 1847, the conservation of energy was originally a law in physics that says that in a closed system energy is neither created nor destroyed. It is not a description of a mechanism but an abstract idea based on mathematical principle. Physical energy changes form (heat energy, kinetic energy, gravitational energy, etc.), but it always remains constant.

Gustav Theodor Fechner, a trained physician and physicist of the 19th century, introduced the principle of conservation of energy into psychology (Sulloway, 1979, p. 66). A convert to *Naturphilosophie*, Fechner had a revelation one day in 1850 that there was a correspondence between the physical and the psychical worlds. He performed experiments to discover the mathematical formula that would demonstrate this law and eventually wrote *Psychophysik*, acknowledged as the starting point of experimental psychology (Ellenberger, 1970, p. 217). Fechner's ideas were later influential to Helmholtz (Cahan, 1993) and Wundt in their own physiological and psychological research. Wundt in his work *Principles of Physiological Psychology*, for example, makes the argument that the nervous system obeys the principle of the conservation of energy because it is the seat of chemical processes as well as psychical ones.

The principle of constancy in psychology was described by Freud in an 1893 lecture:

> If a person experiences a psychical impression, something in his nervous system which we will for the moment call the 'sum of excitation' is increased. Now in every individual there exists a tendency to diminish this sum of excitation once more, in order to preserve his health. . . .
>
> (SE 2, p. xxn)

He would later define the principle of constancy in *Beyond the Pleasure Principle* thus: "The mental apparatus endeavors to keep the quantity of excitation present in it as low as possible or at least to keep it constant" (SE 18, p. 9). In both of these descriptions there is the assumption that psychic energy will seek a return to a previous, lower, state of excitation or at least prevent further increases. This seeking a return to a lower level of excitation has more in common with the principle of entropy than the conservation of energy principle. In general, both principles see energy as lacking development or teleology. Energy behaves quantitatively and the movements between excitation and diminution, or from one form to another, have no ultimate purpose.

Jung adapted the law of conservation of energy for his own uses in *Symbols of Transformation* (1912) and *On the Nature of the Psyche* (1948). He agrees in general with the assumption that psychic energy cannot be destroyed; it may disappear but will emerge somewhere else. He preferred, however, to call it a "principle of equivalence" after Ludwig Busse's suggestion (CW 8/34). Jung said,

> Anyone who has had practical experience of this field knows that the equivalence principle is of great heuristic value in the treatment of neuroses. . . . For instance, when a conscious value, say a transference, decreases or actually disappears, you immediately look for the substitute formation, expecting to see an equivalent value spring up somewhere else.
>
> (CW 8/35)

For Jung, this movement of energy between forms had a goal: "The theory of development cannot do without the final point of view. Even Darwin . . . worked with final concepts, such as adaptation" (CW 8/42).

Jung also considered the principle of constancy, or entropy. For him, entropy was complementary to the principle of equivalence. Whereas the principle of equivalence concerned the *movement* of psychic energy, entropy concerned its *intensity*. Jung saw the equalization of intensities as stabilizing. For example, he wrote,

> The principle of entropy is known to us only as a principle of partial processes which make up a relatively closed system. The psyche, too, can

> be regarded as such a relatively closed system, in which transformations of energy lead to an equalization of differences. . . . Psychologically, we can see this process at work in the development of a lasting and relatively unchanging attitude.
>
> (CW 8/49)

Jung saw this as a "leveling process" which brings stability to the oscillations between opposites in the psyche.

Conflict as dynamic energy

In the energic paradigm, energy exists in a polarized structure that is inherently in conflict. Conflict, and the vicissitudes of the tension arising out of these opposing forces, defines the energic frame of reference.

The notion of 'conflict' in depth psychology has two roots. The first is the general movement in psychology in the 19th century away from philosophy to medical and physiological models of the mind, and more specifically, the model Freud developed in his *Scientific Project*, which ascribes qualities of the physiological system to the mental system. Although this work was never published in Freud's lifetime, he nevertheless retained its energic assumptions in all his later work. The second root involved the focus on one-person psychology at this point in history; the emphasis on intrapersonal dynamics rather than interpersonal or relational dynamics reinforced a model of the mind as functional components that emphasized the mechanical nature of the psyche.

In Jung's work, he approaches the psyche from both the relational (two-person psychology) and the 'mechanical' (one-person psychology) although there is a tendency in his use of the ego to follow the conflict model in a structural theory of the mind. This is especially evident in his early work when his theory is based in an energic paradigm. However, even as he emphasizes a more philosophical attitude in his works and speaks of 'opposites', there is still the underlying assumption of conflict. Even in his last long work, *Mysterium Coniunctionis*, for example, he characterizes the dynamic nature of the psyche as confrontational (CW 14/1).

Psychological determinism and causality

This is a basic assumption that the work of the psyche is reactive; in other words, the psyche reacts to noxious stimuli and produces a reaction of either discharge or repression. The energic paradigm then looks at the psyche as historical – that what has come before leaves its traces in the mind through repressions or other defensive actions. Another principle of an energic paradigm would be, then, *causality*: the idea that behavior and emotions are caused by an internal (or external experience internalized) effect that occurs prior to that effect.

The sense that whatever emotion or behavior happening now has an antecedent was also a topic in philosophy. Especially influential to Jung was Kant's category of causality, which Jung cites in his *Zofingia Lectures*. As Nagy (1991) writes,

> By the term 'category of causality' Jung means the inner need to feel that there is an orderly life process and that there are explanations for things that happen. . . . [Jung] is aware of Hume's challenge concerning the meaning of causal terms and responds on one level by insisting that whether or not we can perceive causal sequences we nevertheless need to believe in their existence.
>
> (p. 88, n. 28)

Physicists and Darwinian biologists did not adopt 'causality' as a principle, according to Nagy, because it implies a 'divine order' that they rejected for the notion of randomness and 'chance' in nature. As she states, "Schopenhauer and more especially Von Hartmann subsumed both teleological final causes and mechanistic causality under the higher aegis of the Will, thinking thus to solve the problem" (Nagy, 1991, p. 88, n. 28).

Freud derived his assumption of psychological determinism and causality from his observations of hysterical symptoms but also from his background in Helmholtzian principles (Meissner, 2000): as stated earlier, Helmholtz was a physiologist whose works on biophysics Freud admired (Sulloway, 1979). In the Helmholtzian model, there was an emphasis on the individual cell or organism. Evolutionary biology and physics of the 19th century (as well as the modern physics of chaos theory, I might add) were concerned with the concept of chance, as opposed to causality, because they were dealing with the actions and reactions of species and elements interacting in groups. In complex systems, they suggest, randomness is a greater factor than causality. This difference in viewpoint between randomness and causality has its parallel in the intrapersonal versus interpersonal/relational viewpoints.

Experimental theorists

Gustav Theodor Fechner

Gustav Theodor Fechner, born in 1801 in Großsärchen, Prussia, and educated in medicine in Leipzig, combined his interest in physiology and physics with metaphysics when he began experiments in psychophysiology in as early as 1850. He published his groundbreaking work, *Elemente der Psychophysik*, in 1860. The aim of this work was no less than the establishment of an exact science that could describe the functional relationship between physical and mental phenomena. His philosophical message, which he believed he had found a way to demonstrate but was largely ignored in favor of his methodological innovations, was that mind and matter were in essence different ways of conceiving of the same reality. He was cited by Jung as the father of experimental psychology (CW 7/407) and one of the first scientists to recognize the existence of an unconscious and view it as an empirical concept. It has also been said that Gustav Theodor Fechner introduced the principle of conservation of energy into psychology.

Fechner, according to Ellenberger (1956), was one of the major influences on Freud as he developed an energic concept in psychoanalysis. Fechner reworked the theories of Helmholtz into a form that could be applied to organic life (Sulloway, 1979, p. 66). Jung would have inherited Fechnerian concepts from Freud as he adopted more medical/materialistic concepts of science and psychology and allied himself initially with Bleuler and Freud.

Nagy (1991) sees Fechner's influence on Jung as naturally occurring, "in as much as depth psychology as a field is partly defined in terms of its concern for the interaction between conscious and the unconscious psyche". The influence of Fechner is especially evident in three areas. First, in the economic view of the psyche, that it is a relatively closed system of energic potentials; second, in the dynamic view, that there is an interaction between the components of the psyche; and third, in the topographical view, that there is a "threshold of excitation marking a boundary between known (conscious) and unknown (unconscious) psychic areas" (p. 283).

H.L.F. von Helmholtz

It has been said that Helmholtz profoundly altered the scientific disciplines of physiology and physics in the second half of the 19th century, an influence that extended to the fields of medicine and psychology. Even more influential than his specific contributions to science (which were considerable), however, was his articulation of the nature of scientific inquiry itself. Heidelberger (1995, p. 835) described him as a leading figure in shaping the philosophy of science during the second half of the 19th century.

His basic and essential theoretical and philosophical approach to scientific investigation was empiricism. Empiricism for Helmholtz meant "experimental interactionism" (Cahan, 1993, p. 463): only by actively interfering with nature through experimentation can one determine its true reality and cause. Observation alone does not inform the scientist about external reality because it was too subjective. Phenomenological data did not offer information as to man's true nature (Cahan, 1993, p. 185).

The scope of psychology for Helmholtz, however, did not extend beyond what could be observed and measured; anything else was experimentally inaccessible:

> Matter as such does not exhibit qualitative differences. If we talk of different matters we posit their diversity as resulting from the diversity of

> their effects, i.e., their forces. The only change that matter as such can therefore undergo is a spatial one, i.e., motion.
>
> (Cahan, 1993, p. 467)

Wilhelm Wundt

Another pioneer in experimental psychology and one whom Jung described as one of his primary influences (CW 18/1737) was Wilhelm Wundt. Born in 1832 in Neckarau in Baden-Württemberg, Wundt completed his medical studies in Heidelberg in 1855. After a year of further studies in Berlin, he returned to Heidelberg and became an assistant to Hermann von Helmholtz. After experimental work on sense perception, Wundt published a series of articles in 1862 *(Beiträge zur Theorie der Sinnwahrnehmung)*, which introduced his plan for experimental psychology. He rejected the metaphysical methodology of the philosophers, and instead argued for an empirically based study of consciousness with a particular emphasis on experimentation.

In 1873, Wundt published his first volume of *Principles of Physiological Psychology*, the first textbook on the subject. Eventually to run to four volumes for a total of 2,035 pages, *Principles* was even called 50 years later "the most important work in modern psychology" (Boring, 1929, p. 317). In his introduction, Wundt described the book as an attempt to "show the connexion between two sciences": physiology and psychology. He went on to say,

> Physiology is concerned with all those phenomena of life that present themselves to us in sense perception as bodily processes, and accordingly form part of that total environment which we name the external world. Psychology, on the other hand, seeks to give account of the interconnexion of processes which are evinced by our own consciousness, or which we infer from such manifestations of the bodily life in other creatures as indicate the presence of a consciousness similar to our own.
>
> (Wundt, 1902, p. 1)

Wundt went on to propose this 'new science', which stood at the border of physiology and psychology, be known as 'experimental psychology'.

Principles was often cited by Jung, and in important ways. For example, Jung followed Wundt in his definition of *affect, apperception*, and *assimilation*, and in the distinction between *feeling* and *sensation*. In a more direct fashion, Jung adopted Wundt's psychophysiological model through his work with the galvanometer and the pneumograph in his association experiments, which led to the complex theory.

In understanding Wundt's concepts of psychic energy, it is important to keep in mind his subtle comparison of physical and psychical energy. Matter and mind do not mirror each other or act in corresponding ways, but rather follow the same global laws with the difference that the energy of the physical world is objective while the energy of the psychical world is subjective:

> Physical measurements have to do with objective masses, forces, energies. . . . Psychical measurements, which are concerned with the comparison of psychical components and their resultants, have to do with subjective values and ends. The subjective value of the whole may increase in comparison with its components; its purpose may be different and higher than theirs without any changes in the masses, forces, and energies concerned.
>
> (Wundt, 1902, p. 400)

The crucial difference according to Wundt is that while physical energy deals with quantitative values, psychical energy deals with qualitative values. Wundt thus equates psychical energy with subjective psychological values (as Jung would many years later). Because of the nature of psychological values, as opposed to objective physical measurements, there can be psychical effects that contradict the laws of physical reality but still are reconciled with it. The connection between mind and matter is a relationship, not an equivalence:

> We can not only reconcile the increase in psychical energy with the constancy of physical energy as accepted in the natural sciences, but we find in the two reciprocally supplementary standards for the judgment of our total experience. The increase of psychical energy is not seen in its right light until it is recognized as the reverse, subjective side of physical constancy.
>
> (Wundt, 1902, p. 401)

Wundt points out there are no contradictions between the law of conservation of energy in the natural sciences and the idea of a "creative synthesis" in the psyche; they are simply different ways of looking at the same content of experience (p. 399).

It cannot be said that Wundt equates the laws of the psyche with the laws of natural science in the same way Freud did later, for example. However, Wundt does emphasize a relationship between matter and mind in which corresponding fundamental principles are observed. These principles would be causality (the idea that all experience, physical and mental, has reason and consequence), constancy (physical and mental experience do not contradict one another when physical energy remains constant and psychical energy increases, but rather express different aspects of an identical experience), and opposition (the fundamental division of experience into subjective and objective components).

Medical and psychoanalytic theorists

In the same period that this work of building up experimental psychology was proceeding, clinicians in asylums were confronted by desperate cases and had little in the way of concrete treatment to offer these patients. In 1900 when Jung began his professional training as a psychiatrist, the psychiatric asylums in Europe were mainly warehouses for chronic schizophrenics and for dements and paretics suffering from the effects of neurosyphilis and alcoholism (Shorter, 1997, Ch. 2 and p. 65). At the turn of the century at the Burghölzli, for example, nearly a quarter of the patients had irreparable brain damage (Hayman, 1999, p. 54). Not only was treatment not available beyond the use of restraints and isolation cells, the wards themselves could be dangerous places due to violent or agitated patients. Clearly there was a gap between the human situation for the severely ill in the asylums and the discoveries of the psychophysiology laboratory.

Emil Kraepelin

In this environment, a revolution of sorts was taking place in the latter part of the 19th century in the field of psychiatry led by Emil Kraepelin. A northern German who studied brain physiology in Munich, Kraepelin became interested in psychology and studied with Wilhelm Wundt at his famous psychological laboratory in Leipzig in 1882. He became an asylum physician and later a professor of psychiatry at Heidelberg University. There at the university clinic, as I have described earlier, Kraepelin began keeping notes on his patients' histories and their clinical outcomes, as well as later incorporating measures of mental functioning into his patient workup. With these innovations he developed a system of classification of mental disorders based on clinical course and outcome.

This shifted the focus of the psychiatry profession away from simple physical management and toward collecting and categorizing data about patients (Kraepelin's, 1893 textbook, *Psychiatrie: Ein Lehrbuch Fur Studerende und Aertze*, included, for example, the diagnosis 'Dementia Praecox' which was altered by his student Eugen Bleuler in 1908 to the present term 'schizophrenia'). The emphasis on categories and course and outcome descriptions moved the psychiatric profession toward a medical model (as opposed to the emerging biopsychosocial model of the physiology labs, an area that was later to become the province of the psychoanalysts; Shorter, 1997, p. 108). Within the medical model, insanity became another form of illness for the medical practitioners to study, to diagnose, and in time, perhaps, to treat. This possibility of treatment offered hope to patients and their doctors.

It was in this professional atmosphere in general and at the Burghölzliklinik in particular where Jung began his apprenticeship. In 1900 the Burghölzli was, in his words, where, "[p]sychiatry teachers were not interested in what the patient had to say but rather in how to make a diagnosis or how to describe symptoms and to compile statistics" (Jung, 1983a, p. 135). Kraepelin's revolution had thus reached Zürich, an attitude of medical cataloging later to be an object of Jung's disdain.

Eugen Bleuler

The newly installed chief at the hospital, Eugen Bleuler was an exception to the status quo in 19th century Europe. He was progressive, open to new ideas in the understanding and treatment of mental illness, and he became a leader in his field, even cultivated by Freud as an ally. His prominence as well as his role as Jung's first teacher of psychiatry proved him to be a major influence on Jung's developing attitudes toward mental illness in general and psychic energy in particular.

Eugen Bleuler, born in 1857 in Zollikon near Zürich, had studied with Charcot in Paris before returning to Switzerland. After a series of staff psychiatrist positions at various Swiss mental hospitals, he was appointed director of the Burghölzli in 1898. Bleuler was known as a humane doctor who instructed the assistant doctors to see their patients twice a day and write done what was said (Hayman, 1999, p. 55). Bleuler was even receptive to the new theories of Freud and had, for example, written a review of Breuer and Freud's *Studies on Hysteria* in 1896 prior to his position at the Burghölzli (Donn, 1988, p. 56). Freud's ideas seemed to offer a way to understand and, more important with his talking cure, to treat the seemingly hopeless mentally ill.

Bleuler led Jung back to Freud. Although he had read *Interpretation of Dreams* in 1900, Jung laid it aside at that time because, as he said, "I could not grasp it" (Jung, 1983a, p. 169). In 1903 he became reacquainted and deeply interested in Freud's book after being asked by Bleuler to report on it for a staff meeting. Hayman (1999) quotes Jung from an interview in 1957 describing his reaction to rereading *Interpretation of Dreams*: "I studied the book very attentively . . . I thought 'this is a masterpiece – full of future'. I had no ideas of my own; I just was beginning" (p. 56).

Supported by Bleuler, Jung set up a laboratory for experimental psychopathology at the Burghölzli in 1902 and began listening to patients as they were attached to the galvanometer and the pneumograph, a kind of early lie detector–type apparatus. These experiments were to investigate the physiological reactions to psychical stimuli, specifically words deemed to provoke varying degrees of arousal.

These researches, called the association experiments, brought Jung attention for his work but also led Jung to researchers with similar outlooks, most notably one of his early mentors, Sigmund Freud. Freud became another one of Jung's strong influences in using an energic frame of reference to think about the mind.

Sigmund Freud

Freud had begun his career as a neurophysiologist but turned to psychology by way of neurology. Because of Freud's professional background and training in physiology in the Helmholtz school of medicine, his understanding of the energic mechanisms of the psyche were grounded in the scientific principles of the day, especially late 19th century biology and physics. As opposed to Jung, whose energic paradigm was partly influenced by the bio-experimental and Kraepelinian interests of Bleuler and from his own clinical experience at the Burghölzli with the mentally ill, Freud's early theoretical works display a more purely medical and physiological orientation.

Because of Freud's particular influence on Jung's ego concept, I will briefly summarize Freud's ego theory. The ego concept in Freud's works was not born fully worked out and elaborated, but rather evolved over time as his thinking about the psyche developed. Meissner (2000) has divided the historical development of Freud's ego concept into four phases:

1 A phase ending in 1897 that coincided with the development of his early psychoanalytic formulations.
2 A phase from 1897 to 1923 in which Freud developed his psychoanalytic theory proper. (This phase and the previous would have been the theoretical material available to Jung as he collaborated with Freud.)
3 A phase from 1923 to 1937 in which Freud elaborated a specific theory of ego and in which in fact the ego held a prominent position in his overall psychoanalytic theory.
4 A phase after the death of Freud in which a general psychology of the ego was developed by his followers.

PHASE I — WORK UP TO 1897

In this phase of his work, Freud was still working out his ideas. He had not abandoned his sexual seduction and trauma hypothesis as the origin of neurosis and so there was an emphasis on the role of external reality rather than instinctually derived and fantasy-driven experience.

At this stage the ego was not precisely defined, but rather it was part of the area of consciousness distinct from the wishes and impulses of the repressed unconscious. According to the topographical model of the psyche held by Freud at this time, there existed a barrier between the conscious and unconscious area. This barrier was a defense against unacceptable wishes and impulses, and acted as the repressing agent. In his manuscript *Project for a Scientific Psychology*, Freud describes the ego as "an organization . . . whose presence interferes with passages [of quality (of excitation)]" (SE I, p. 323). The ego, according to Freud stores the psychical, or drive, energy (p. 323) – that is, cathexis – needed for specific action as it arises from the unconscious.

The ego can then act to inhibit the drive energy and repress it, repression being synonymous with defense in Freud's theory at this stage. In this way the ego had a regulatory role in upholding conscious moral ideals against the unacceptable sexual impulses and wishes stimulated by sexual seduction and trauma. Thus in this phase of Freud's theory, the ego was essentially the agent of, if not the barrier between, conscious and unconscious.

PHASE 2 – 1897 TO 1923

In these years, Freud was working out several contradictions and inconsistencies inherent in his topographical model, which would lead later to a clearer definition of ego. The first problem concerned the vicissitudes of the instincts (SE 14, 1915) and narcissism (SE 14, 1914). Instincts could be repressed, reversed, sublimated, or turned onto the self. The two issues here are (1) what is the psychical agent effecting these actions and (2) what is the difference or similarity between this agent and the self. A second problem is Freud's introduction of the ideas of 'ego-instincts' into his theory in 1910 (SE 11) and its elaboration in his essay 'On Narcissism'. Finally, the issue of anxiety brought Freud back to the role of defenses in the formation of neurosis. As he initially formulated his theory, anxiety was a return of repressed ideas through somatic channels. In this first model, then, by removing the repression there would be a reduction in anxiety. However, his patients felt more anxious as their repressions were stripped away, not less, and Freud needed an explanation for this.

Problem 1 – The vicissitudes of the instincts and narcissism Freud arrived at the conclusion that there were four actions the instincts could take when blocked. Three of these (reversal into the opposite, repression, sublimation) raise the question of the agent responsible, the 'motive force', in Freud's words, for these defensive actions. Here the ego is implied because of its opposing position to the instincts and yet the topographical model assigns the censoring functions to the region of the subconscious.

The last vicissitude of the instincts, turning on the subject's own self, raises a separate issue about the relationship between ego (the opposing force) and self. In his essay on the vicissitudes of the instincts, Freud refers to the ego as *das ich*, the 'I', and refers to 'one's own self' as *die eigene Person*. There is an implied differentiation between the intra-psychic defensive agency that interacts with the instincts, and the subjective representation of oneself, the self. However, there is no sense at this stage that one is subordinate to the other; indeed there is no clear sense of what is the relationship of the ego to the self.

Problem 2 – 'Ego-Instincts' At this stage in his work, Freud makes a distinction between instincts of the unconscious, the 'libidinal drives', and the ego-instincts. In his 1915 essay 'Instincts and Their Vicissitudes' (SE 14), Freud describes the ego-instincts as instincts for self-preservation and aggression. The later quality is based on the ego's reaction to all that causes unpleasure, "The ego hates, abhors and pursues with intent to destroy all objects which are a source of unpleasurable feeling for it . . ." (p. 136). Self-preservation is an instinct of and for the individual, as opposed to the libidinal instincts, which are directed toward preservation of the species. In Freud's theory, therefore, the root of neurosis (p. 121) was a conflict between "the claims of sexuality" (a collective phenomenon) and "those of the ego" (the individual factor).

The concept of ego-instinct was problematic, however. One problem was the aggressive instinct. By placing aggressive impulses (impulses to control, defensive tendencies) in the ego sphere, Freud would be altering his basic criterion of an instinct – a mechanism for discharge of energic tension. As an ego-instinct, aggression was now an aim rather than a primal source. A second problem with aggression as an ego-instinct was that destructive tendencies did not always serve self-preservative purposes. They were at times, as in masochistic and self-injuring patients, directed toward the self. These problems were worked out in the next phase of Freud's work.

PHASE 3 – 1923 TO 1937

Freud's work *The Ego and the Id* was published in 1923. In this work he introduced the ego for the first time as a structural entity: as an organization of mental processes and functions that was primarily organized around the perceptual-conscious system. Also, he conceived of structures in the ego for resistance and unconscious defense. The ego at this stage was passive and weak, functioning as a result of pressures from the id, the superego, and reality. Freud (1933, p. 77) wrote, for example, regarding the ego, that its relationship to the id was "that of a rider to his horse". In this formulation, the ego was dependent on id's forces, but somehow differentiated out of id.

The radical changes Freud made in theory of ego in this phase were as follows:

1 In *Inhibitions, Instincts, and Anxiety* (SE 20, 1926) Freud repudiated the conception of ego as subservient to the id.
2 The reality principle is now elaborated and an adaptation function is added to the ego concept. This allows the ego to curb instinctual drives when drives would lead to real danger. In this way the ego could convert passively experienced anxiety into active anticipation.
3 The ego at this point is therefore conceived:

   - As a powerful regulatory force responsible for integration and control of behavior.

- In terms of its adaptive function. The role of reality is brought to center stage: the concern now is with the adaptive function of the ego – but this is limited to ego's role in avoiding danger.
- In terms of its roots. In 1937 in *Analysis, Terminable & Interminable* (SE 23), Freud makes explicit the idea that the ego has independently inherited roots that are free of the inherited roots of the instincts. This idea would be taken up later by Hartmann as the basis for his theory of primary ego autonomy.

PHASE 4 – AFTER 1937

After Freud's death in 1939, his daughter Anna took up the Freudian mantle, concentrating on the psychology of ego defenses. Hartmann would focus after Freud's death on issues surrounding ego autonomy and the problems of adaptation. Meissner calls this period the 'egoization' of psychoanalysis. With the focus on adaptation and ego autonomy, the emphasis became normal development rather than pathology.

The symbolic paradigm

In 1935, Jung wrote an introduction to a book about the dream problem in modern psychology. In his introduction, he summarizes the rationale for the transition from an empirical to a phenomenological view of the psyche:

> For a long time it seemed as though experimental and medical psychologists could get along with purely scientific methods. But the view gradually gained ground that a critique of certain ideals originating in the humanistic disciplines was not out of place . . . it turned out that the principles which had hitherto held unlimited sway over men's minds were of a purely rationalistic or materialistic nature and, in spite of their 'scientific' pretensions, had to be subjected to a philosophical criticism because the object of their judgment was the psyche itself. The psyche is an extremely complex factor, so fundamental to all premises that no judgment can be regarded as 'purely empirical' but must first indicate the premises by which it judges. Modern psychology can no longer disguise the fact that the object of its investigation is its own essence, so that in certain respects there can be no 'principles' or valid judgments at all, but only phenomenology – in other words, sheer experience.
>
> (CW 18/1738)

According to Thomas Kuhn in his landmark work *The Structure of Scientific Revolutions*, there is a significant shift in paradigm when there is a change not in methods or standards of solution to a scientific problem, but rather a change in the subject of the problem itself. He said, for example,

> Political revolutions are inaugurated by a growing sense . . . that existing institutions have ceased adequately to meet the problems posed by an environment that they in part created. In much the same way, scientific revolutions are inaugurated by a growing sense . . . that an existing paradigm has ceased to function adequately in the exploration of an aspect of nature to which that paradigm itself had previously led the way.
>
> (Kuhn, 1962, p. 92)

Jung saw that the existing energic paradigm of experimental psychology and psychoanalysis did not adequately explain the psyche as he observed it. When he then changed the object of observation in psychology from the objective formulation of psychical phenomena to the phenomenological experience itself, he fundamentally changed the paradigm of psychology; a scientific revolution in Kuhn's sense.

As was described previously, the energic paradigm characteristic of the field of psychology of the 19th century was based on scientific assumptions borrowed from the physical sciences. The psyche itself was 'observed' and investigated 'objectively': the point of reference being outside the subject. Jung turned this around and instead placed the point of reference inside the subject; the images and emotional experiences of the subject became the objects of investigation. These inner experiences were facts just as real as reaction times. This shift in thinking on Jung's part, away from the scientific and medical developments of the 19th century and the energic paradigm, to a paradigm based on psychical phenomenology and inner experience, characterizes the paradigm that was to dominate his mature psychological theory.

From a scientific perspective, the symbol and the symbolic process represent a viewpoint toward the psyche incompatible with the energic paradigm; the symbolic paradigm assumes intentionality and purpose more associated with philosophy and religion than with materialism. Fundamentally, the symbolic paradigm is based on principles of relationship and relatedness rather than the fundamental laws of science. Relational concepts in current psychological thought are based on the basic philosophy that human behavior derives from a powerful need for interpersonal connection to others. Relatedness, in this model, is the environment but also the means for individuals to grow into themselves: we as humans are "a social product" (Mitchell, 1988, p. 18).

The symbolic paradigm shares the basic assumption that relatedness is the means for growth but goes further. Jung describes a theory in which connection itself, interpersonal as well as intrapersonal, is a creative act that has implications beyond the growth of the individual, or even of society. Relatedness leads to manifestation of the symbol: a psychic image, according to Jung, not to be confused with a semeion. To explain the implications of this he wrote at one point: "In a certain sense the symbol has a life of its own which guides the subject and eases his task; but it cannot be invented or fabricated because the experience of it does not depend on our will" (Jung, letter to A. Zarine, 3 May 1939).

Therefore, I have chosen to call this paradigm symbolic rather than relational, because the mechanisms of relatedness and achieving relationship, in Jung's theory, are directed toward manifestation of the symbol rather than an end in themselves. The symbol itself is the therapeutic factor according to Jung: "So is healing given to us in the unlockable and ineffable symbol . . ." (letter to Schmid, 6 November 1915). But also, the symbol is the expression of an inner religious experience that has the quality of an "immanent vital force" (letter to Plachte, 10 January 1929). It wants, "to step over, as it were, into visible life, to take concrete shape. (The spirit shows its effective power only in the reshaping of matter)" (letter to Plachte, 10 January 1929). As Jung would later add in this letter,

> The symbol needs man for its development. But it grows beyond him, therefore it is called 'God', since it expresses a psychic situation of factor stronger than the ego (I call it the self [das *Selbst*]). This factor is pre-existent in the collective unconscious, yet powerless unless I experience it consciously; then it takes the lead.

Relationship, in other words, experienced between the ego and the Other consciously is the prerequisite for creation of the symbol. This approach then, which emphasizes the symbol's creation, is an attitude toward psychical phenomena outside the relational concepts of contemporary psychology and quite incompatible with the energic paradigm.

Lastly, the symbolic paradigm is an approach to psychical phenomenology and inner experience as described earlier, but it is also a way of understanding and working with the psyche. As a consequence, then, the clinical extension of Jung's symbolic approach was the development of methods and techniques for working with patients that focus on the inner experience and spontaneous image with the goal of personal growth and development as well as healing. These innovations of Jung in the symbolic paradigm are relevant to clinical understanding in work with the ego and consciousness.

Jung's influences

In contrast to the energic paradigm, which envisions psychic energy as a factor in the psyche which acts according to laws similar to those of natural science, the symbolic paradigm focuses on the dynamic power of symbols to act as transformers of psychic energy. Rather than energy flowing blindly, obeying mechanistic physical laws, in the symbolic paradigm there is an intention behind the flow of energy in the psyche, which has as its reason and goal the development and evolution of individual and human consciousness.

This is different from the causality of the energic paradigm, which sees the reason and goal of psychic energy as discharge or equilibrium.

Rather than look toward the schools of Wundt, Freud, and Janet for direction in this regard, Jung looked to the Romantic philosophers and alchemists. Philosophy and religious mysticism, that is, pre-scientific thinkers, rather than experimental psychology were for Jung most relevant for understanding the experience of the psyche.

Three pre-scientific systems of thought inform Jung's symbolic paradigm: first, the Christian mysticism of the 12th century monk Meister Eckhart; second, the 19th century philosophical movement *Naturphilosophie*; and third, alchemy and alchemical philosophy. These three 'humanistic disciplines' share certain attitudes and philosophies, which taken together characterize the basic tenets of the symbolic paradigm. These tenets can be summarized as follows:

1 The symbolic paradigm emphasizes the reality of the unseen world (psyche). In contrast to the energic paradigm that dismisses as unknowable that which is not available to the five senses, and beyond the Rationalists in philosophy who saw truth as knowable through human reason, the symbolic paradigm in various ways accepts and even values experience which is beyond physical reality or human understanding. This view gives weight and value to the unconscious, for example, as a reality in itself and not as a repository of conscious experience forgotten or repressed.
2 The symbolic paradigm also emphasizes the nature of man as a microcosm of the macrocosm. The secret of the soul of man lay in understanding the fundamental elements of nature and mankind. The romantic philosophers, such as Heyne, Schlegel, Creuzer, and Schilling, saw the universal symbols in myths and folklore, in dreams, and mental illness as "living forces and realities" (Ellenberger, 1970, p. 200). By understanding these universal elements in nature and man, one could approach the essential truth of the individual. Likewise, the spontaneous manifestations of nature in man (dreams, visions) were ways to study and understand nature and mankind.
3 Whereas the energic paradigm sees psychic energy as following a course dictated by quasi-physical laws (conservation of energy, the constancy principle) the symbolic paradigm sees psychic energy as having a teleological quality. The psychic energy in the individual is directed toward a purpose, has a reason unknown to consciousness. This idea of life following a course that demonstrated an unfolding of the personality or a series of metamorphoses was reflected, for example, in the popular novel form of the 19th century, the 'Bildungsroman'. One's life history had a developmental story behind it and this attitude may be, according to one author (Ellenberger, 1970, p. 200), what shapes the view of life as a whole.

4 The symbolic paradigm emphasizes the concept of polarity and complementarity as basic forms, as the basic mechanisms of nature and life. This concept is seen not only in the *Naturphilosophie* of von Schelling and others, but in eastern religion, in alchemy, and in Gnosticism and Christian mysticism. The corollary to this concept of polarity is the concept of unity resulting from union of opposites. For Jung the opposites were the most elemental structure of the psyche. The energy in the psyche was generated from opposites (CW 14/759–792).

Meister Eckhart

As an example of mystic literature that influenced Jung's ego concept, I will highlight the work of Meister Eckhart. A key figure in the history of Western mysticism, this 12th century monk and theologian had a revival of interest in his unconventional writings in the 19th century. Jung in his Collected Works refers to Eckhart's writings more than to those of any other Christian mystic and seems to have incorporated Eckhart's thinking into, among other things, his own concept of God and man. In Meister Eckhart, Jung saw a mind that understood what he himself was wrestling with (letter to Herbert Read, 12 September 1960). Jung appreciated Eckhart's insights into the relationship of man and God. He called him, in Psychological Types, the greatest thinker of the Middle Ages (CW 6/410).

Eckhart was part of "the bridge of the spirit" which spanned the "morass of world history" (Jung, letter to Max Rychner, 28 February 1932). In a 1958 letter (to Herbert E. Bowman, 18 June 1959), Jung, in a discussion of the Self, states, "In Europe . . . Meister Eckhart is about the first where the self begins to play a noticeable role".

The writings of Meister Eckhart especially influenced Jung in his reflections on the nature of God and the religious function in the psyche (CW 6/411). This influence can be seen in the paradigm Jung adopted as he sought to understand the phenomenology and inner experiences of the psyche.

The Dominican monk Meister Eckhart was born in a village near Thuringia, Germany, around 1260. He studied at the Dominican monastery in Cologne and later at the University of Paris. He returned to Germany about 1294 and had positions as vicar or administrator in various towns and provinces thereafter and was also a spiritual leader in the Dominican order. An inquisitional process was begun against him in the 1320s for his alleged heretical teachings, although the accusations were in the context of political intrigues within the church. A vast dossier was compiled, composed of extracts from his teachings and sermons, and in 1327, he was found guilty of heresy. His appeals and responses to the charges, part of his collected writings today, were rejected by the papal tribunal in Avignon and he died about 1329, an "unyielding heretic" (Colledge and McGinn, 1988, p. 15).

Eckhart's writings were not suppressed after his death but rather were copied and studied by the Dominicans and later by the Carthusians throughout the Middle Ages. His works were preserved, despite the papal declaration of heresy, because he remained revered by members of his order who saw the papal judgment as profoundly wrong. His works were rediscovered in the early 19th century as interest in religious mysticism returned to the mainstream.

ECKHART'S IMPORTANCE TO JUNG

The reality of the unseen world Eckhart saw no fundamental contradiction between the truths of revelation and truths that are arrived at through reason. This distinction, argued at the time by Thomas Aquinas and supported by the philosophy of Aristotle, differentiated between what is known in the world through science and through reason, and what is inaccessible to human reason but nevertheless 'truth' because it is revealed in scripture (for example, that Jesus is the son of God). Eckhart believed natural and revealed truths coexist. He followed the great Jewish thinker Maimonides in his idea of finding proof of revealed truth in the 'hidden meanings' of sacred text, a kind of early literary deconstructionism. Eckhart said for example in his commentary on Exodus: "Sacred scripture frequently tells a story in such a way that it also contains and suggests mysteries, teaches the nature of things, furnishes and sets in order moral actions" (Colledge and McGinn, 1988, p. 29).

In this sense Eckhart's thoughts support the concept in the symbolic paradigm of the reality of the world beyond that known through empirical study or arrived at through reason. While philosophy emphasized knowledge through reason, Eckhart accepts as valid and true that which is revealed, whether in scripture and beyond human reason to grasp (such as the concept of the Trinity, or Jesus as son of God) or, even further, that which is hidden in scripture and reveals an inner meaning. As another example of his method of assigning reality to what is not visible, Eckhart wrote in the introduction to his 'Commentary on the Gospel of Saint John':

> This is what is said here: 'In the beginning was the Word' [John 1:1]. In interpreting this Word and everything else that follows my intention is the same as in all my works – to explain what the holy Christian faith and the two Testaments maintain through the help of the natural arguments of the philosophers. 'God's invisible attributes are seen and understood from the creation of the world in the things that he has made, as well as his everlasting power (that is, the Son), and his divinity (that is, the Holy Spirit)', as the Gloss on Romans, chapter one says. . . . It is the intention of this work to show how the truths of natural principles, conclusions and properties are well intimated for him 'who has ears to

> hear' [Matthew 13:43] in the very words of sacred scripture, which are interpreted through these natural truths.
>
> (Colledge and McGinn, 1988, p. 122–123)

In this passage Eckhart emphasizes the notion that truth is not just what one is told explicitly ("the Word"), but also what one senses ("has ears to hear") and intuits ("God's invisible attributes"). Jung wrote that Eckhart was the greatest thinker of his age, a time when "a belief in the efficacy of individual revelation and individual knowledge" replaced regula fidei (conformity to dogma). Jung takes this point to develop his idea about the religious function (CW 6/411). Jung saw Eckhart as restoring man's "inner affinity with God"; that man and God have a "reciprocal and essential" relationship "whereby man can be understood as a function of God, and God as a psychological function of man" (CW 6/412). God was not an abstract or distant principle, but an unseen psychological reality.

Man as microcosm of macrocosm A central point in much of Eckhart's writings, and what brought him official condemnation during his life, was his doctrine of 'the birth of the Son in the soul'. In his 'Commentary on the Gospel of Saint John', Eckhart makes the argument that God, because He is eternal and beyond temporality, is eternally giving birth to His Son. The soul's ground is also God's ground and therefore God is always giving birth to the Son in the soul. For Eckhart the soul is individual and so therefore each of us has the divine born in us: "The Father gives birth to his Son in eternity, equal to himself . . . yet I say more: He has given birth to him in my soul" (Eckhart Sermon 6, in Colledge and McGinn, 1988, p. 187).

This was so controversial to the Church at the time because it implied a union between God and man. This contradicted the Church's official dogma, which stated man was God's creation in his likeness, that is, separate. Eckhart's idea of the 'individual', each of us, containing God, that in addition to our individual existence there was an eternal and divine element – this was a revolution.

Jung cites just this idea, of man containing the universal, eternal, divine element, in his discussions of man as microcosm of macrocosm. In his essay 'The Philosophical Tree' (CW 13, 1945), Jung writes,

> Zosimos's 'whole' is a microcosm, a reflection of the universe in the smallest particle of matter, and is therefore in everything organic and inorganic. Because the microcosm is identical with the macrocosm, it attracts the latter and thus brings about a kind of apocatastasis, a restoration of all individua to the original wholeness. Thus 'every grain becomes wheat, and all metal gold', as Meister Eckhart says; and the little, single individual becomes the 'great man', the homo maximus or Anthropos, i.e. the self.
>
> (CW 13/372)

This attitude, that man contains the divine element, and even further that man can have a relationship with this 'other' element, has unmistakable implications for Jung's ego theory. The system of the psyche would necessarily contain an individual conscious element, embodied by the center of consciousness, the ego, which would be the personal element that relates to the divine element. This takes the ego out of a structural role, one in which it perceives, reacts, and processes experience, to a role where it is a partner to God. Man as a microcosm of the macrocosm also means that God and man create the world together, whether this creation resides in the soul of man, or as outer values and meaning in the world of man.

Teleological aspect Eckhart's idea of man containing God as elemental in his soul has a teleological aspect. Simply put, man is completing God's work on earth. Eckhart wrote that there is a reason and purpose in man's soul:

> One ought also to know that beyond any doubt even natural, human virtue is so excellent and so strong that there is no external work too difficult for it or great enough for it to manifest itself in it and through it and to form itself in it. And there is an interior work, which can not be confined or comprehended by time or place; and in this work is what is divine and like God, whom neither time nor place confine, for he is everywhere and present in all time. . . . And no one can hinder this interior working of virtue, anymore than anyone can hinder God.
>
> (Eckhart, in Colledge and McGinn, 1988, p. 225)

Eckhart makes the point in this passage that the source of man's virtue and good works is God, and that even more, these works are a manifestation of God in human reality. He expands this by discussing the parable of the stone:

> Man is like the stone that fulfills its function as it was created – he can not turn away from the inclination in him to want what is good and flee what is evil. Man's nature is not a random act, in other words, but a direction instilled by God.
>
> (Colledge and McGinn, 1988, p. 225)

Jung said in 1935, "[T]he psychic process, like any other life-process, is not just a causal sequence, but is also a process with a teleological orientation" (CW 7/210). Just as Eckhart saw a reason and goal in the life of man, that is, to glorify God by continuing His work on earth, so too Jung saw a reason and goal in man's psychological life: "The creator sees himself through the eyes of man's consciousness" (letter to Kelsey, 3 May 1958). In the symbolic paradigm this teleological orientation, the inner purpose that directs one's life toward a goal, is connected to this incarnation of God in the world of consciousness.

Polarity as basic force In physics the concept of polarity describes an electro-dynamic system that can create energy through dynamic polarization. It is a dynamic of mere mechanical value, however, and cannot evolve beyond its positive–negative valance. In contrast, the concept of polarity and complementarity in the symbolic paradigm includes the qualities of emotion and human development. Jung emphasized the emotional component, for example, in the first sentence of his work *Mysterium Coniunctionus*: "The factors which come together in the coniunctio are conceived as opposites, either confronting one another in enmity or attracting one another in love" (CW 14/1). Human development flows from this encounter. The central polarity in Eckhart was likewise a pair infused with emotionally meaningful dynamism as well as an implicit path toward a goal: the transcendent-immanent relationship between God and man.

For Eckhart, God's creations can only exist in and of this relationship. He wrote in his 'Sermons and Lectures on Ecclesiasticus', for example, "Every created being radically and positively possesses existence, life and wisdom from and in God and not in itself" (Eckhart, in Colledge and McGinn, 1988, p. 33). In other words, all beings are inextricably linked to the divine reality. God in the God–man relationship has two aspects according to Eckhart. First, He is transcendent; that is, His being is beyond existence in the same way or manner that his creations exist. Second, however, God is also immanent in that His existence is indeed the existence of all things and therefore residing in nature and the human soul. In his sermon 'Justi vivent in aeternum', Eckhart made his famous heretical statement, "What is life? God's being is my life. If my life is God's being, then God's existence must be my existence and God's is-ness is my is-ness, neither less nor more" (Colledge and McGinn, 1988, p. 187). The notion of unity of God and man was even more forcefully expressed by Eckhart in Sermon 15, "Truly you are the hidden God (Is. 45:15) in the ground of the soul, where God's ground and the soul's ground are one ground" (Colledge and McGinn, 1988, p. 192). Rather than advocating pantheism, which the idea of God residing in all his creations suggests, Eckhart consistently makes a distinction between the God of absolute transcendent reality (*ens absolutum*) who does not have 'formally inherent existence' (since God is beyond questions of existence or non-existence), and the immanent God who is the cause of all existence.

Thus there is a paradox in the relationship between God and man. Man exists in relation to God as His creation and as such, separate, and yet man is of God, part of God's totality. Rather than looking at the God–man relationship as a straightforward polarity, Eckhart sees God and man as simultaneously relating to each other as separate entities and at the same time one in unity. God is the Other; there is a 'categorical gulf' (Colledge and McGinn, 1988, p. xiv) between man and God. But also, God alone is real, in Eckhart's thought, and we are real only where we partake in His presence or being.

Therefore, following Eckhart, there is a paradox between the part of us that is continuous with God and the part that is categorically different.

This paradox described by Eckhart between our inner divine nature, where we are 'the hidden God', and our profane being absolutely separate from God, expresses the nature of polarity and the ego–Self relationship as Jung uses it in his symbolic paradigm. It is not a simple on–off, positive–negative dynamic, but rather a living struggle between man as man and man as God's expression of existence. God is equally the Other and the 'I'. There is no final resolution to the problem of this type of polarity, only a deeper grasp of it, a sense of being in and out of this experience. For Eckhart, to realize what cannot be realized is to begin to enter into the inner experience of one's own divine ground (Colledge and McGinn, 1988, p. 31).

For Jung, Eckhart's concept of the God–man relationship explains the creative nature of the relationship between man's consciousness and the unconscious. In Eckhart's description of God, Jung sees the concepts "God as a psychological value" (CW 6/417) and "God as a psycho-dynamic state" (CW 6/418). Jung quotes Eckhart thus:

> If any should ask me, Wherefore do we pray, wherefore do we fast, wherefore do we all manner of good works, wherefore are we baptized, wherefore did God become man, I would answer, So that God may be born in the soul and the soul again in God. Therefore were the scriptures written. Therefore did God create the whole world, that God might be born in the soul and the soul again in God. The innermost nature of all grain is wheat, and of all metal, gold, and of all birth, Man!
>
> (CW 6/427)

Jung interprets this passage as describing the essential creative nature of the God–man relationship. Since Jung associates (in 1920 when *Psychological Types* was written) the nature of the God–man relationship in Eckhart with the relationship between conscious man and the unconscious, this serves to emphasize the creative nature of the psychic polarity.

For Jung, what is created in this psychic polarity is the symbol: "The organ of perception, the soul, apprehends the contents of the unconscious, and, as the creative function, gives birth to its dynamis in the form of a symbol" (CW 6/426). The symbol then offers the conscious man an image that may be employed to form a new attitude and a "renewal of life" (CW 6/427), which Jung equates with Eckhart's previously mentioned idea of the soul giving birth to God.

There is one other aspect of Eckhart's God–man polarity that Jung uses to characterize the nature of the psychic polarity: God as immanent and God as transcendent. Jung notes the distinction Eckhart makes between God and the Godhead: God is a function of the soul, whereas the Godhead is the All, an all-pervasive creative power that does not know itself. For Eckhart, there is a movement of man between his relationship with God (God as immanent) and his relationship with the Godhead (God as transcendent; CW 6/428–429). Jung then associates this movement with the psychodynamic action of the ego and the unconscious. The ego relates to the unconscious as an object and separate, and then regresses and reunites with the unconscious to immerse itself in the "flood and source" (CW 6/430). This is the creative movement of the psyche according to Jung, similar to the idea of systole and diastole, but a movement that creates not only a new personal perspective or attitude in man, but also gives birth to God out of the Godhead, i.e. the unconscious dynamis is objectified.

Naturphilosophie *and Romantic philosophy*

Naturphilosophie, an offshoot of German Romantic philosophy, was founded by Friedrich Wilhelm von Schelling (1775–1854). Its influence on Jung's symbolic paradigm can be seen in the importance he gives philosophers of this school, such as Schelling, Carus, and von Hartmann, in his arguments for the understanding of the psyche in his 1933 *Modern Psychology: Notes on Lectures Given at the ETH*: Schelling formulated the idea that "the unconscious is the absolute foundation of consciousness" (Jung, 1933, p. 15), Carus "is the first to call the universal soul the unconscious and his works contain highly modern points of view with regard to it" (Jung, 1933, p. 22), Hartmann "conceives of the unconscious as the unity of will and idea, at the same time it is the active purposive foundation of the world of a divine and absolute nature" (Jung, 1933, p. 23). The eminent historian Ellenberger quotes Liebbrand for example as stating "C. G. Jung's teachings in the field of psychology are not intelligible if they are not connected with Schelling" (Ellenberger, 1970, p. 204).

THE REALITY OF THE UNSEEN WORLD

The idea of an unseen world in nature was central to *Naturphilosophie*. "Nature is visible Spirit, Spirit is invisible Nature" (Ellenberger, 1970, p. 202) sums up this attitude. Nature is not understood through physical or mechanical laws such as were being developed during and after the Enlightenment. Rather, *Naturphilosophie* saw an invisible world soul (*Weltseele*) as the origin of the concrete visible world as well as the world of man and consciousness. In this realm spiritual laws were analogous to physical laws and exploring one world led to understanding of the other (Ellenberger, 1970, p. 203).

Integral to this concept of *Weltseele* was the concept of primordial phenomena (*Urphänomene*). This harks back to the myth in Plato of the primordial human possessing both male and female characteristics. *Urphänomene* also refers to the world of the unconscious and its universal quality linking mankind to one another as well as to the natural world. For

Naturphilosophie the unconscious was no longer the place of "forgotten perceptions" (Ellenberger, 1970, p. 204) or memories but a realm of dreams and mysteries. C.G. Carus (1789–1869) wrote, for example, "The key to the knowledge of the nature of the Soul's conscious life lies in the realm of the unconscious" (Ellenberger, 1970, p. 207). Von Hartmann (Ellenberger, 1970, p. 210) describes the unconscious as three layers: (1) an absolute unconscious that was the substance of the universe, (2) a physiological unconscious out of which arises living beings, including man, and (3) a psychological unconscious that is the source of our mental life. Jung's later concepts about the collective unconscious and psychoid unconscious are clearly evident in these ideas.

MAN AS MICROCOSM OF THE MACROCOSM

Implied in the concepts of *Naturphilosophie* of *Weltseele* and *Urphänomene* was the idea that man had an inner or universal sense which enabled him to intuit or sense and to know the nature of the universe. The Romantic philosophers were keen to explore dreams as a way to know universal truths, for example (Ellenberger, 1970, p. 204). For this reason, cultural myths and fairy tales were also of interest in part for revealing general patterns of culture common to all mankind. Not surprisingly, collections of fairy tales and myths became popular and were studied scientifically beginning in the 18th century (von Franz, 1970, p. 3).

In this way man was seen not only as participating in a universal cosmic movement, but also as containing a universe within. Jung quotes Schelling: "And although the unconscious never becomes the object, yet it stamps its identity on all free actions, being the same for all intelligences; it is the invisible root of which all intelligences are only potentials . . ." (Jung seminar, 1933–1935, p. 15). Jung goes on to comment, "The primeval foundation is not differentiated, but universal".

TELEOLOGICAL PERSPECTIVE

'Becoming' was a central feature of *Naturphilosophie*: that one's life is a process, not of progressive aging toward ultimate death, but rather an unfolding, a story being written and developing toward a meaningful conclusion. Much like Jung's later concept of individuation, 'becoming' was a process inherent in man's nature, just as it was inherent in societies and cultures. It was an ultimate natural or spiritual law.

POLARITY

Another basic concept in *Naturphilosophie* was the idea of polarity (Ellenberger, 1970, p. 203). Polarities were seen everywhere by the Romantic philosophers: day/night, male/female, acid/base, waking/sleeping, and so on.

The polarities of opposites were the dynamic forces in nature and the origin of life energy. For example, one scientific contemporary of the *Naturphilosophen* wrote, "Nature is the struggle of forces, the conflict of a positive and negative force" (Ellenberger, 1970, p. 203).

The human form of polarity in the Romantic Movement was the conflict and attraction between men and women. Whereas in the Enlightenment relations between men and women emphasized reason (Ellenberger, 1970, p. 201), in Romanticism emotional and spiritual qualities in the relationship were emphasized. The marriage as a quasi-business arrangement was replaced in the late 18th to early 19th century by the marriage for love.

This meant relationships emphasized love and spiritual development. Ellenberger quotes the Romantic philosopher Novalis, for example, that love should impart "the drive to perfect oneself with the beloved one and help her to reach perfection" (Ellenberger, 1970, p. 201). For the Romantic philosophers, then, polarity was a natural dynamic force but with a goal in man of spiritual development, of man 'becoming'.

This is very much the sense Jung had of opposites in his symbolic paradigm. Polarities exist to drive a process forward. The polarity of male and female was the central idea behind Jung's anima/animus concept, for example. And as will be described later, the polarity of ego–Self in Jung's psychology was a dynamic force that was a process of development for both ego and Self.

Alchemy

A science which reached its height in the 17th century (Jung, 1963, p. 230) but which reached back 2,000 years, alchemy was only on a superficial level a chemical process to make gold out of common substances. It was also, as Jung proposed, a psychology of the psyche and psychical transformation.

Jung came to alchemy in 1926 after studying Gnostic writers from 1918 onward (Jung, 1963, p. 226). He had looked at alchemical texts before that but after reading The Secret of the Golden Flower, a Taoist text and alchemical treatise given to him by his sinologist friend Richard Wilhelm, Jung felt he had found the link between Gnosis and the processes of the collective unconscious in modern man (CW 13/4). Alchemy became Jung's principle research source thereafter.

REALITY OF THE UNSEEN WORLD

In Jung's psychology the concept of the reality of the psyche is presented as the reality of the transpersonal or collective psyche. The personal psyche can vary as much as any individual's life story can vary, whereas for Jung the collective psyche is a factual, objective reality. Alchemy describes the processes of this transpersonal reality because as Jung understood it, alchemy was an endeavor in which its practitioners projected these unconscious collective psychical processes into their work with chemicals. He presents his rationale for this approach in his *Alchemical Studies:*

> It is often impossible to establish [the] full range of meaning from the associative material of a single individual. . . . [Hence] the necessity of comparative research into symbols. . . . For this purpose the investigator must turn back to those periods in human history when symbol formation still went on unimpeded, that is, when there was still no epistemological criticism of the formation of images, and when, in consequence, facts that in themselves were unknown could be expressed in visual form. The period of this kind closest to us is that of medieval natural philosophy. . . . It attained its most significant development in alchemy and Hermetic philosophy.
>
> (CW 13/353)

Therefore, the first principle of the objective psyche according to Jung's alchemical studies is that it is transpersonal or collective.

As Jung studied the alchemical texts and condensed or abstracted their varied, even vast, literature, he saw the objective psyche as presented through these works as a world of images. Chemical processes, for example, were described through metaphors such as the interaction of beings or creatures; vivid pictures of destruction and creation illustrated reactions. The second principle of the objective psyche then is that it consists of images. As Jung stated,

> The psyche consists essentially of images. It is a series of images in the truest sense . . . a structure that is throughout full of meaning and purpose; it is a 'picturing' of vital activities. . . . Mind and body are . . . the expression of a single entity. . . . This being appears outwardly as the material body, but inwardly as a series of images of the vital activities taking place within it.
>
> (CW 8/618ff)

As Jung studied these images in alchemy he saw organized patterns and recurring basic processes. These uniformities of pattern and process were, according to Jung, archetypal – that is, transpersonal forms of psychical movements with reason and goal. Therefore a third principle of the objective psyche would be that it consists of universal, transpersonal transformational processes. While the images in the psyche can be considered its anatomy, these processes can be considered its physiology. What processes did Jung identify in the objective psyche? The following can be identified from his writings on alchemy:

1 The psyche arranging itself into pairs of opposites or quaternities.
2 A mediator appearing, which reconciles the opposites and produces unity.

3 A change process: separation, loss and parting, abandonment, destruction, death (the opposite of constancy).
4 A uniting process: forming, concretization, building, filling up, joining together, coagulation.
5 An emptying process: kenosis, making room for, letting go, a centering: "[W]e can see that the *retorta distillatio ex medio centri* results in the activation and development of a psychic center, a concept that coincides psychologically with that of the [S]elf" (CW 13/189).

MAN AS MICROCOSM OF MACROCOSM

In alchemical texts, according to Jung, symbols in parables and as metaphors are used to refer to universal principles. As an example of how Jung used such texts to find psychological meaning, here is an especially inscrutable passage from Paracelsus that he quoted:

> But if this [i.e. the *anima iliastri*] should be wholly filled with that [air] which renews itself again, and is then moved into the center, that is, outside that under which it lay hidden before and still lies hid [i.e. in the heart capsule], then as a tranquil thing it is not heard at all by anything corporeal, and resounds only as Aniadus, Adech, and Edochinum. Whence comes the birth of that great Aquaster, which is born beyond Nature (i.e., supernaturally).
>
> (CW 13/201)

What could that possibly mean? In order to interpret this 'laborious' text, Jung takes the attitude it is a metaphor for qualities in the psyche: "The meaning of this . . . seems to be that by psychic means the soul is not only prevented from escaping but is brought back into the heart region" (CW 13/202). Metaphors in alchemy, then, are the 'code' for interpretation of psychological meaning.

In alchemical texts there is frequent mention of one particular metaphor, the *aqua permanens*, a kind of divine water with powers beyond the physical properties of ordinary water. One alchemist, Zosimos, said of *aqua permanens*: "This is the great and divine mystery which is sought, for it is the whole. And from it is the whole and through it is the whole" (CW 13/370). Like the alchemical Philosophers Stone, the *aqua permanens* as a metaphor conveys the image of a universal psychological force. Jung interprets the preceding passage from Zosimos thus:

> Zosimo's 'whole' is a microcosm; a reflection of the universe in the smallest particle of matter, and therefore found in everything organic and inorganic. Because the microcosm is identical with the macrocosm,

> it attracts the latter and this brings about a kind of apocatastasis, a restoration of all individua to the original wholeness.
>
> (CW 13/372)

Jung uses the alchemical idea of the microcosm being identical to the macrocosm to make two points about psychic energy:

1 The individual who as individual is necessarily incomplete or one-sided psychologically will be restored to wholeness by contact with his collective nature ("and from it is the whole and through it the whole"; CW 13/170).
2 Jung implies it can be deduced that man as an organic (physical) or inorganic (spiritual) being has within him a nature which is inherently whole, a microcosm of the macrocosm. The question of the nature of this macrocosm also arises in Jung's writings. Jung has been criticized for idealizing the collective unconscious (Fordham, 1985, for example) but in fact he emphasizes over and over in his alchemical writings the negative and destructive potentials in the unconscious. In his discussion of the individual's encounter with the collective unconscious, he emphasizes the necessity for maturity and ego strength. He says, for example, in a discussion about the ego–Self encounter, "The ego enters into the picture only as far as it can offer resistance [to the Self], defend itself, and in the event of defeat still affirm its resistance. The prototype of this situation is Job's encounter with Yahweh" (CW 14/778).

The universal or collective nature of man stands in opposition to the individual nature. This relationship is not a simple polarity however, but a 'mutuality'. The individual is a part of the whole but also contains the whole within him. Alchemy then, or rather more accurately as Jung interprets alchemy, attempts to describe the dynamics of this relationship between microcosm and macrocosm that exist in man. The mechanisms or principles of the psyche described earlier are aspects of this relationship.

TELEOLOGICAL ASPECT

The mutuality present in the microcosm–macrocosm relationship, according to Jung's understanding of alchemy, has a reason and a goal. The general reason is psychological development (individuation), and the general goal is expanding individual and universal consciousness. He states, for example, "The alchemical idea of transformation is rooted in a spiritual concept of value which takes the 'transformed' as being more valuable, better, higher, more spiritual, etc., and the empirical psychologist has nothing to set against this" (CW 14/613). In alchemy then, Jung saw a detailed exposition of the two principles of development of the individual out of collective attitudes and values, and toward consciousness:

> To one familiar with our psychology, it may seem a waste of time to keep harping on the long established difference between becoming conscious and the coming-to-be of the [S]elf (individuation). But again and again I note that the individuation process is confused with the coming of the ego into consciousness and that the ego is in consequence identified with the [S]elf, which naturally produces a hopeless conceptual muddle. Individuation is then nothing but ego-centeredness and autoeroticism. But the [S]elf comprises infinitely more than a mere ego, as the symbolism has shown from of old. It is as much one's self, and all other selves, as the ego. Individuation does not shut one out of the world, but gathers the world to oneself.
>
> (CW 8/432)

Jung's work *Mysterium Coniunctionis* contains his evidence from alchemy of the four-stage course of psychological development and development of consciousness. These stages in alchemy are separation of man's soul, spirit, body, from the world in four stages and then another four-step process of reintegration of man and world to form the *Unus Mundus*.

Details of the meanings and manifestations of these stages of development in man comprise a substantial portion of *Mysterium Coniunctionis*. Relevant for this discussion of the teleological aspects of alchemy, however, is the final goal. The ultimate goal of psychological development in the alchemical tradition as interpreted by Jung is emergence of a transpersonal consciousness: "The thought Dorn expresses by the third degree of conjunction is universal: it is the relation or identity of the personal with the suprapersonal atman, and of the individual Tao with the universal Tao" (CW 14/762). In other words, individual consciousness ultimately touches the universal consciousness and brings about a broader, more comprehensive world perspective to the individual.

POLARITY IN ALCHEMY

The opposites are the basic structure and process of the world according to alchemy. Already in his pre-alchemy work *Psychological Types*, Jung pointed out the union of opposites is not an act of will but rather an autonomous process of psychic development (CW 6, Ch. 5).

Jung's (1956) work, *Mysterium Coniunctionis*, is an analysis of the actions of the opposites in alchemy. The action of opposing forces in alchemy is quite different than the actions of opposites in, for example, Helmholtz's energic paradigm. In alchemy the opposites do not respond mechanistically but rather act as if there existed a living, feeling relationship between the two entities.

Jung makes the point in *Mysterium Coniunctionis* that the opposites in alchemy do not represent ego qualities and are not ego images. Rather, the opposites are characteristic of the transpersonal psyche, the Self.

> The elevation of the human figure to a king or a divinity, and on the other hand its representation in subhuman, theriomorphic form, are indicators of the trans-conscious character of the pair of opposites. . . . They do not belong to the ego-personality but are supraordinate to it. . . . The pairs of opposites constitute the phenomenology of the paradoxical Self, man's totality.
>
> (CW 14/4)

What this means in terms of energic dynamism is that first, the actions of the psyche concerned with transformation are non-personal, that is, collective, and second, the dynamic of transpersonal opposites nevertheless occurs in the psyche of the individual.

This idea of the third is a theme that Jung also develops in his alchemical writings. The third is a mediator acting as a creative reconciler to opposite energies. Jung says, for example,

> But if a union is to take place between opposites like spirit and matter, conscious and unconscious, bright and dark, and so on, it will happen in a third thing, which represents not a compromise but something new, just as for the alchemists the cosmic strife of the elements was composed by the λίθος οὐ λίθος (stone that is no stone), by a transcendental entity that can be described only in paradoxes.
>
> (CW 14/765)

In alchemy, the mediator is identified as Mercurius, a figure Jung analyzed in two lectures given at the Eranos Conference in Ascona in 1942. By reviewing centuries of alchemical texts, Jung concluded,

> The fact that Mercurius is interpreted as spirit and soul, . . . indicates that the alchemists themselves conceived of their arcane substance as something that we today would call a psychic phenomenon . . . from the phenomenological point of view they are psychic structures.
>
> (CW13/266)

Because Mercurius is represented in the alchemical literature as having contradictory properties and qualities (such as being simultaneously matter and fire) Jung concluded, "The psychologem Mercurius must therefore possess an essentially antinomian dual nature" (CW 13/266). He is dualistic not only in his properties but also is a universal entity: "a spirit of the macrocosmic as of the microcosmic world" (CW 13/263).

Besides Mercurius' duality, Jung notes the emphasis on his unity and trinity. He is thus related in symbolism to the Godhead (CW 13/271). This does not imply the goodness of the Christian Godhead, but rather Mercurius as Godhead for Jung contains the highest and lowest, or most evil, divine qualities. Jung says, "[H]is nature is more exactly defined . . . if one conceives him as a process that begins with evil and ends with good" (CW 13/276). Transformation of Mercurius occurs, then, just as much as Mercurius interceding to transform the conflict of opposites. As Jung wrote,

> Besides being the prima materia of the lowly beginning as well as the lapis as the highest goal, Mercurius is also the process which lies between, and the means by which it is effected. . . . Therefore he is called the Mediator, Servator [preserver], and Salvator [healer].
>
> (CW 13/283)

In his role as mediator of the process of the reconciliation of opposites and the progenitor of the process of psychic development, Mercurius was in the alchemists' view "a divine emanation harmonious with God's own being" (CW 13/283) and "a principle co-eternal with God" (CW 13/283). In Alchemy, Jung saw the ultimate source of growth and transformation in the human psyche as this 'hidden' God-like life force. This force as Mercurius "becomes the one animating principle of all created things . . . the suprapersonal Self" (CW 13/287).

In alchemy, then, Jung saw the process of psychological development as a "work of conciliation between apparently incompatible opposites" (CW 14/790) that had as its goal "a symbol which had an empirical and at the same time a transcendental aspect" (CW 14/790). For Jung, the reconciling symbol was a force with a concrete, that is, psychotherapeutic, action that brought greater individual consciousness. But also, the symbol worked as a transcendent entity in that it was ultimately valid but irrational. He said, for example, regarding the Transcendent Function,

> The process of coming to terms with the unconscious is a true labor, a work which involves both action and suffering. It has been named the 'transcendent function' because it represents a function based on real and 'imaginary', or rational and irrational, data, thus bridging the yawning gulf between conscious and unconscious. It is a natural process, a manifestation of the energy that springs from the tension of opposites.
>
> (CW 7/121)

Comparing the two paradigms in practice

Returning to the story of my client 'Valentina': how could I understand what occurred between us in our interaction using principles of the energic paradigm and the symbolic paradigm? From the energic perspective, traditional psychoanalysis from the early works of Freud would speak of the transference: in the analytical relationship, the analyst has taken on the characteristics of the mother. Freud introduced this concept in his 1912 work 'The Dynamics of Transference' (SE 12). He describes this phenomenon as a libidinal impulse that

> has been held up in the course of development; it has been kept away from the conscious personality and from reality, and has either been prevented from further expansion except in phantasy or has remained wholly in the unconscious so that it is unknown to the personality's consciousness.
>
> (p. 1)

This is psychical energy, in other words, that had been directed inward but is now directed outward in the transference in order to become conscious and therefore "serviceable for reality" (SE 12/1).

In this context, the psychical energy has no purpose except to develop the reality stance of the individual. This illustrates the perspective of a one-person psychology: as the analyst, I function simply as a stimulus of this energic dynamic, the purpose of which is development of the reality principle. What is interesting from the analyst's perspective, Freud asserts, is the extent to which the client resists this transference. By resisting this energic dynamic, the client is blocking his or her own opportunity to develop consciousness. The work of analysis according to Freud thus becomes analysis of the resistance.

Viewing my client from this energic perspective, it could happen that my client articulates the feeling she has developed in our relationship that she experiences me as a judgmental mother-type. This would require a level of self-awareness she did not as yet possess. Alternatively, I could inquire, responding out of my covert awareness of the nature of her transference, about her feelings regarding her mother's critical comments and then see what follows. It may also happen that my client would begin to react to me as very critical of her out of this transference, which indeed began to happen soon after the incident described earlier. With this, the ambivalent feelings toward her mother were no longer 'out there' in her failed relationships but rather, in the 'here and now' of the consulting room. As well, we could begin to look at what happens to her in relationships. The psychical energy can be followed thus from transference to a mother-imago (the analyst) back to the original mother, and then to a template for present-day relationships. This is an appropriate technique using transference in depth psychotherapy based on the energic paradigm. Consciousness of this dynamic is the goal and for the client it is a lifesaver.

What perspective does the symbolic paradigm bring to the clinical vignette described? In the earlier scenario, I remained a screen for her to project her inner drama. As an intra-psychic process, this was my role. However, one can see from the clinical vignette that my own feelings and attitudes were involved; this was a two-person process.

The most striking phenomena in the interaction were my thoughts and feelings which coincided with my client's experience of her mother in a particularly specific way. It had the effect of startling me (my client remained unaware of this coincidence) and alerting me to a level of psychical interaction I hadn't felt with her up to that point (indeed, I had felt actively excluded from her inner world). This effect on me brought to mind Jung's concept of the reality of the psyche and of the unseen world. This felt like more than the energic exchange of transference but rather a communication from something different than her conscious ego stance that wanted me to know her. Freud attributed the transference to the repetition compulsion – that unconscious libidinal energy persists in attempts at conscious expression. This experience felt numinous and purposive and to see it as only transference of libidinal energy felt cruel and pathologizing.

Freud himself said in a letter to Jung, "[P]sychoanalysis is in essence a cure through love" (Freud/Jung Letters, 8F). I believe he recognized in analysis there are at a basic level two people in the therapy relationship whose engagement in a mutual endeavor is the mutative factor. I would also suggest that Jung saw in his concept of the Self a reality at the core of psychological life that had as its purpose the developmental process of individuation and concomitant growth in consciousness and relatedness. A polarity, two people facing each other, is a necessary element of this process; Jung said no one can individuate alone on a mountain top. The mutative factor becomes the possibility for transformation with the addition of the third factor: Mecurius in alchemy and God for Meister Eckhart.

The Self as this third presence represents the reality of the unseen world, the phenomenon not explained by the senses but nevertheless constituting a fact. The presence of a polarity constellates the Self as the mediator in the form of a symbol or as a synchronous event which shocks and delights its targets, or in the case described, two individuals meeting each other in a therapeutic endeavor given a gift through love of connection and understanding.

Chapter 3

1896–1912

Historical development

Beginnings

It has been a common assumption in the history of depth psychology that Carl Jung came to depth psychology as an original supporter of Sigmund Freud's model but that he then broke away from Freud over differences in theory, going on to develop his own psychological ideas. The facts are, however, rather different. Before he had even heard of Freud, indeed before Freud had even written the book *Interpretation of Dreams* which would later arouse Jung's interest, Jung was very much occupied with the scientific issues of the day concerning psychology and did in fact have his own model of the mind. From 1896 to 1899, as a young medical student, Jung gave a series of lectures at his university fraternity that contain the essential elements of many of his later ideas. The Zofingia lectures contain not only Jung's standpoint regarding the vitalist–materialist controversy of the day, but also offer indications on his views on consciousness, the unconscious, and the ego.

Jung's work at the Burghölzliklinik in Zürich under Eugen Bleuler was a major step in his subsequent embrace of Freud's theories; theories whose scientific assumptions would seem to contradict Jung's earlier philosophy. As was discussed previously, Bleuler's influence brought Jung closer to a medical model of mental illness that made the transition to Freud's empirical/materialistic model easier. However, before his contact with Bleuler, Jung was tending toward a vitalist philosophy.

At this stage in Jung's career then, the two paradigms that formed the background to Jung's ego concept were in evidence. Jung takes a definite stand for philosophy, especially Kant, and Spiritualism during the Zofingia years. During the Burghölzli and Freud period of Jung's life, empiricism and the energic paradigm enter the mix and begin to bear upon Jung's theoretical formulations.

This chapter then will focus on these historical developments in order to answer the following questions: What were Jung's ideas about consciousness and ego in this first phase of his work? What were the key concepts developed in this period that were to become the foundations of his later work as they relate to his theory of ego?

The Zofingia years

Jung's Zofingia lectures (part of the activities of the Zofingia fraternity to which he belonged while a student at the University of Basel) were first made available to the public in 1975, when Jung would have been 100 years old. These lectures had been put away and forgotten by Jung, never mentioned in his writings, and probably not something he would have cared to see published (Von Franz, 1983, p. xiii). Because these lectures, presented to fellow fraternity members, were expected to meet a high scientific standard expressed in an open and outspoken manner (p. xiii), they represent Jung's best scientific thought at ages 21 to 23. Also, because the topics of the lectures were left to the discretion of the lecturer, one can see from these particular lectures what issues preoccupied Jung at this time in his life.

There are five lectures in all, four of these five concern scientific or religious controversies. Lecture 3, Jung's inaugural address upon assuming the chairmanship of the Zofingia Club, is more concerned with his political stance and has little relevance for this work. Therefore I would like to examine the four other lectures in detail.

Lecture 1: 'The Border Zones of Exact Science' (November 1896)

In this lecture Jung critiques Materialism in the scientific discourse of the day: 'Materialism Versus Vitalism' was the focus of spirited debate in scientific and philosophical circles. In this lecture, Jung clearly takes the side of the Vitalists. He not only attacks the materialist perspective itself as an "absurd colossus with feet of clay" (CW A/14), but also denigrates those who adhere to Materialism as "bearing witness to their own intellectual poverty" (CW A/14).

Of particular interest is the argument he constructs against Scientific Materialism. Although Jung's specific critique of certain concepts in physics is outdated – he defends the theory of ether, for example – his overall perspective reveals his fundamental orientation toward the phenomenological world. As he examines the intellectual inconsistencies in the theory of ether, he points out that by following its assumptions to their logical conclusion, one realizes that "[the] most elementary train of reasoning has suddenly transported us from the realm of the most concrete phenomena, into a realm where we must confront the most despised word in the field of applied science, namely 'metaphysical'" (CW A/45). As he argues for the existence of a non-physical or non-material entity that possesses a force contradicting the laws of physics, he concludes, "[T]his notion is so baffling that we have finally returned to a metaphysical hypothesis" (CW A/46). In a final thought deleted from the lecture as presented, he states, "Moreover, we have reached the border of something that simply leaves science behind" (CW A/46).

For Jung, science explains nothing and in truth ignores the greater question of 'why' (CW A/59). He states that once one has reached this point at the limits of knowledge one is not at the end of understanding but rather, "we are only at the beginning. We think that the gate is locked, when we have the key" (CW A/62). Jung concludes his argument with the logical principles to be included in the realm of material nature: "We have seen that ether, with its transcendental properties, constitutes an essential means of explaining certain physical phenomena, just as a preexistent vital principle is necessary to explain the world of organic phenomena" (CW A/63). In other words, there is a force in the natural world with a non-physical nature, and there is a life-essence that precedes physical life.

Rather than focus on the merits of Jung's scientific arguments against Materialism – arguments that were made in the climate of late 19th century scientific debate and are certainly dated – I want to highlight his general philosophical perspective. It has been said that Jung's understanding of what is scientific is non-traditional and even at times unmistakably in the philosophical realm. In his lecture on the border zones of science, Jung was grappling with phenomena (such as light passing through a vacuum) that he felt did not fit into the scientific explanations of the day. Rather than try to fit these observations into known scientific theory, Jung instead expanded the definition of science to fit his view of the natural world. Jung's scientific method is descriptive and phenomenological; empirical science or science that emulates the principles of classic Newtonian physics, for example, is only one part of Jung's scientific sense. He had no difficulty seeing beyond physical reality to another realm. As Jung says in his lecture, when the observed phenomena do not correspond to physical principles, then one must consider metaphysical ones.

Jung's embrace of the reality of the metaphysical is one of the central arguments against him as a scientist. Beginning with Freud, Jung was criticized for his 'mysticism' and 'occultism'. Yet these criticisms, however valid, miss the point about his scientific perspective. In this first Zofingia lecture, Jung rejects the 'practical reason' of scientific empiricism that demands consistency according to eternal laws. Rather, he advocates 'pure reason': the fact that something exists makes it true. It is therefore immaterial to Jung whether what exists has a physical nature. His second lecture at the Zofingia Club would develop this line of thinking further.

Lecture 2: 'Some Thoughts on Psychology'

In 1897, at the time Jung gave this lecture, psychology was a new discipline striving to be scientific. As was discussed previously, Wundt and others were developing a 'scientific psychology', and it is clear from Jung's multiple citations of Wundt in these lectures that he was familiar with this evolution. Therefore, when Jung focuses his attention on 'rational' versus 'empirical' psychology in this lecture, he is choosing to take the debate about psychology out of the scientific realm and instead place it in the philosophical. Like Kant before him who arrived at a new philosophical position, Jung uses these two categories of major historical philosophical movements (the 'Rationalists' versus the 'Empiricists') to arrive at a new understanding of psychology beyond the arguments of the scientists.

Jung begins with 'Rational Psychology'. Just as the Rationalists discovered knowledge through reason, the Rational Psychologists, according to Jung, search for man in his physiology. They are quickly dismissed by Jung: "Physiologists are struggling to explain life in terms of natural laws, when all the time it is clear that life exists despite these laws. They try desperately to force life into the system of natural laws, when life contradicts every law of nature" (CW A/91). But, Jung goes on to argue, "if one applies the 'category of causality correctly – then it is necessary for us to postulate the existence of a vital principle . . ." (CW A/93). Using 'rational' epistemological methods then, Jung justifies the existence of a "life force" as proposed by ancient physiologists (and contemporary Vitalists).

Following this argument, Jung links the 'life force' to the function of consciousness as well as the unconscious, vegetative, functions of the body and then makes a bold assertion. There is a common root, he argues, that links the conscious and unconscious life, and it is, as he quotes Schopenhauer, "a transcendental idea" (CW A/93): he writes, "Let us boldly assign to this transcendental subject the name of 'soul' [*Seele*]. What do we mean by 'soul'? The soul is an intelligence independent of space and time" (CW A/96).

By 'rational' reasoning then, Jung arrives at the criteria of soul: it is *intelligent* due to the purposefulness of its acts, it is *independent of space and time* because it has no material force and is therefore not subject to the basic mechanical laws of physics, and it is *immortal* because of its independence of space and time. Because it is the function upon which consciousness depends, consciousness is *ein Akzidens* compared to the soul, which is "substance" (CW A/96). Here Jung alludes to the distinction made by Aristotle in his philosophy of nature between 'substance' and 'accident' (Aristotle, *Categories*). According to Aristotle, 'substance' is whatever is a natural entity and exists in its own right, whereas an 'accident' is the modification that the 'substance' undergoes, but that does not change the essence of the 'substance'. Jung is also echoing the *Naturphilosophie* of von Schelling, who described consciousness in 1803 as a contingent (*Akzidens*) of something more formal (Schelling, 1988, p. 215).

In the next part of his lecture, Jung addresses 'Empirical Psychology'. Empiricists, in the philosophical tradition, derive all knowledge from what can only be known through the senses. Quoting Kant, Jung argues for another sense beyond the five physical senses, or 'external' senses, of the Empiricists. There is an 'inner sense' possessed by all and exemplified by the phenomenon of 'Spiritualism'. The practical experience of the soul is through telekinetic and telepathic effects, according to Jung, as well as through prophetic dreams and phenomena such as 'second sight' (CW A/112–134).

Jung felt his arguments supporting Spiritualism provided "empirical evidence substantiating [his] definition of the soul" (CW A/135). Through empirical means, he contends, one could establish the reality of the soul as well as the fallibility of the 'empirical' laws of nature and Materialism. Mankind indeed lives at "the boundary of two worlds", between the material worlds of matter and the soul in contact with "a higher order of being" (CW A/142).

In this lecture, then, Jung further elaborates his fundamental philosophy of science in general and psychology in particular. He again takes the side of the Vitalists and defends the existence of forces in nature that cannot be deduced through reason, or revealed through the senses. Jung goes further still and sides with a controversial cultural phenomenon of the latter half of the 19th century: Spiritualism. He uses arguments that favor Spiritualism to support his hypotheses about Soul. The basic assumptions behind his defense of Spiritualism, that the phenomena such as telekinesis and telepathy observed in séances of the period are real and not chicanery, tarnishes his vision of the soul and may have contributed to critics' accusations of occultism. On the other hand, it has been observed that this conflict between scientific inquiry and interest in Spiritualism may have "sharpened his scientific curiosity about the psyche" (Hayman, 1999, p. 46). He would later return to the theme of Spiritualism in his doctoral thesis and examine the phenomenon as an instance of cognitive dissociation and multiple states of consciousness, turning his back on this occultist aspect.

The science of psychology at the time was trying to distance itself from philosophical speculation and to establish truths about the mind through physiological experimentation. Jung returns in this lecture, however, to philosophical roots, particularly Kant, to locate his own vision of psychology. Although at times his arguments against science and physiology descend to simple name-calling (Wundt is "stubborn", Ludwig "slippery", and so on.), Jung does try to fashion a logical argument for his support of a 'vital force' he calls 'soul', in human psychology.

At this point, Jung views consciousness as a state connected to and dependent on the 'soul' for its essential nature. Consciousness is only an epi-phenomenon of this soul, the unconscious not addressed. In his fourth lecture, however, he does address the issue of instinct and the unconscious.

Lecture 4: 'Thoughts on the Nature and Value of Speculative Inquiry'

After giving his inaugural address upon assuming the chairmanship of the Zofingia Club, Jung returned in 1898 to the topic of philosophy and elaborates in this fourth lecture what has been described as his "scientific credo"

(CW A, p. xxi). In this lecture he again draws on the philosophy of Kant to attack the science of the day. However, in this lecture he wishes to address two deeper questions: what brings happiness and what is the organic root of man?

He begins by describing alienation in modern man: "The process of perfecting external relations has torn man away from his bond with nature, but only from the conscious bond, not from the unconscious" (CW A/170). Jung goes on to argue that this separation due to technological progress and material success is an illusion; the road to happiness is not through material and scientific achievement but "up and down into the unfathomable depths of our own being" (CW A/171). Following Kant's "categorical imperative" that to do 'good' and eschew evil leads to happiness, Jung cites Hartmann in arguing that the gratification of the causal instinct is an "inexhaustible source of happiness" (CW A/171). Causal instinct in this instance is used by Jung to mean the instinctual need to think in causal terms (CW A/179). He wrote regarding this instinct, "It is that ardent desire for truth which impetuously breaks down all barriers and is even capable of crushing the will to live" (CW A/179). For Jung, then, the search for truth, to understand, was the source of happiness.

Jung would base his scientific philosophy on this conclusion. He wrote, "Our philosophy should consist in drawing inferences about the unknown, . . . on the basis of real experience, and not in drawing inferences about the inner world on the basis of the outer . . ." (CW A/175). For Jung, then, the search for truth, experienced as a drive to understand, meant to accept as true even those inner experiences not explained by natural laws. The inner world, the world of instincts and the unconscious, is purposeful in the same sense as the laws of nature, *but does not necessarily adhere to those same laws*. Jung's scientific philosophy is in essence that truth is what one finds, not what one concludes.

What is the purpose of this underlying causal instinct? Jung cannot say, and even thought it unimportant to know (CW A/186). He believed the purpose was ultimately transcendent: it is "a world of the invisible and incomprehensible, a continuation of material nature into the incalculable, the immeasurable, and the inscrutable" (CW A/184). Because the instinct had a purpose did not then also mean we could know it.

The search for truth and need to understand (causal instinct) did have a use, however, besides bringing the greatest happiness: "[I]t is the infinitely subtle agent that frees man from his animal nature" (CW A/191). In other words, the search for truth, as an instinct, removes the searcher from his subjective state and leads him to ask why, to search for ultimate rather than proximate meaning. Jung said,

> Man is a Prometheus who steals lightening from heaven in order to bring light into the pervasive darkness of the great riddle. He knows

> there is a meaning in nature, that the world conceals a mystery which is the purpose of his life to discover.
>
> (CW A/194)

There is, then, in this lecture, a view of the instinctual world very different from the scientific community of the day. Jung sees 'his' instinct, the 'principle of causality', in religious terms: "In every healthy, reflective person the simple need to satisfy the principle of causality develops into a metaphysical longing, into religion" (CW A/181). The causal instinct has metaphysical purpose just as other instincts have physical purpose. Man as a reflective being assumes importance for an as yet unknown reason. There is an implied significance and value, then, to man's reflective ability – his consciousness.

Jung develops this theme of observing and reflecting as a path to truth and knowledge by discussing dualism. He begins by quoting the medieval mystic and philosopher Jakob Böhme: "Without opposition no thing can become apparent to itself . . ." (CW A/202). There are two "radically different powers" in nature that struggle for domination, one representing all those forces that oppose change and movement forward, and the other striving to create life and color and to "liberate matter from the crushing embrace of matter" (CW A/205). After examining the physical and biological variations of these forces, Jung concludes they have two chief characteristics: the one striving toward "passivity", the other striving toward "unceasing activity" (CW A/208–211).

Jung then makes the connection between this principle of opposition and the acquisition of knowledge and truth. There is an inner dualism in man that is a direct continuation of the dualism present in nature, he argues. The external environment (matter) represents and is inwardly experienced as the passive, blocking force, whereas the force toward truth in the individual arising from the inner world is the active animating force. Jung concludes, then, that because mankind's true nature is one of activity, striving toward the transcendent and away from the material world, the causal instinct is superior (CW A/225).

Jung is making three arguments in this lecture relevant to his concept of ego and consciousness. First, he constructs a model of the mind that is based on dualism. Second, he assigns primacy to the inner instinct or force directed toward truth and knowledge. Lastly, he emphasizes the teleological importance of individual reflection.

Dualism

Jung cites the ancient Greeks, philosophers von Schelling, Hartmann, and Kant, contemporary science, and even the Bible to support his argument that dualism is a universal principle "grounded in the depths of nature" (CW A/225).

Dualism is seen in two areas: first, opposition between the individual and the environment, and second, within the individual, "an inner reflection of this struggle [individual/environment], in the form of a feeling of psychical schism" (CW A/223). The inner inertia is the "direct continuation" of the environmental forces blocking activity and progress. Only the inner causal instinct leads away from these inertial forces toward "the inwardness of transcendental causes" (CW A/224). Jung uses "transcendental causes" here to mean the teleological element of the causal instinct.

Dualism is a fundamental part of Jung's model of mind. By taking up this view here Jung establishes a dynamic-structural view of the mind rather than a topographical one. It is dynamic in the sense that the unconscious force directed toward knowledge and the inertial forces of nature continually counter truth. It is structural in that the elements of the dynamic are placed in specific non-spatial areas (inner versus outer world). The development of knowledge is seen less as a consequence of the dynamic but more as a triumph of the inner causal instinct over inner and outer environmental inertia.

Causal instinct

Jung offers the search for truth and need to understand as a universal principle. He elevates this undoubtedly personal concern of his to a primary force ("If we wish to avoid falling prey to idle fancies, we must regard this organic antagonism as the real, empirical basis of all speculation on the nature of the world", CW A/220). He bases this on Kantian philosophy of nature: "I have employed no forces other than those of attraction and repulsion to elaborate the greater order of nature, two forces which are both equally certain, equally simple, and, at the same time, equally *primary and universal*" (CW A /212).

By characterizing this inner dynamic force as an instinct, Jung is implying he too, following Kant, sees it as impersonal and universal. With this formulation, then, he establishes the basic and fundamental structure for all his work that follows: the instinctual inner and outer forces of nature opposing change and the counter-forces directed toward change.

There are two elements as yet undeveloped in this model: the subjective personal equation, that is, the ego, and the economics of the causal instinct. Jung implies the individual is the vessel of this dynamic and notes the personal suffering involved and in this sense a personal factor exists. However, there is as yet no accounting made of the action of the ego, no discussion of will. Also not pursued is the effect of the dynamic forces on the ego of the individual beyond subjective happiness and a sense of being more and more oneself, although an increase in consciousness ('knowledge') is implied.

Despite Jung's focus on the importance of the causal instinct, he does not offer a complete explanation for the source of its energy or the consequence of its energy being blocked. He envisions it as a force – likening it to forces in physics – and yet connects this force to the 'vital force', his anti-scientific formulation. In the end, he sidesteps the issue, concluding, "The living organism is, quite simply, a miracle, in that it lifts itself above all those laws of physics that approach absolute reliability" (CW A/223).

Teleological importance of causal instinct

Jung describes a greater consequence of the dynamic action of dualism, beyond individual happiness, as the creation and redemption of the world. He cites Genesis to describe a world without active forces, cold and dead, that is transformed by the action of the forces of light: "'And God said, let there be light'. When a creative act illuminated the dark chaos, the redemption of the world began" (CW A/217). Later Jung summarizes what this fundamental antagonism in nature means:

> This primal and fundamental opposition between living and dead, active and passive, is the mighty minor chord with which the song of the world begins. It is this antagonism, which out of two conflicting elements composes the third, and the forth, and the tenth, and the hundredth, and the thousandth.
>
> (CW A/218)

Here already is the beginning of the formulation to be found later in the first sentence of his late work (CW 14) completed in his 81st year, *Mysterium Coniunctionis.*

The happiness that results from the causal instinct is not simply a kind of joy at acquiring knowledge or feeling one has found truth. Jung implies in this lecture a sense of individuation:

> The pure contemplation of nature supplies us with unconditional affirmation of the causal instinct. Here we also have the objective reason for the subjective appearance of the greatest source of happiness, which is attained through gratification of the need for causality. No man feels well and happy until he finds others of his own kind. The closer we approach to the roots of our own being, the more unalloyed and the more enduring our happiness becomes.
>
> (CW A/225)

This for Jung is ultimately the teleological element of the causal instinct: to become oneself.

Lecture 5: 'Thoughts on the Interpretation of Christianity, With Reference to the Theory of Albrecht Ritschl'

In this last lecture delivered in January 1899, Jung focuses on religious questions in a critique of the German Protestant theologian Albrecht Ritschl. Ritschl, one of the most influential protestant theologians of the 19th century (Jodock, 1995, p. 3), was known for his emphasis on faith through assimilation into the community of the Church (Nagy, 1990, p. 447). He was against another dominant form of Protestantism of the time, Pietism, which saw faith as a result of a direct subjective experience of God. Ritschl criticized these subjective experiences as 'mystical visions' and 'sentimentalities' (Nagy, 1990, p. 447) due to their emphasis on the individual looking inward rather than outward to Church institutions. Ritschl, then, represented for Jung the theological equivalent of the Scientific Materialists: an acceptance of orthodoxy embodied by an institutionalized creed rather than individual discovery of truth through inner experience.

In attacking Ritschl's theology in this lecture, Jung further establishes his vision of the personal equation in three ways. First, by defending mystical experience Jung in this lecture begins to link the enlightening personal experience to feelings and emotional value. Second, Jung begins to describe a sense of self born out of the conflict between these personal feelings and institutions. Finally, Jung emphasizes the act of will as a form of freedom to pursue one's personal truth.

At the time Jung delivered this lecture, he had been participating in séances with his cousins for four years. Mysticism and Spiritualism, as was seen in the previous lectures, were strong elements in his model of the world. Jung defends these elements here in this lecture as "illuministic" (CW A/257) and the way to experience God directly, without Him being "compelled to go through official channels whenever he wishes to do something good for man" (CW A/248). In fact, Jung had his own experience and understanding of the sclerotic nature of the official Church through the problematic faith of his own Protestant minister father, Paul Jung.

Jung the son focuses on the emotional aspect of the personal experience of God not available when intermediaries exist: "No religion has survived, or ever will, without mystery, to which the devotee is most intimately bound" (CW A/289). One must seek out the *unio mystica*, "experience personally the heights and depths of emotions" (CW A/249), and "live out [one's] own truth" in order to "detect its results" (CW A/249). Jung derides those scholars such as Kant and Wundt whose works of scientific knowledge contain "so little depth of feeling" (CW A/248).

Only knowledge generated through an individual emotional encounter with the unknown has value. Jung maligns Ritschl's emphasis on consciousness: "Thus according to Ritschl, no effect can be exercised on a man's consciousness except by way of conscious sensation. . . . Man draws the entire content of consciousness from the sphere of conscious sensation, of sensory perceptibility. Thus he also acquires all motivation for ethical action by way of conscious sensation, in other words from the communications of other human beings" (CW A/261). Jung argues that post-hypnotic suggestion (and in a deleted passage, premonitions) would be impossible if Ritschl were right. For Jung there is instead an inner source of motivation: "the mystery in the human heart" (CW A/280–283), in other words, by the personal experience of feeling. The individual is moved less by what he experiences through the five senses or by what he is told outright, than by his emotional life, which remains an enigma.

The emotional life, however, is linked to the experience of consciousness. Jung wrote,

> Everything real, that is, every object of cognition, arouses a sensation. It is the function of memory to store up such sensations. At any time memory can reproduce for us the image of an event that originally was real. The image of memory consists of two distinct objects. The first is the image of the original event, and the second is the image of the feeling aroused in us by the original event.
>
> (CW A /253)

Jung then proceeds to link these emotional components of memory with values. This linkage of consciousness in the form of memory with emotional experience and value was counter to the prevailing scientific psychology of the day. As was discussed earlier, Wundt, for example, linked cognition to physiological processes. This linkage of consciousness with feeling prefigures Jung's later work on the psychological complex.

The personal self as a factor becomes now a part of Jung's argument. As the individual pursuit of personal value and truth conflicts with the established institutions conveying value, Jung envisions in this opposition the birth of a personal power. He wrote,

> Everything takes second place to the one great question, that of the inner spiritualization of the individual and the concomitant disintegration of the existing order of nature. Christ came to bring not peace but a sword, for he unleashes the conflict of the dualistic, divided will.
>
> (CW A/290)

In the tension between the individual drive and the tendency toward inertia of the Church, the individual wields equal power. This implies a separateness of the individual from God that is necessary and intended by God.

In addition, Jung emphasizes the freedom of this individual self by contrasting it with the Ritschlian world of renunciation of personal relationship to God and obedience to social and political institutions. Nagy (1990, p. 448) compares Ritschl's doctrine with the Stoics of ancient Greece, in which free will was limited to a choice of resisting or following one's fate. Ritschl links God's will to the will of the Church, whereas Jung wants to restore the Gnostic idea of a personal relationship with God. In this way Jung stresses the personal will as a path to personal truth. Jung would return to this image of man and God over and over throughout his life in his writings in order to address the issue of self versus other and self versus group.

Summary of main points

These Zofingia lectures represent Jung's nascent thinking about science, psychology, and religion and are his only writings that precede the influence of Bleuler and Freud. Although the ego as a function of the psyche is not elaborated, a number of themes emerge relevant to a Jungian theory of ego. First, his early ideas in these lectures are contrary to the energic paradigm and approximate the basic tenets of the symbolic paradigm. Second, ideas about the development of a personal self are introduced. Third, an attitude toward adaptation, another key component of an Ego Psychology, emerges.

Symbolic paradigm

In these lectures, Jung explicitly rejects the basic tenets and philosophy of the Materialists (i.e. psychology derived from Newtonian laws of nature, energic conflict) and instead argues repeatedly for a view that corresponds with the symbolic paradigm. In Lecture 1, Jung defends the idea of a non-material, 'vital' force which acts beyond the reach of scientific instrumentation. He emphasizes in Lecture 5 the creative dualism inherent in man that has a teleological purpose. In Lecture 4 he makes his case for a non-organic universal instinct toward the search for truth and he describes in Lectures 2 and 4 his vision of the soul in mankind. Jung understood these views were outside the scientific mainstream, and one gets the sense reading these lectures that he was indeed pleased to do battle with the scientific orthodoxy of the time.

Development of a personal self

In Lecture 5, Jung begins to describe the dialectic of the individual with the Godhead and the individual with the group. Ritschl proposes in his theology faith through adaptation to dogma of the Church. There is an explicit rejection, in Ritschlian theology, of knowledge of God through personal experience. Jung on the other hand sees no other path to faith and knowledge of God then through the personal, even mystical, encounter. For Jung, there is a further consequence to this encounter: a 'disintegration' of the established order and the creation of personal value and personal truth. The individual self, as a counterforce to the collective institution of the Church, becomes a vehicle for power and value. As Nagy argued, this viewpoint conveys a sense of personal freedom and free will. Jung's position implies that the individual is indeed separate from God and necessarily so in order to encounter God and know Him.

There is purpose to this separateness beyond the development of knowledge; it is the means for a 'new order of nature' to emerge. Established religion is sclerotic and cannot evolve without the 'inner spiritualization of the individual' but it is a calling the individual is free to pursue or not. Therefore, Jung implicitly places the burden on the individual self to further the 'progress of civilization' (CW A/290).

Even at this early phase of his work, Jung takes the position that the individual self develops out of an encounter with the numinous (the *unio mystica*). Freud and later ego psychologists would take the position that the ego develops because of conflict and frustration. Again, Jung's perspective reflects the symbolic paradigm, in which the unseen world, the encounter with the numinous, is considered a source of growth and possibility. In contrast, the energic paradigm has a vision of the natural world and the unconscious as essentially in conflict with the rational ego. Here then are the seeds of Jung's theory of ego development: the ego develops (not merely differentiates) through its encounter with the numinous Other.

Adaptation

Just as the development of the individual self has the highest value and purpose in Jung's thought, there is consequently little value placed on adaptation. Jung's entire lecture on Ritschl deprecates the latter's emphasis on Church allegiance: "[W]e can feel nothing but pity for Ritschl's Christian . . ."; his God exists "only in church, school, and home" based on the memory of Christ presented and sustained by the official Church. The 'inner spiritualization', in other words, the individual encounter with the numinous, is the decisive factor in the individual and the world for Jung.

This emphasis on the mystical experience is in one sense a polemic by Jung against the larger issue of materialism in the intellectual currency of his day. However, Jung emphasizes the individual mystical experience over the group faith for a particular purpose: it is the means to find one's own truth and to become one's own self. There is the implication in this emphasis that being and becoming oneself has value over adapting to the group. Jung appears to place these two processes, adaptation and individuation, in opposition, as if to adapt is against the path to knowledge and truth. One of the issues that would occupy Jung throughout his career – individuation versus adaptation – is thus seen in this first student work.

On the Psychology and Pathology of So-Called Occult Phenomena (1902)

Jung's next significant work was his doctoral dissertation completed two years after he began his training at the Burghölzli clinic under Eugen Bleuler. It is an extended examination of a case of somnambulism, multiple consciousness, and automatic behaviors in a teenage medium. This first case description is in fact a disguised record of Jung's séance experiences with his cousin Hélène Preiswerk, and it is impossible to evaluate his conclusions without understanding the context of this experience for him, as well as the audience for whom this dissertation was intended: Professor Bleuler.

Hélène Preiswerk and the séances

The historical record for these experiences has been examined in the literature (Goodheart, 1984; Hillman, 1976; Oeri, 1970). These works have relied on the semi-fictionalized biographical sketch written by Hélène's niece Stephanie Zumstein-Preiswerk (1975) and Jung's own description in his autobiography for their factual background. Both these sources unfortunately are suspect: Jung's because of its self-serving nature (Hayman, 1999) colored by age and possibly altered by family members (Hillman, 1976), and Zumstein-Preiswerk's because it is a second-hand account from her father (Hélènes brother) and her mother (Hélènes best school friend). The Zumstein book also remains suspect because it is less an historical document than "personal family memories, fantasies, and resentments" (Hillman, 1976, p. 123), a mythology rather than a history. What is not disputed is the fact that Jung and his cousin 'Helly' and other family members, including Jung's own mother, held séances from June 1895 until 1899, the period when Jung was 20 to 24 years old.

Jung describes the séances this way:

> At the beginning of August 1899, I witnessed the first attacks of somnambulism. Their course was usually as follows: S.W. grew very pale, slowly sank to the ground or into a chair, closed her eyes, became cataleptic, drew several deep breaths, and began to speak. At this stage she was generally quite relaxed, the eyelid reflexes remained normal and so did tactile sensibility. She was sensitive to unexpected touches and easily frightened, especially in the initial stage.
>
> (CW 1/39)

One can see Jung's style in this work is quite different from his Zofingia lectures. The lectures were talks he gave to fellow fraternity members, deliberately provocative. In this dissertation, his first scientific work, Jung writes, as the preceding example shows, with a noticeable detached academic tone. He strives for empirical exactitude and rejects the mysticism of occultism. Throughout his dissertation he cites literature and clinical examples to illustrate his scientific argument. His audience is primarily Professor Bleuler, the advisor for his thesis and the director of his training program, whose strait-laced character and professional scientific standing has been discussed earlier. Jung wanted approval as a scientist and scholar, and so he approaches his subject with detachment rather than the passion seen in his lectures.

Goodheart (1984) talks about the "puritanically repressive" nature of Jung's professional milieu as he wrote his dissertation. This characterization, however, more accurately describes Jung's experience at Burghölzli rather than his personal history. In Jung's social and family milieu it was more complicated and certainly less ordinary. Late 19th century Europe was taken with the Spiritualist and séance phenomena, and although his family had nine Protestant ministers in its number, this did not repress the family's strong psychical and spiritualistic tendencies: most notably for Jung in the person of his mother. One could say the split in his society was present at home for Jung in the personalities of his Protestant minister father and his irrational mother, who he described as "like a priestess in a bear's cave" (Jung, 1983a, p. 68).

The séances

According to Jung's account of these séances, they occurred within a period of four to eight weeks (CW 1/134), although according to Hayman (1999) they went on over a period of three to four years (June 1895 to 1899). Jung himself organized the initial sessions with his mother's encouragement (Hayman, 1999, p. 33). In his dissertation Jung describes seven séance sessions. In general they would follow a certain pattern: "S." would enter a trance and begin to communicate messages from spirits. As she awoke from these trances she would fall into an ecstasy state followed at times by catalepsy (a loss of voluntary motion in which the limbs remain in whatever position they are placed) until she was fully awake. Whether there was amnesia after the attacks was not clear. Jung had his doubts (CW 1/41) and assessed that some of her performance was hysterical in origin (CW 1/42).

During her trances, S. would speak in the person of various spirits. At first it was of her paternal grandfather, Samuel Preiswerk, who was also Jung's maternal grandfather. Then another spirit, Jung's paternal grandfather the first Carl Gustav Jung, began to communicate. These grandfather spirits were opposite in temperament in these trances as well as in life. Over time more spirits appeared and the séances became more and more fantastical. There were astral journeys, sojourns to the spirit world, exotic and fantastical romances and liaisons, a complete mystical system of the universe was revealed to her. One spirit, called Ivenes, emerged as a voice of reason and maturity that controlled S.'s 'semi-somnambulistic' state.

In analyzing these somnambulistic states, Jung concluded these were an example of hysterical splitting of consciousness (CW 1/131). The spirit personalities represent 'secondary complexes of consciousness' that appeared to S. at first as visions of her two grandfathers. Jung speculated that the splitting of consciousness this way was due to physiological changes of character due to puberty (CW 1/113) – S. was 15 ½ years old at the time the séances began – but these changes in character can also be due "on rare occasions" to hysteria (CW 1/112).

Jung distinguishes between these 'complexes of consciousness', and the ego, and the ego-complex. Complexes of consciousness are personalities that dominate consciousness during the somnambulistic experience, and they have access to the whole of the medium's memory, including the unconscious

(CW 1/58). There was partial and inconsistent amnesia for these episodes upon 'awaking', and it appeared a part of the ego (the waking personality) remained connected to the experiences of the complex (CW 1/58).

Jung uses the term 'ego' in this dissertation when referring to the waking, rather immature, personality of S. as the "everyday ego" (CW 1/114). Jung wrote, "Ivenes is the direct continuation of her everyday ego: she comprises its whole conscious content" (CW 1/114). Ivenes is the "calmer, more composed personality, and her pleasing modesty and reserve, her more uniform intelligence, her confident way of talking, may be regarded as an improvement on the patient's whole being" (CW 1/116). "She [the patient] embodies in Ivenes what she wishes to be in twenty years time – the assured, influential, wise, gracious, pious lady" (CW 1/116). Jung associates the invention of the personality Ivenes with a dream situation: "One cannot say that she deludes herself into the higher ideal state, rather she dreams herself into it" (CW 1/116). Jung is making, therefore, a distinction between the S. waking ego (CW 1/116) that comprises the day-to-day here-and-now personality, and a dream, or dreamlike, ego that she has built up through her fantasies. This fantasy ego is not like an ideal state (Jung cites Janet's case of Léonie I and Léonie II to illustrate the difference) but rather a product of "hysterical identification" with a fantasy mystic (the Clairvoyante of Prevorst). Jung concludes this occurs because of decreased consciousness. He states, for example, "[T]he less the waking consciousness intervenes with its reflection and calculation, the more certain and convincing becomes the objectivation of the dream" (CW 1/117).

Jung explains the two ego personalities this way:

> The patient herself is a peculiar mixture of both [the two grandfather complexes]; sometimes timid, shy, excessively reserved, at other times boisterous to the point of indecency. . . . This gives us the key to the origin of the two subconscious personalities. The patient is obviously seeking a middle way between the two extremes; she endeavors to repress them and strives for a more ideal state. These strivings lead to the adolescent dream of the ideal Ivenes, beside whom the unrefined aspects of her character fade into the background. They are not lost; but as repressed thoughts, analogous to the idea of Ivenes, they begin to lead independent existence as autonomous personalities.
>
> (CW 1/132)

In other words, he highlights the role of repression in the formation of complexes but also points out the autonomous nature of the unconscious personalities. The role of repression is not as exclusive for Jung as it was for Freud.

The ego-complex is described as something enduring, a psychical entity that underlies other psychical phenomena. "Here we come upon the characteristic feature of all hysterical splits of consciousness. They are disturbances that only touch the surface, and none of them goes so deep as to attack the firmly knit basis of the ego-complex" (CW 1/130). The ego-complex is like a central station and the 'site' of experiencing continuity (a concept Bleuler elaborated in 1895; see later discussion). Jung wrote, for example,

> After all, an important idea is linked by numerous associations to the ego-complex; it has been thought about at different times and in different situations and therefore has innumerable connecting threads leading in all directions. Consequently it can never disappear so entirely from consciousness that its continuity is lost to the sphere of conscious memory.
>
> (CW 1/139)

In a reply to a review of *On the Psychology and Pathology of So-Called Occult Phenomena* published in 1904 (CW 1/89), Jung further characterizes the ego-complex in a discussion of S.'s hysterical misreading of proper German words as the dialect words:

> In the normal and sick persons who are distractible but not hysterical, these feeble accentuated psychic processes give rise to misconstructions based on phonetic or formal likeness, so that reproduction is falsified at the cost of sense. It is the other way around with my patient: the formal connection breaks down completely but the sense connection is preserved. This can only be explained on the hypothesis of a split consciousness; that is to say, besides the ego-complex, which follows its own thoughts, there is another conscious complex which reads and understands correctly, and allows itself various modifications of expression, as indeed is frequently the case with complexes that function autonomously.
>
> (CW 1/157)

Here, Jung is describing an ego-complex that steps aside to another complex, one which has hold over consciousness and which directs the mistakes made in misreading. The hysterical misreading, in other words, is due to the autonomous complex taking over control of consciousness (awareness and perception) while the ego-complex 'has left the building'.

Jung's developing ego concept

A number of issues are presented for the first time in this work. First, there is the question of how the unconscious personalities are generated. What constitutes an unconscious personality? What are their characteristics? What purpose do the personalities serve? Second, Jung discusses the relationship of these unconscious personalities to the ego-personality. What are the dynamics involved? Finally, what is the nature of ego-consciousness as opposed to the ego-complex, both being terms Jung uses seemingly interchangeably?

Unconscious personalities

Jung is describing autonomous complexes in his description of the somnambulistic personalities of S. In his dissertation one can discern four broad conclusions about these complexes. First, they arise out of the unconscious. Second, they consist of memories, perceptions, and feelings of the conscious personality. Third, they result from an intolerable ego stance, and finally, they are a result of repression.

Ego-consciousness and the ego-complex

Jung saw Helly's somnambulism as an example of unconscious personalities related to ego-consciousness:

> We have discussed two secondary complexes of consciousness and followed them into somnambulistic attack, where, owing to loss of motor expression, they appeared to the patient in the second séance as a vision of the two grandfathers. [. . .] It was really only a question of two different subconscious personalities appearing under various names, which had however no essential significance. [. . .] According to our previous explanations, the attack can in these circumstances be thought of as partial hypnosis. The ego-consciousness which remains over, and, as a result of its isolation from the external world, occupies itself entirely with its hallucinations, is all that is left of the waking consciousness.
>
> (CW 1/126)

Critique of Jung's ego concept in occult phenomena

There are a number of points of criticism to make in looking at Jung's dissertation. Goodheart (1984) points out that Jung avoided acknowledging the interpersonal aspect of his description of 'S.W.' – who was his cousin and deeply attracted to him – as a defense against the "enormous erotic and emotional realities underlying the entire relationship" (p. 27). Jung saw the subpersonalities as autonomous phenomena rather than as 'interactionally determined'.

Similarly, Jung failed to see that his giving S. the book *The Clairvoyante of Prevorst* may have influenced the emergence of this ego figure, and that in fact she was trying to please him by this. It may simply be the case that in the late 19th century when these séances took place, the concept of transference was not yet articulated and that Jung was naively assuming he could be objective. This is a missed opportunity on Jung's part, but not unexpected. Hillman (1976) makes the point that the new case study in psychoanalytic literature demands a new form of writing closer to the roman à clef than a historically honest account because the reality of the case is best expressed in psychological facts rather than historical accuracy.

One can see from this dissertation that Jung is beginning to affiliate himself with Freudian theory, but retains a fascination with the concept of an autonomous psyche. He is developing an outline for a theory of complexes – the emergence of autonomous feeling and image as a result of conflict – while for Freud psychopathology was a result of repression only. Jung conceives of the ego then as having an ability to split in response to conflict.

Burghölzli and the association experiment (1902–1910)

Bleuler introduced research into word associations to the Burghölzli clinic in 1901, and Jung began investigating the associations of his patients in 1902. Wilhelm Wundt in Leipzig had developed a technique more than 20 years earlier (Meier, 1984, p. 71) for measuring the physiological reactions such as respiration rate to a given impression or word, and to measure the time elapsed between perception and physiological reaction: the 'reaction-time'. Wundt's student, Emile Kraeplin, introduced this technique into psychiatry in the late 19th century, a technique studied and refined further by his pupil Gustav Aschaffenburg. These experiments were particularly concerned with the association between the stimulus – a word in this case – and the reaction response. Following this method, Édouard Claparède of Geneva published a prizewinning paper called 'L'Association des Idées' in 1903 which contained a classification of associations found in this research.

What did Jung conclude about the nature of the ego with these association experiments? Three major ideas emerged which began to form the basis of his thinking on this subject. The first was the idea of the complex and the ego-complex. The second had to do with the nature of what he called ego-consciousness. The third idea dealt with the mechanisms of repression and displacement, that is, defensive actions in the psyche. These topics have as their background, however, assumptions about the nature of the psyche that constitute Jung's own emerging structural theory of the psyche and the place of the ego in this structure.

The complex

In looking over the words with disturbed associations for a given individual, Jung noted certain reactions grouped together, whether through theme or particular disturbance, and that the grouping had as a unifying subject two things: a particular idea and a feeling-tone. In other words, the disturbed reaction had as its background a particular emotional experience for the individual such as 'unhappy love affair' or 'guilt'.

How unconscious are these complexes? Jung would conclude very much so. In 1906 he wrote,

> Everybody, of course, has one or more complexes that manifest themselves in some way in associations. The background of our consciousness (or the unconscious) consists of such complexes. The whole material that can be remembered is grouped around these. They form higher psychic units analogous with the ego-complex. They constellate our whole thinking and acting, therefore also our associations.
>
> (CW 2/664)

The complex, then, is not only unconscious, but also directing conscious thought and action. This is a strong assertion indeed. Complexes in this formulation constitute the hidden hand in the function of personality.

Groupings of psychical material around a psychological theme were first associated with the word complex, according to Christoffel (Meier, 1984, p. 173), by Eugen Bleuler himself at the Burghölzli. Jung picked this usage up then, and indeed Jung cites Bleuler's sense of the word 'ego-complex' in his early association experiment papers (CW 2/664). Bleuler introduced the idea of ego-complex some years earlier.

Bleuler and the ego-complex

In 1894, while director of the mental hospital in Rheinau near Basel, Eugen Bleuler wrote for the leading psychiatric journal of the day an essay entitled 'Toward a Scientific Examination of Fundamental Psychological Concepts'. This was a unusual article in a journal more accustomed to publishing treatises on syphilis or imbecility, but it was especially remarkable because Bleuler, in a very careful, clear way, not only describes the relationship of the ego to the neurological functioning of the brain, but he also introduces the concept of and describes the ego-complex.

His thesis is summarized in the first paragraph (my translation):

> Mind, soul, and consciousness are still metaphysical concepts. The question as to whether a soul exists, and what it is, is still as unanswerable as ever. However, our knowledge of neurology allows us, it seems to me, not only to construe a conscious 'ego', but also to show that this conscious 'ego' (personality with consciousness and self-consciousness) genuinely exists and is composed of well-known functions of the nervous system. It must be left open if this 'ego' is the same we observe in ourselves: but

> because it fulfills all the requirements that we assign to the mind, soul, and consciousness, it is at least quite unnecessary to adopt a second metaphysical 'soul' independent from the nervous system.
>
> (Bleuler, 1894, p. 133)

He begins his discussion by describing the neural pathways of the brain that comprise the experience of continuity. When these are activated repeatedly over time, there develops a 'dynamic pathway' to which slightly different experiences get associated. This is experienced consciously as a sense of unity that continually incorporates new experiences. Each new experience, then, is incorporated into an associated pathway. This group of associated experiences is a 'complex'.

According to Bleuler, the complex is associated with a particular physical or physiological feeling and he emphasized this point:

> [The] concomitant constancy and enduring nature of the different experiences of the body [breathing, heartbeat, for example] necessitates an especially close relationship between the individual arriving emotions and their dynamic pathway. . . . All our experiences and their 'dynamic pathways' must therefore be connected to physical sensation [conscious or unconsciously experienced].
>
> (Bleuler, 1894, p. 137; my translation)

He goes on to conclude that personality and physical sensation create a new centralized complex that acts as a 'central station' for all the other complexes: the 'ego-complex'. The ego-complex is, according to Bleuler, "formed from the accumulated stores of physical sensation and the memory images of the individual" (1894, p. 141; my translation). He concludes that the ego-complex represents the conscious experience of 'I'.

The three characteristics of the ego-complex described by Bleuler – that it is conscious, that it is composed of mental images and physical sensation and emotional experience, and that it is the 'central station' for all other complexes – were incorporated into Jung's schema of the ego-complex in his association experiment work, and more importantly, all his later thinking on the ego.

Ego-consciousness and defensive actions in the psyche

Jung differentiated between the ego-complex and ego-consciousness in his experimental researches. In speaking of the association process, he said,

> To our ego-consciousness the association-process seems to be its own work, subject to its judgment, free will, and concentration; in reality,

> however, as our experiment beautifully shows, ego-consciousness is merely the marionette that dances on the stage, moved by a concealed mechanism.
>
> (CW 2/609)

The individual is compelled, in other words, in his feelings and associations by unconscious complexes. So ego-consciousness therefore amounts to the sense of oneself as an 'I'.

This conscious 'I', however, rests upon a partly conscious, partly unconscious component – the ego-complex. Jung wrote,

> The feeling-toned complex . . . exercises an influence that constantly and successfully competes with the intentions of the ego-complex; in spite of the rejecting and repressing attitude of the ego-complex, it brings about subjective and treacherous reactions and arouses associations the meaning of which is utterly unexpected by the ego-complex.
>
> (CW 2/610)

Jung implies two different aspects to the ego-complex in this passage. First, there is the part that comprises the conscious will ('intentions') and usual conscious sense of oneself (self-consciousness). The other aspect, however, is the implied unconscious defensive role of the ego-complex. In this capacity the actions are less intentional than reactive. In a discussion of the mechanism of 'not-wanting-to-betray', for example, Jung states, "This not-wanting-to-betray is, as we have become convinced from numerous experiments, by no means always a conscious not-wanting but quite often an unconscious inhibition . . ." (CW 2/417, n. 42). Also, in another passage he describes a defensive function but is more equivocal about its stance in consciousness or unconsciousness:

> The concealment of an emotion is always characterized by a quite particular attitude, a particular state of feeling. Without conscious censure, the emerging part of the complex is suppressed by the feeling of being directed not to betray, which is present in consciousness and from which specially attuned inhibitions arise. Of course the process of suppression may take place at a considerably more conscious level (or more unconscious, as in hysteria!).
>
> (CW 2/417)

So Jung unintentionally builds a model of two forms of the ego in these early association experiment researches. There is a conscious sense of selfhood, of identity and will, which Jung associates with the term 'ego-consciousness'. This use of the term 'ego' emphasizes that it is a conscious experience. By using the term 'ego-complex', however, Jung stresses the aspect of the ego which is not wholly conscious and which rests on unconscious, even somatic and autonomous processes, but which is experienced by the conscious personality.

Collaboration with Freud (1906–1912)

Jung's personal and professional association with Sigmund Freud in the years between 1907 and 1912 has been extensively documented in the literature on the history of depth psychology (cf. Ellenberger, 1970). Jung's close association with Freud came about in the context of the influence of Eugen Bleuler and the growing application of the scientific, or energic, paradigm to Jung's work and writings. Freud represented for Jung, the young psychiatrist, by his own admission an 'honored teacher' and 'a source of illumination'; Jung even compared Freud at one point to the scientific genius Galileo (CW 3, p. 4). Jung would later describe himself during this period as a Freud 'partisan'. His passion for Freud is clearly evident in their letters, for example, despite the differences of opinion Jung reserved throughout their relationship.

This period collaborating with Freud was at an early career point for Jung – as he himself admitted in his autobiography, he had much to learn – and yet it is worthwhile to remember that Freud, although a mature clinician, still had major revisions in his theories before him. The major work Freud would devote to the psychology of the ego, for example, would not occur until after World War I (Freud, 1923, 1926), several years after the Freud–Jung split. Freud's work *On Narcissism*, which would introduce the theory of ego-libido, was not formed in his mind until 1913 (Gay, 1988, p. 338). Freud's theory of the mind had not progressed to a structural theory but rather, during his period of collaboration with Jung, he was still working out his theory of sexuality. *The Interpretation of Dreams* had just been published in 1900, after all, and during the years of Freud and Jung's association, Freud would also be preoccupied with the "exhausting demands" of psychoanalytic politics, as well as writing case histories and essays on literature, art, education, for example, alongside clinical papers on technique (Gay, 1988, p. 306).

So in evaluating Freud's influence on Jung's theory of ego, it is well to remember that this topic was very much nascent in both as these two men were developing their own theories. Although for Freud during this period the emphasis was on the theory of sexuality and the instincts, for Jung the focus became the issue of libido in a more general sense. By looking beyond Bleuler's ego-complex theory and the nature of psychical energy beyond Freud's theory, then, Jung formed his initial ego theory.

Because of his differences with Freud, Jung began to develop his alternative theory in a more systematic way. It is as if he was forced to structure his dissentions in order to articulate and argue these differences to Freud and others. His psychological theories arising out of this period are therefore more structured and elaborated for two reasons: first because of his general move toward a scientific and therefore more structured, outlook in general, and second, because he had an opponent, an opposite, in the person of Freud, with whom Jung was to conduct an intense inner as well as outer debate about fundamental concepts.

I have chosen to focus on three works by Jung in my discussion of his collaboration with Freud. Their association began formally when Jung sent Freud the book *Diagnostic Association Studies*. Freud remarked in his reply to Jung that he was most pleased with the paper in it by Jung, 'Psychoanalysis and Association Experiments' (Freud/Jung Letters, 1F). In that paper Jung defended, and sought to support with empirical evidence, the etiological theories of hysteria developed by Freud in his *Studies on Hysteria* (1895). They began their correspondence.

The next work discussed, 'The Psychology of Dementia Praecox' (1907), has been described as the culmination of Jung's work at the Burghölzli on the nature of psychosis, the publication of which made his reputation as a psychiatric investigator (CW 3, p. v). In this book, Jung cites Freud repeatedly and with "marked appreciation". In it Jung uses the association experiment to again support Freud's theoretical conclusions. The two were able to meet in person finally in 1907, and their friendship and professional collaboration was thus well underway.

Regarding the third selection to be discussed: Jung's trip to America to speak at Fordham University in 1912, in order to deliver the lecture series 'The Theory of Psychoanalysis', came at a time when strain between the two men was becoming difficult to contain. The period of theoretical and personal differences leading up to the delivery of these lectures has been well documented elsewhere (Gay, 1988; Hayman, 1999). Rather than dwell on the minutiae of the breakdown of the personal relationship between Freud and Jung, I would like to instead examine the content of these lectures in order to outline Jung's emerging ego theory as he was breaking away from Freud. The theoretical differences with Freud evident within are the foundation of Jung's preliminary Ego Psychology.

'Psychoanalysis and Association Experiments' (1906)

Background

In 1902 in his doctoral dissertation, Jung already recognizes the phenomena of repression described in Freud's *Interpretation of Dreams* and in Freud and Breuer's work *Studies on Hysteria*. Later, he describes himself as "indebted" for the "valuable stimulus" the latter work provided for his association experiment research (CW 2/490n). In particular, Jung felt the concept of repression was the key to understanding the complex phenomena he was observing in the association experiment. He returns again and again to the concept of repression in his analyses of association experiments. The concept of repression represented a key bridge to Freud's work for Jung.

In 1905 (in his *Habilitationsschrift*, the piece of academic writing required for a university appointment) Jung subtly differentiates his understanding of repression from Freud's. He wrote in a footnote:

> In Freud's work this concept [repression] . . . has the character of an active function, frequently a function of consciousness. In hysteria one may, however, get the impression that repression equals deliberate forgetting. With normal subjects it might, however, be a more passive 'sliding into the background'; at least here repression seems to be something unconscious, to which we can only indirectly attribute the character of something willed or something *wished* [emphasis added by Jung, possibly as a reference to Freud's dream theory]. If, nevertheless, I speak of 'repressing' or 'concealing', this use of language, according to one's taste, can be taken as a metaphor from the psychology of consciousness. Essentially it comes to the same thing because objectively it does not matter one way or the other whether a psychic process is conscious or unconscious. (cf. Bleuler, 'Toward a Scientific Examination of Fundamental Psychological Concepts', 1894)
>
> (CW 2/619n)

In discussing the relative consciousness or unconsciousness of the repression process here, Jung is alluding to Bleuler's concept of the ego-complex possessing relative consciousness. According to Bleuler, the conscious subject 'I' is only partially in control of one's actions. He wrote,

> When conscious perceptions, thoughts, and actions all become associated with the ego-complex, it follows that the ego-complex, the personality, gets the greatest meaning from conscious action; and that only with one's conscious action does one throw one's 'full weight on the scale'. With unconscious, or less conscious, activity, the ego-complex has no, or very little, connection to one's actions and therefore has very little influence.
>
> (Bleuler, 1894, p. 146)

From Bleuler's point of view, then, a psychical phenomenon such as repression could be associated with consciousness or the unconscious depending on the degree to which it is associated with the ego-complex. A conscious action would more accurately be called suppression rather than repression, although as Jung said earlier, it does not matter in the end because phenomenologically the result is the same.

Freud's attitude toward the conscious or unconscious nature of repression evolved. In *Studies on Hysteria* (1893), repression has a conscious character. He wrote in the discussion of one case history, for example,

> Now I already knew from the analysis of similar cases that before hysteria can be acquired for the first time one essential condition must be fulfilled: an idea must be *intentionally repressed from consciousness* [emphasis Freud], and excluded from associative modification. In my view this intentional repression is also the basis for the conversion. . . .
> (SE 2, p. 116)

He later modified his opinion and stated in a subsequent paper 'Further Remarks on the Neuro-Psychoses of Defense' (1896, in SE 3), that the repression of ideas incompatible with the ego were unconsciously repressed as a defense.

Although Freud would call the repression defense "the cornerstone on which the whole structure of psycho-analysis rests" (SE 14, p. 16, 1914), he does not identify a repressing agency at this point in his theory (and would not until his later work on the ego concept, after his break with Jung). The repressing 'cause' is characterized as a mechanistic process:

> I should like, finally, to dwell for a moment on the working hypothesis which I have made use of in this exposition of the neuroses of defense. I refer to the concept that in mental functions something is to be distinguished – a quota of affect or a sum of excitation – which possesses all the characteristics of a quantity (though we have no means of measuring it) which is capable of increase, diminution, displacement and discharge, and which is spread over the memory-traces of ideas somewhat as an electrical charge is spread over the surface of the body.
> (SE 3, 1894, p. 60)

For Jung, as he explores the theory of complexes and the phenomena of repression in this work, the mechanics of the process interest him less than the meaning of the contents repressed. The complex retains a meaningful, that is, emotion-laden, unconscious bond with the ego demonstrated through associations. Jung begins to see that the cause of hysteria, the repression defense, in a subtly different way from Freud's mechanistic view – rather than a sum of affect or excitation displaced, the act of repression is, for Jung, a struggle between two personalities, one the ego-complex, the other the neurotic complex.

The paper

This paper is a defense of psychoanalysis as well as a confirmation of the usefulness of the association experiment in Freud's new treatment method. As Jung approached writing this, however, he had already developed differences with Freud in the area of repression. Another difference emerges in Jung's elaboration of the ego-complex – a concept Freud did not use. Also, while Freud was thinking in terms of "the topography of the mind" (Freud, 1900) and working out his theory of sexuality, Jung was beginning to develop in parallel his own theory of psychic structures and processes in general and a theory of ego and consciousness in particular distinct from Freud.

Psychoanalysis and Association Experiments begins with a summary of Freud's theory of hysteria and the role of repression. Jung agrees with Freud that sexual trauma and the subsequent repression of associated sexual ideas is the origin of hysteria. Hysteria occurs, according to Jung, because ideas too painful ('charged with painful affect') for ego-consciousness are repressed. The repressed cause, or trauma, is revealed 'symbolically' through the hysterical symptom or through disturbances noted in the association experiment, which denote 'complexes of ideas'.

Jung's focus in establishing the origin of hysteria in particular and of neurosis in general is the complex. He says,

> Every psychogenic neurosis contains a complex that differs from normal complexes by unusually strong emotional charges, and for this reason has such a constellating power that it fetters the whole individual. The complex, therefore, is the *causa morbi* [source of illness].
>
> (CW 2/665)

Jung then presents the case of a patient with an obsessive neurosis in order to illustrate the connection of psychoanalysis to the association experiment. His case is of a 37-year-old woman, a teacher with problems with insomnia and "inner restlessness and excitement, irritability toward her family, impatience and difficulty in getting on with people". The obsessive symptom manifested itself as the problem that "each time she started going off to sleep the thought came that she certainly would not be able to sleep, she would never be able to sleep until she was dead" (CW 2/666).

Jung performed the association experiment with her and after detailed analysis of the reaction times and recollection disturbances and so on identified the dominance of an erotic, or sexual, complex. When he informed the patient of his conclusions, she denied the explanation for her difficulties "with affect and sincere conviction". Jung took her denial as confirmation he was correct in his assessment. After several long and tumultuous analytic sessions, Jung observed that the "sexual complex" began to replace the original obsessional ideas. He saw that there was a struggle between the ego-complex and the sexual complex:

> Her everyday person and her sexual person are just two different complexes, two different aspects of consciousness that do not want to or must not know anything of one another. The split of the personality here

> is, however, only hinted at (as in every vigorous complex, the peculiarity of which is a striving for autonomy).
>
> (CW 2/712)

He goes on to say later, in a discussion of the sexual complex and her "gently disposed character", that "they [complexes] actually have a separate existence, they form a state within the state, they constitute a personality within the personality. Expressed in other words, there are two mental attitudes present, kept apart by strong emotional barriers" (CW 2/719).

Jung then discusses the dynamic relationship between the ego- and neurotic complex:

> But even if a complex is still so far repressed, it must yet have a constellating influence on the contents of normal consciousness, for even the deepest split of consciousness does not reach the indivisible basis of the personality. Thus the repression must leave a certain imprint on the conscious processes; the normal consciousness must somehow explain away the emotional condition that a repressed complex leaves behind.
>
> (CW2/720)

Jung wishes to account in this passage for the obsessive symptoms as a displacement 'explanation'. At another level, however, he is implying something quite different. Jung is also saying that there is ultimately an 'indivisible basis' of the personality and that there is a dynamic interaction. A 'constellating effect' compels the ego-complex and the repressed complex to interact with each other: consciousness to 'explain away' the emotions (thus activating the ego defenses), and the complex to 'strive for autonomy'. This interaction is evidenced, according to Jung, by the associations. This implies a level of engagement and interaction beyond the energic level, something purposive.

In his conclusion Jung is unable to reach further in this line of thinking, however. He writes that 'abreaction' of the 'submerged pathological idea' is the cure. "The split-off contents of the mind are destroyed by being released from repression through an effort of the will. So they lose a great deal of their authority and therefore of their horror, and simultaneously the patient regains the feeling of being master of his ideas" (CW 2/725). In this passage Jung acknowledges that by opening up the repressed complex to consciousness its "horror" is overcome ("destroyed"). Jung adds finally that it is the "arousing and strengthening of the will" he would emphasize in treatment, and not merely abreaction. He believes this helps the patient regain "the feeling of being master of his ideas" (CW2/725). So it appears that Jung values consciousness and fails at this point to see an advantage or any growth in the ego-complex because of the ego–unconscious complex engagement.

Critique

Although Freud and Jung agree that repression lies behind the neurosis, in this work Jung also differs from Freud. In Freud's view, repression is a mechanistic response to unpleasure;

> it turns out to be a sine qua non for the acquisition of hysteria that an incompatibility should develop between the ego and some idea presented to it. . . . The hysterical method of defense . . . lies in the conversion of the excitation into a somatic innervation.
>
> (SE 2, p. 122)

Although Freud describes at another point in this passage that the ego has a role in this defensive maneuver, Jung in the paper discussed, in contrast, focuses on repression as the outcome of a struggle between two psychical entities – the ego-complex and the neurotic complex.

The nature of the neurotic complex in Jung's concept is subtly different from Freud's formulation. Complexes have the characteristics of a separate personality, for example. Jung writes, "They [complexes] form higher psychic units analogous with the ego-complex [reference to Bleuler's ego-complex concept made here]. They constellate our whole thinking and acting, therefore our associations" (CW 2/664). Because Jung equates the ego-complex with the conscious personality according to Bleuler's formulation, the complex would also constitute a personality in its organization ("higher psychic unit") and power ("They constellate our whole thinking and acting").

Critiques of Freud's theory of repression would be relevant here for assessing Jung's theory. Macmillan (1991) points out a "fatal" inconsistency in Freud's concept:

> For an affect to be converted and for its idea to become unconscious the separation of the two has to be complete or near complete. However, for abreaction to take place, the idea has to be recovered with its affect still attached. Symptom formation thus requires repression to separate the idea from its feeling but symptom removal requires they remain attached.
>
> (p. 161)

Jung, however, does not separate the idea and the affect in his complex theory. A complex is defined as a split-off or repressed idea with an affective core.

A further criticism of Freud is that the mechanism of repression is uncharacterized (Macmillan, 1991, p. 160). Freud can say what it is but does not describe, at this point in his writings, the mechanism of how it comes about. Jung also fails to offer an explanation at this point but refers to the mechanisms of repression in a way that implies contradictory ego functions. For example, he states that "crucial ideas charged with painful affects" (CW 2/661) are incompatible with ego-consciousness and are therefore repressed. The implication is that 'consciousness' is the inhibiting factor. Yet later he states, "The split-off contents of the mind [the repressed contents] are destroyed by being released from repression through an effort of the will" (CW 2/725). In this instance, there is implied a factor outside or separate from consciousness that is repressing and that this must be overcome by a conscious factor, the will. If Jung intends ego-consciousness to mean personality with consciousness and self-consciousness (following Bleuler), then it cannot contain an unconscious function such as ego defense. However, if he means the ego factor that has conscious and unconscious components, then he really meant ego-complex: that is, as described earlier, the aspect of the ego which is not wholly conscious and which rests on unconscious, even somatic and autonomous processes, but which is experienced by the conscious personality. Thus to make sense of the preceding quotes: the ego-complex does the repressing, but ego-consciousness releases the repressed through will.

'The Psychology of Dementia Praecox' (1907)

This work is important historically for the development of a Jungian Ego Psychology in two ways. First, Jung for the first time uses the term 'psychic energy' and explores a nonsexual libido concept to explain the psychotic impairments seen in 'Dementia Praecox'. By moving away from (but not rejecting) a straightforward energic repression explanation, he can propose a dynamic interaction between the ego-complex and the pathological complex that he now begins to describe in greater detail. Second, he begins to describe not only the dynamic aspect of this psychical system, but also the nature of its components. This leads to a more defined structural system that gives the ego a fundamental role.

Jung's purpose in writing this essay was to show a new view of the "individual psychological basis of Dementia Praecox". As he states in the foreword, even as he utilizes Freud's mechanisms of dreams and hysteria to analyze the phenomena of Dementia Praecox, he does not therefore subscribe to the exclusive importance of Freud's infantile sexual trauma hypothesis. As Stepansky (1976) points out, Jung was not using this essay to disagree with or rebel against Freud. He was at this point still striving to utilize Freud's concepts or expand them in a way acceptable to Freud.

Jung begins with a survey of theoretical views of the psychology of Dementia Praecox. In this section, he reviews the 'lowering of attention' seen in this disorder, and introduces a discussion of 'perception' versus 'apperception'. Based on Wundt's research, and others, 'perception' would be the subjective side of attention, the subjectively experienced feelings and sensations. 'Apperception', on the other hand, is "the more objective consequences, the alterations in the conscious contents (CW 3/19). Although Jung feels Wundt's concept of apperception is enormous in scope, he nevertheless agrees with others that characteristic of Dementia Praecox is deterioration in apperception but not perception. In other words, memory and comprehension in general are unimpaired but active attention (i.e. consciousness) toward the immediate environment is diminished.

Also, Jung reviews the well-known incongruity between 'idea and affect' in Dementia Praecox: there may be 'disproportionate and incomprehensible' affects, or a poverty of emotional reactions. He acknowledges it remains unknown why this occurs (CW 3/35) but later cites work by Otto Gross (CW 3/55) as a means to understand this as a dissociation of consciousness. Ideas are split off from consciousness and lead a life of the own "as separate chains of association occurring simultaneously" (CW 3/56). Jung sees the 'cement that binds' these chains of consciousness together is some definite affect. With the chains loosened, disintegration of consciousness sets in and "the complexes coexisting with it are simultaneously freed from all restraint and are able to break through into ego-consciousness" (CW 3/59). Affects, however, become 'fixed' because the patient has less and less control over the idea, Jung quotes Neisser: "The affects which are normally meant to regulate our relations with the surrounding world and to implement our adaptation to it . . . these affects become alienated from their natural purpose" (CW 3/73). In Freudian terms then, Jung says, "the repressed complexes (the carrier of affects) can no longer be eliminated from the conscious process" (CW 3/74).

Jung presciently concludes this first review section by speculating that there may be an organic factor that injures the 'higher psychic functions' (such as the coordinating and controlling functions of the ego-complex). This may ultimately be the reason for the emergence of Dementia Praecox rather than hysteria when there is a strong complex.

In his own analysis of the psychology of Dementia Praecox, Jung returns to the theory of complexes. He begins to describe in this essay the structure and dynamics of the ego-complex and the autonomous complexes as well as the mechanisms of interaction.

Structure and dynamics of the complex

The ego-complex and the autonomous complexes have differing origins and characteristics. The ego-complex, understood as "the highest psychic authority", is based on and rooted in the ongoing "powerful and ever-present feeling-tone of our body" (CW 3/82). Jung defines this feeling-tone as "an affective state accompanied by somatic innervations" (CW 3/83). He goes on to say that "[t]he ego is the psychological expression of the firmly associated combination of all body sensations. One's own personality is therefore the firmest and strongest complex . . ." (CW 3/83). The ego-complex directs attention (CW 3/83), wishes, and interests (CW 3/86); controls one's mood, thoughts, words, and deeds (CW 3/93). There is a feeling of wholeness of personality associated with it (CW 3/102). At its barest essentials the ego-complex is concerned with survival (CW 3/86).

The autonomous complex, on the other hand, arises out of strong affect and endures through its powerful connection to the physical effects of the affect. Jung wrote, for example,

> [L]arge complexes are always strongly feeling-toned, and conversely, strong affects always leave behind very large complexes. This is due simply to the fact that on the one hand large complexes include somatic innervations, while on the other hand strong affects constellate a great many associations because of their powerful and persistent stimulation of the body.
>
> (CW 3/87)

Complexes of this type have certain characteristics. They 'constellate' and sap psychic energy from the ego-complex (CW 3/ 109). Jung wrote, for example, "When we are dominated by a complex only the ideas associated with it have full feeling-tone – all other perceptions within and without are subject to the inhibition" (CW 3/174). The autonomous complex can erupt into consciousness in 'symbolic' ways (symbolic refers here to a 'feeling-image' rather than a 'thought-image'; CW 3/136), and act like 'little secondary psyches' when the ego-complex has less control (in sleep, for example), or when the complex is particularly strong (CW 3/109). An example of this would be the case of an individual with a strong victim complex.

Because the ego-complex is rooted in the body, it is not eliminated by the autonomous complex but instead is pushed aside. Jung suggests that the ego-complex is modified by a strong complex into an "affect-ego" (CW 3/86). He writes in a footnote,

> By 'affect-ego' I mean the modification of the ego-complex resulting from the emergence of a strongly toned complex. In the case of painful affects the modification consists of a restriction, a withdrawal of many parts of the normal ego. Many other wishes, interests, and affects must make way for the new complex, so far as they are opposed to it.
>
> (CW 3/86, n. 9)

This affect ego, or ego remnant, persists in hysteria or Dementia Praecox as a "correcting voice" heard in the mind (CW 3/180). This "correcting, ironical, semi-normal ego-remnant" (CW 3/314) may come about as a compensation for the one-sidedness of the autonomous complex (see CW 3/304, for example).

Complex mechanisms

Jung describes four types of mechanisms characteristic of the ego-complex and the autonomous complex. First, as mentioned earlier, there is a *Mechanism of Constellation*, characteristic of the autonomous complex. Jung demonstrated this mechanism in his work on the association experiment and describes it here in relation to the complex at the nucleus of Dementia Praecox. Because of its link to neurological pathways in the brain, any association or feeling that touches the neurological pathway of the complex causes the complex to gain control of consciousness at the expense of the ego-complex. Jung, following Bleuler, attributes this constellating power of the feeling-toned complex to the fact that "the essential basis of our personality is affectivity" (CW 3/77). By affectivity, he means feeling, sentiment, and emotion. Jung quotes Bleuler in his assessment that the basis of affectivity is ultimately a reaction to pleasure/unpleasure (CW 3/78, n. 2).

A second mechanism characteristic of the autonomous complex is the *Mechanism of 'Contrast'*. Jung wrote,

> [W]e must mention another characteristic effect of complexes: the tendency to contrasting associations. As Bleuler has demonstrated [. . .] all psychic activity that strives toward a goal must be accompanied by contrasts. This is absolutely necessary for proper co-ordination and control. Experience shows that in every decision these contrasts appear as the nearest associations. Normally they do not hinder reflection; on the contrary they promote it and are useful for our actions. But if for any reason the individual's energy is impaired, he easily becomes the victim of the counterplay of positive and negative, since the feeling-tone of the decision is no longer sufficient to overpower the contrasts and restrain them.
> (CW 3/138)

Jung demonstrated this tendency empirically in the association experiment where a 'complexed' association reaction would take the form of a subjective, or internal, contrasting association ('sweet' in response to the stimulus word 'sour', for example).

As a mechanism, there is much implied here. There is the assumption that psychic activity, that is, the dynamics of the ego-complex/autonomous-complex system is not merely seeking a balance, which would be the case in a psychology based on energic principles. Rather, psychic activity is 'striving toward a goal' – a teleological perspective – and that the mechanism of contrasts is an inherent part of that activity. It is the means of 'coordination and control'. What would be the objective of this coordination and control? Jung writes that contrasts 'promote reflection' and are therefore 'useful for our actions'. It appears, then, that Jung is suggesting the work of the ego-complex (the seat of 'reflection' and 'action' – and *handlung* in the original German) needs the mechanism of contrasts in order to participate in some unspecified teleological function. When it is impaired due to 'lowered energy' the ego-complex cannot act in its normal coordinating function, and the individual is then 'overpowered' by the contrasts. There is along this line also the possibility of a 'double personality' or double consciousness; the ego-complex retains some strength but the powerful split-off complex acts as a second personality. Noll (1989) explored this same phenomenon of split-personality-as-opposing-complexes in a discussion on multiple personality disorder.

This interactive and teleological perspective contrasts, as I said, with the energic paradigm. (This theme would be developed further in the lectures in America where Jung discusses the mechanism of compensation.)

In addition, Jung mentions another mechanism in this essay that was to become a topic for Freud almost two decades later: *Repetition*. In *Beyond the Pleasure Principle* (1920), Freud introduced the concept 'compulsion to repeat', and overturns one of his basic principles. In a discussion on transference phenomena Freud wrote,

> If we take into account observations such as these [instances of reoccurrences leading to unpleasure], based upon behavior in the transference and upon the life-histories of men and women, we shall find courage to assume that there really does exist in the mind a compulsion to repeat which overrides the pleasure principle.
>
> (1920, p. 23)

Freud later characterizes this compulsion as giving "the appearance of some 'demonic' force at work" (1920, p. 35). Freud would describe this force as having an instinctual character comparable to the sexual instinct.

Jung looks at repetition from another perspective. Stereotypy, "the persistent and constant reproduction of a certain activity" characteristically seen in Dementia Praecox, is according to Jung and others (CW 3/182), in fact a normal and necessary part of our psychical development.

> In order to perform a certain activity we direct all our attention to the ideas related to it, and through this strong feeling-tone we engrave the various phases of the process on our memory. The result of frequent repetition is that an even smoother 'path' is formed, along which the activity comes to move without our help, i.e. automatically.
>
> (CW 3/182)

Jung then relates repetition to the formation of a complex because of the strong feeling-tone associated with the 'engraving process'. Complexes have "a greater tendency to persistence and reproduction than ordinary and therefore automatic repetition is a complex indicator" (CW 3/182–183).

Jung, however, hints at a purpose to these repetitions. He cites a 1906 work by Pfister (CW 3/185, n. 43) and wonders if "some ideational content is at the back of the stereotypy, but that it comes out in a distorted way"; that the stereotyped ideas "are struggling to express themselves". Jung is thus moving away from a purely organic explanation for these repetitions (a neurological pathway hypothesis) and suggests instead a psychological explanation related to the complexes' efforts to be conscious ("struggling to express themselves"). In this formulation Jung recognizes repetition as a mechanism for complex formation at the organic level, but there may be an additional psychological purpose for its eruption into consciousness beyond the organic explanation. The key element that differentiates the organic from the psychological is the emotional content. A mechanism of repetition then would represent a drive or need to bring the repressed unconscious emotional content into consciousness.

Jung also discusses specific *mechanisms of the ego-complex*. The first is a *mechanism of defense*. There are a number of defenses Jung specifically describes, including negativism and blocking (CW 3/179), as well as displacement and reversal (CW 3/105). These all arise when the complex is touched (by the stimulus word in the association experiment, for example) and the individual resists, that is, 'draws back' from the complex. These mechanisms arise to maintain the distance and separation of the (conscious) individual from the contents and emotions of the complex. It can also occur that the emotions arise from the complex but the content is resisted (CW 3/93): a form of splitting.

Jung appears to place this 'rejecting', that is, managing, activity in the ego-complex. For example, he states, "The complex functions automatically in accordance with the law of analogy [i.e. dreamlike]; it is completely freed from the control of the ego-complex, and for this reason the ego-complex can no longer direct associations" (CW 3/218). At another point he says, "During the normal activity of the ego-complex the other complexes must be inhibited or the conscious function of directed association would be impossible" (CW 3/135). In a discussion of the inhibiting action of sleep on the ego-complex, Jung states, "[t]he autonomous complexes are no longer under the direct control of the ego-complex . . ." (CW 3/137). In all of these statements, there is the assumption that in waking consciousness the ego-complex directs and controls, like a psychical guard, the influence of the unconscious complexes.

The key to the ego-complex's strength is the quantity of psychic energy. The dominance of the ego-complex is overcome when the autonomous complex gains in intensity of psychic energy. This is at the expense of the ego-complex (CW 3/102) so Jung here implies a law of conservation of energy, that psychic energy is not created or destroyed but rather, transferred.

Is this action by the ego-complex conscious, i.e. deliberate and fully mindful, or is it an unconscious function? Jung is not clear on this. Although there is no direct statement one way or the other, he certainly implies that there is an aspect of the ego-complex that will act in an unconscious or less than fully mindful way. In his discussion of the "affect-ego" (CW 3/86) described earlier, for example, Jung describes an ego that reacts instinctually and without thought. The reaction of the affect-ego is directed toward personal survival above all else: a "primitive ruthlessness" dissolves the layers of adaptation and civilization when the individual is gravely endangered.

It also appears as if Jung describes the defense 'displacement' as an unconscious ego process in his discussion of 'double personality' (CW 3/105). A complex is "disguised" by the "superimposition of a contrasting mood". He goes on to say that "these displacements and disguises may as we know, produce real double personalities' which manifests itself in 'double consciousness'" or "dissociation of the personality". It hardly seems possible it is a conscious action on the part of the ego-complex to keep two consciousnesses separate. It only makes sense logically if there is a third, unconscious element aware of these two complexes that can sustain the separation.

Lastly, Jung appears to place the mechanism of adaptation in the ego-complex in opposition to the dream-mechanisms seen in the unconscious complex. When there is a strong complex present, Jung says, for example, "all progress adapted to the environment ceases and the associations revolve entirely around the complex" (CW 3/184). In a discussion of the disturbed associations seen in Dementia Praecox (CW 3/216–18), Jung implies or characterizes the ego-complex as directed toward adaptation to reality, while the unconscious, autonomous complex lacks this ability and functions according to the mechanisms of the unconscious described by Freud (such as condensation, indistinctness of ideas, etc.). The action of the autonomous complex impairs "the *fonction du réel*, or adaptation to the environment" (CW 3/298), necessary for conscious awareness and 'direct thinking'.

One notable aspect of Jung's formulation of the ego-complex is that the ego-complex and the autonomous complex are not simply psychic entities, but possess mechanisms, that is, dynamic functions, which complement each other. These opposing, or complementary, functions are the instruments of some kind of psychic process – the goal of which Jung implies is consciousness (see earlier discussion). So while Freud, at this point in his theory, has placed the opposing forces of the psyche, consciousness, and unconsciousness, in a process directed toward repression, Jung implies the process is two-way: repression of unacceptable psychic contents but also a drive toward consciousness of these same contents.

In formulating the ego-complex and autonomous complex as he does, Jung is building up a structural theory of the mind in which psychic entities have specific and complementary mechanisms and functions. In contrast, at this point (1906), Freud has a view of the psyche dominated by an energic and topographical model. Freud only finally formulated the ego as the organizing, controlling, and adapting mental structure in 1923 (SE 19). As stated earlier, Freud was more interested in these early years of psychoanalysis with "establishing the existence of unconscious mental processes and elucidating their nature. Concomitantly, he concerned himself with demonstrating the values of psychoanalysis as a potential technique for exploring the depths of the mind" (Meissner, 2000, p. 155).

'The Theory of Psychoanalysis' (lectures delivered at Fordham University, 1912)

Jung was invited to deliver a series of lectures on the topic 'Psychoanalysis' in September 1912 at Fordham University, a small Catholic University in New York. This came at a time when there were considerable personal and professional tensions between him and Freud that were beginning to poison their collaboration, although a formal break had not yet occurred (Hayman, 1999). Jung took the opportunity of these lectures to present for the first time a substantial critique of Psychoanalysis rather than a description (Hayman, 1999, p. 156). In these lectures, however, are not just criticisms of Freud's theory but also the outline of Jung's own emerging psychological theories.

The revisions Jung made to Freud's theory in these lectures can be said to center around three topics: the nature of libido, the nature of individual development, and the nature of the unconscious. Libido was not exclusively sexual, but of a more general character according to Jung. The individual is therefore not exclusively directed in his personal growth and development by the sexual instinct but by other factors as well, such as the parental complexes. The nature of the unconscious that Jung had begun to explore in his research on autonomous complexes now was a more fully elaborated theory. Jung would therefore see the psychic energy held in the unconscious complex as useful (CW 4/416). These reformulations of Psychoanalysis would lead to the later work in which Jung fully commits himself to a transpersonal view of the unconscious, and to his work on archetypes.

In assessing Jung's divergence from Freud's theories in general and in these lectures in particular, however, the focus has historically been their disagreements about libido and Freud's emphasis on damaging childhood experiences as the origin of neurosis (CW 4/377). What has not been examined in these lectures is Jung's developing ego theory. He is able to present in these lectures a more elaborated formulation of the concepts that were introduced in his works on complexes as well as a picture of psychic processes that enlarge and extend the role of the ego.

Repression, psychic energy, and adaptation

Although one critic believed Jung had suggested repression was under conscious control (Glover, 1950), it appears that Freud himself gave that same impression early in his work. As was discussed earlier, Jung did acknowledge that repression seemed at times under conscious control but in certain individuals (hysterics, for example) it appeared to be a more unconscious action. In the lectures at Fordham, Jung answers the question of whether repression is a conscious or unconscious action directly. He states, for example,

> We might ask if repression is due to a conscious decision of the individual, or whether the reminiscences disappear passively, without conscious knowledge? In Freud's writings you will find excellent proofs of the existence of a conscious tendency to repress anything painful. [. . .] we must not forget that there are any number of cases where it is impossible to show, even with the most careful examination, the slightest trace of 'putting aside' or of conscious repression, and where it seems as if the process of repression were more in the nature of a passive disappearance, or even as if the impressions were dragged beneath the surface by some force operating below. Patients of the first type give us the impression of being mentally well-developed individuals who seem to suffer only peculiar cowardice in regard to their own feelings. But among the second you may find cases showing a more serious retardation of development, since here the process of repression could be compared rather to an automatic mechanism.
>
> (CW 4/212)

This clearly shows that Jung proposes an unconscious structural, that is, autonomous, element to repression.

Samuels (1985, p. 68) speculates that the confusion between the consciousness or unconsciousness of repression may be due to a linguistic problem or a weakness in Jung. Jung writes about conscious repression (*Verdrängung*), for example (CW 4/212), in a way that implies suppression. It is true the German word *Verdrängung* can be translated as either 'suppression' or 'repression'. *Unterdrückung*, another possible German word for 'suppression', is used by Freud in *The Interpretation of Dreams* to stress less an attachment of dream-wishes to the unconscious and more a specific conscious action, so the role of the ego is unclear. Jung would make a distinction between *Verdrängung* and *Unterdrückung* for the first time only in 1924 (CW 17/199a), calling 'suppression' a conscious act that is easily reversed, while 'repression' is forgetting that cannot easily be reversed. It is described at this later time, however, in terms of effects on the ego rather than any specific action of the ego, and this may reflect Jung's theoretical interests turning away from the conscious processes at this point in his work.

This brings up the issue of whether an unconscious part of the ego is the repressing agent or is a force from the unconscious itself. Jung makes his argument about repression in the Fordham lectures in the context of discussing Freud's trauma theory of neurosis and therefore is not arguing the case for or against unconscious elements of processes in the ego. Despite this context, it appears, at least at this point in his theory, that Jung distinguishes between an ego that represses consciously and an automatic process of repression "from below" (CW 4/212).

Jung relates the action of repression to the "reality function" (CW 4/284–286). The individual adapts to reality by transferring libido ("the energy of growth in individuals") from the sexual function, which is directed toward continuation of the species, to other functions (those directed toward enhanced adaptation to reality, the "reality function"). When this transfer of energy, that is, adaptation, runs smoothly, it is called "sublimation" – sexual energy not used for reproduction is put to use for the care and rearing of children, for example. The transfer or diversion of libido into "other destinations" detrimental to the reality function is called repression. Jung uses the example of schizophrenia to illustrate this: the schizophrenic "withdraws his libido from the outside world and in consequence suffers a loss of reality compensated by an increase in fantasy activity" (CW 4/289).

What Jung is proposing, then, is an energic system of libido based on the principle of conservation of energy (explicit in CW 4/254) in which the reality principle develops by taking energy away from the unconscious (CW 4/255). Jung does not relate the reality function, concerned with adaptation, to the ego because throughout these lectures he remains in Freud's conceptual universe; the topographical model which describes energic relationships between areas of the mind rather than psychic entities with functions.

If one looks at the assumptions behind statements Jung makes in these lectures, it is possible to 'deconstruct' a meaning of ego. Jung says the following:

1. Emotional rapport is a feature of the reality function and lack of it is characteristic of Dementia Praecox (CW 4/272).
2. Reality is replaced by complex contents in Dementia Praecox (CW 4/274).
3. Reality is linked to adaptation, and when adaptation disappears so does reality (CW 4/274).
4. The withdrawal of libido from the ego does not impair the reality function (CW 4/276).

In these statements, Jung is assuming a distinct mental construct that is absent or overwhelmed in Dementia Praecox. This construct is the seat of adaptation and the reality function. We know from Jung's previous work that he calls the mental construct absent in Dementia Praecox and which is associated with adaptation and the reality principle the ego. I would suggest, therefore, that Jung is implying a mental construct he associates with previous uses of the term 'ego', which is the seat of the reality function (emotional rapport, adaptation). Jung places this construct in opposition to the unconscious and also assumes a kind of zero-sum, conservation of energy dynamic between these two entities.

Psychological development

Jung does not explicitly propose a theory of ego development in these lectures, nor, in fact, in any other work of this period. However, he presents a theory of psychological development here for the first time as a response, it appears, to Freud's theory of psychosexual stages as outlined in *Three Essays on the Theory of Sexuality* (1905, in SE 7). This account of development reveals his thinking about the progress from infancy to adulthood and what are the psychical processes at work. Implications for an ego theory can therefore be constructed.

Freud proposed three developmental stages based on the theory of libido: progression through the body in infant and child maturation. Although he agreed that libido existed before puberty, Jung disagreed with Freud's formulation of infant and early childhood physical phenomena such as suckling as sexual. Jung wrote, "I [. . .] must admit that I can find no ground for regarding the pleasure-producing activities of the infantile period from the standpoint of sexuality, but rather grounds to the contrary" (CW 4/262).

Jung therefore proposed his own theory, "the three phases of life" (CW 4/263):

1 *The Presexual Stage* – "characterized almost exclusively by the functions of nutrition and growth".
2 *The Prepubertal Stage* – "[g]ermination of sexuality takes place in this period".
3 *Maturity* – "the adult period from puberty on".

Development is contingent on the "change in localization", that is, movement, of libido in the child. Because libido in the child is "occupied far more with subsidiary functions of a mental and physical nature than with local sexual functions" (CW 4/268), Jung concludes that libido itself cannot be exclusively sexual in nature, and that Freud's sexual definition of libido must be abandoned. What Jung does not reject but, rather, embraces is the energic paradigm for libido: "I do not think I am going astray if I see the real value of the concept of libido not in its sexual definition but in its energic view, thanks to which we are in possession of an extremely valuable heuristic principle" (CW 4/270).

In his development or phases of life model, Jung is establishing the background assumptions for a later ego development theory. First, there is the assumption of movement toward a goal. Regarding the task of the first life stage, for example, Jung states, "It seems as if, at this stage, an essential step forward is taken in the emancipation and centering of a new personality" (CW 4/266). The "discontinuity of consciousness" is replaced with "continuity of memory" (CW 4/266).

"Affective development" (CW 4/297) is a goal of maturation. Jung associates poor affective development with "the intemperate psychic attitude of the child to reality, his precarious judgment, his lack of orientation, his dislike of unpleasant duties" (CW 4/298), which can lead to "an unreal and completely unadapted attitude to the world" (CW 4/298).

There is also an assumption of a separation from the unconscious world. The infantile stage is a world of fantasy (CW 4/298), and to remain there leads to neurosis, the assumption being that development demands that one face 'stern reality' and separate from fantasy (which Jung associates at this time with the unconscious, as I have already shown).

So we can conclude from these passages that Jung assumes psychic energy taken up with fantasy and an unadapted attitude moves into and is replaced by, in the developmental phases, adaptation and the reality function. Jung places value, therefore, in this arc of development. To do otherwise, to remain in the fantasy and unadapted world of childhood, is associated with the neurotic.

What are the implications for an Ego Psychology then? First, normal non-neurotic growth and development is a flow of this energy away from the unconscious to the elements or qualities Jung associates with ego (the reality function, adaptation). It is a zero-sum energic exchange: energy that flows into one mental construct is taken from another. Second, Jung assumes the movement of psychic energy away from the unconscious to qualities he has associated with the ego builds up those qualities. Consciousness becomes more continuous, for example, and adaptation proceeds.

Clinical implications

Developing the concept of the complex was a major focus for Jung in this period of his life. From his early musings in the Zofingia lectures, through his dissertation on occult phenomena, to his association experiment work and his collaboration with Freud, themes of ego-consciousness, ego-complex, and autonomous complex were beginning to solidify. These concepts would remain substantially intact as he developed his psychological theory and are some of the best known in a wider audience.

Overall then, ego-consciousness would represent the ego as the center of consciousness associated with the sense of identity, will, agency, and personal self. This could then be characterized as the subjective ego. The ego-complex is a structural entity, the 'central station' of the ego that has conscious awareness but also mechanisms outside conscious control. These mechanisms are the mechanism of defense and the mechanism of adaptation. The ego-complex can be described, then, as the structural ego. The autonomous complex, sometimes referred to as the neurotic complex, is a mix of conscious and unconscious elements – similar in this regard to the ego-complex – except that the autonomous complex functions as a split off personality that can supplant the primacy of the ego-complex. It can be that an individual's personality is so dominated by the autonomous complex and for so long that this split-off personality forms the basis of one's personal self.

Issues around complexes are often the starting point for work in analysis. How does the ego-complex manifest, that is, what values and beliefs and identity inform the ego-complex? What distressing psychological symptoms are related to an autonomous complex? How does the ego- and autonomous complex present in a client's behaviors, emotions, and dreams? A clinical example can serve to clarify these questions:

> 'Marcus' was a young banker, originally from a small village in the Alps, who had studied economics at university and was making his career in the financial world of Zürich. After a few months into his employment, he was developing anxiety around tasks such replying to emails, answering the phone, or speaking in meetings. He found, however, that by quickly checking his bank balance on the computer, he would feel relief. As well, the extravagant lifestyles of his fellow young bankers perplexed him at first – wearing suits of several thousand Swiss Francs, dining out mid-week at expensive restaurants, for example – yet he felt over time more and more comfortable adopting this lifestyle. He began looking at his bank balance many times a day, however. Confused by his compulsive behavior, and shocked by a particular incident at the bank, he decided to go to therapy.
>
> The incident which precipitated his seeking out therapy occurred on an otherwise routine day. After several months of employment he began a new orientation to the various banking departments at the international headquarters. He described seeing the large, cathedral-like bank tellers hall, the currency traders' area filled with computer screens and ringing telephones, the quiet plush offices of the private banking division, and so on until he was brought to the vaults underground where the stores of gold were kept. After the thick steel doors were opened, he saw a grille, like an iron rood screen, through which he could see massive blocks of stacked gold bars. He was stunned to see that the bank employees in this area spoke only in whispers.

This vignette illustrates three ego states for 'Marcus'. First, his ego-consciousness is demonstrated by his growing identity as a banker, his awareness of his experiences in the bank both distressing and gratifying, and his access to memories presumably of his life before Zürich in the mountain village of his youth. Second, his ego-complex appears to act at the unconscious level by the mechanisms of defense and adaptation to create a split between his ego-consciousness and something unknown. Finally, the autonomous complex in the form of a money complex, exhibits the characteristic mechanisms of constellation and contrast, as well as repetition.

Ego-consciousness

Jung's theory is based on the premise that psychical development requires dynamic opposing forces; this is a key characteristic of the energic paradigm. Ego-consciousness represents in this model of the psyche one side of this duality which is acted upon by the inner and outer world. Ego-consciousness is closely tied to the ego-complex but at this point in Jung's theory, it appears that the ego-consciousness concept is a 'topographical' entity whereas the ego-complex is a dynamic-structural entity which has overlapping qualities with the former. It is unfortunate when these terms are used interchangeably by Jung due to the confusion it creates.

Ego-complex

As the 'central station', the ego-complex would defend against elements of the inner or outer world that were intolerable to ego-consciousness. This defensive action acts to maintain adaptation; for example, 'Marcus' may have repressed his discomfort and misgivings about the values and attitudes of the banking world in order to fit in. This action can be conscious through suppression (e.g. "I just can't think about this right now") or unconscious through repression. Many other defenses are possible in any case and they all have in common the circumstance that they act outside conscious awareness.

Autonomous complex

The constellating effect of the autonomous complex is purposive according to Jung's theory: a key characteristic of the symbolic paradigm. For 'Marcus' the experience of being around serious wealth was experienced as seductive on the one hand but also distressing on the other. According to Jung, through the mechanism of contrast the repressed emotion or knowledge is revealed symbolically through the symptom. For my client this symptom was his anxiety and obsessive checking of his bank balance. This symptom was repetitive, characteristic of the autonomous complex.

The question, then, is how to understand his symptoms and his shock at the reverence toward gold in his adopted community. By focusing on the meaning of the complex, Marcus was able in analysis to see the contrast between the prevailing values and attitudes of the banking world and the world of his rural upbringing. The dominating ultimate value in the bank was money: its acquisition and display. This realization led him to explore his feelings of inferiority and status as an outsider.

A deeper meaning was revealed, however, by a subsequent dream: "I was back in the mountains near [home village]. Out of the forest at the edge of a clearing very close to me, there emerged a great stag. The stag turned its head silently toward me and our eyes met". With this dream, 'Marcus' was given a profound and moving sense of his own individual values and of which he had been consciously unaware. At one level, he experienced the stag as calling him back to the dignity and pride of his mountain home and village origins. On another level the stag represented a contrast to this worship of money. It was a true symbol of his own innate spiritual values that stood at his core: the world of nature and life lived around family, faith, the seasons, and the down-to-earth world of his youth.

Just as the grandfather personalities for Helly represented unrealized consciousness, so too does the autonomous money complex reveal a deeper consciousness for 'Marcus'. In his case, the deeper meaning points to what is sacred. As Jung said, the complex has a constellating effect which compels the ego-complex and the autonomous complex to interact, leading to a symbolic representation of this meaning. As it became apparent to him that the god of Zürich is money, he was led to his ultimate values as well; the money checking was a form of worship of this Zürich god, but his ultimate values were of a god found in nature. At this point in his writing, Jung felt that this kind of realization was the cure, much as Freud viewed abreaction as curative. Due to the influences of Freud and Bleuler, Jung was approaching his formulation about the ego from a predominately energic focus. His later work, when he introduces the concepts of Self and archetypes, would expand the understanding of what stood behind the autonomous complex and the ego-complex to encompass the symbolic paradigm more completely.

Chapter 4

1912–1945

Outer research and inner transformation

Jung ended his relationship with Freud over theoretical differences, although there is much written, and much to acknowledge, about the personal aspect of the break between these two men. There was no love lost when Jung, for example, said,

> One might say Freud consists of bitterness, every word being loaded with it. His attitude was the bitterness of the person who is entirely misunderstood, and his manner always seemed to say, 'If they don't understand they must be stamped into Hell'. I noticed this in him the first time I met him, and always saw it in him. . . .
>
> (Jung, 1990, p. 20)

Freud for his part also maligned Jung, writing later in his 1914 essay 'On the History of the Psychoanalytic Movement' (SE 14), for example,

> It was now my desire to transfer [my] authority to a younger man who would, quite naturally, take my place on my death. I felt that this person could be only C. G. Jung, for Bleuler was of my own age. In favor of Jung was his conspicuous talents, the contributions he had already made to analysis, his independent position, and the impression of energy which his personality always made. He also seemed prepared to enter into friendly relations with me, and to give up, for my sake, certain race-prejudices which he had so far permitted himself to indulge. I had no notion then that in spite of the advantages enumerated, this was a very unfortunate choice; that it concerned a person who, incapable of tolerating the authority of another, was still less fitted to be himself an authority, one whose energy was devoted to the unscrupulous pursuit of his own interests.

It is easy to see, then, their split as a part of a more general personality conflict or power struggle acted out through theory. In many ways, Jung's writings ever after this split would contain as a subtext, arguments directed to Freud regarding why he was wrong. By rejecting materialist arguments, was Jung in part also aiming to reject his former teacher?

Indeed, the theoretical differences were there and were fundamental, setting Jung on a path toward his own theory of analytical psychology. I would like to set aside the considerable personal differences and focus instead on this theoretical aspect: Jung's shift from a materialist–energic orientation to a symbolic orientation as he broke from Freud's view to his own. This shift, really at the root of Jung's impulse to break from Freud, reveals the change in philosophy and paradigm from which Jung would forever after work under and develop. Jung might, perhaps, very well have gone on to develop a theory of ego identical to Freud's later work if he had stayed within the material framework. But because he shifted the paradigm and therefore saw mental structures and mechanisms in a different light, Jung would set an entirely different relevance and emphasis on the ego than Freud did. It can be said that this new paradigm became for Jung, to borrow a phrase from Henri-Bernard Levy, his structuring passion.

Libido and the energic versus the symbolic paradigm

Fundamental in this shift was the basic notion of libido and the assumptions about it. As has been discussed previously, there are two fundamental and irreconcilable philosophies behind the energic paradigm and the symbolic paradigm. The energic paradigm looks at libido as part of a biological function, following the laws of science. This attitude was exemplified by Freud's attachment to the sexual theory. Libido as sexual energy kept the psychological system tied to the biological realm. Jung, with his background in *Naturphilosophie* and interest in Schopenhauer and Kant, among others, could not remain solely in the biological realm as he constructed his theory.

In other words, a major philosophical difference between the two men revolved around a basic attitude toward the nature of life: one side believing we are physical matter in our essential nature and the other side believing we are created in the image of God. Jung took this second position, as Nagy (1991) points out, in *Symbols of Transformation*. His controversial position regarding libido, and for which he more authentically broke with Freud, was not merely that it was not exclusively sexual in nature but rather that libido has an intention.

By taking a teleological position, Jung is therefore forced in his theorizing to understand the structure and mechanisms of the psyche in terms of their place in this philosophy. Consciousness, the unconscious, and complexes must therefore function as elements that lead or develop toward something else when the psychic system is no longer based on equilibrium or discharge. In *Symbols of Transformation* and in other works of the period 1912 to 1917, Jung begins to work out these elements in terms of their teleological functions. Works of this period, notably *Symbols of Transformation* and the two essays that would become Volume 7 of Jung's Collected Works, were revised over time to include these changes as his thinking matured.

Although Freud's dynamic model of the mind (the idea of conflict, that opposing forces in the psyche encounter or clash with each other) remained part of Jung's frame of reference, a new structure for the psyche began to take shape in this period of Jung's work. In seeing the psyche as intentional, Jung needed to account for the source and the goal of this intention, as well as its mechanisms. He would arrive at the conclusion that the source of the psyche – the central regulatory function – is the Self and its archetypes, and that the goal was individuation. The mechanisms of this process were splitting and projection (not in a defensive sense), compensation and enantiodromia, and the Transcendent Function. It is in this middle period of Jung's professional career that he began to describe these structures and mechanisms.

In his model of the psyche, Jung did not place the Self and ego in opposition in order to develop the ego (as is reminiscent of the Freud model). Rather, Jung placed the ego and the Self in opposition in order to create and develop a third entity – the individual. The individual, individuation, is the ultimate goal of the process, an entity that stands in contrast to the collective.

All of the structures and mechanisms Jung created in his new model of the psyche would require the development of a concept that accounts for the subjective, individual standpoint in the psyche and which would stand in opposition to the Self. This new concept would need to act as the equal partner to the Self in the interactive process Jung envisioned. The ego concept up to this point in Jung's work, however, was rather vague and ill defined – more a description than a psychic structure. Therefore, in this phase of his work, Jung needed to structure and define an ego concept really for the first time.

The ego concept in Jung's writings, therefore, essentially grew out of a theoretical imperative. In order for it to fit together and maintain an essential logic, the model of the psyche that Jung built up in this period requires an ego with certain characteristics. The psyche requires an active partner, a collaborator with the unconscious which possesses specific qualities: that it can act as its own agent for or against psychic forces (i.e. it possesses a will, and has defensive capabilities); that it has a capacity to perceive, receive (not an identical capacity), and evaluate the limitations of reality; and that it can change and evolve. As Jung found, these ego capacities are not identical with consciousness.

As described earlier, I am taking a chronological analytical approach to Jung's works as a way to discover the development of his thought. The significant works in this period for Jung in the order they were written were four: *Symbols of Transformation* (CW 5) and *Psychological Types* (CW 6), two books published originally in 1911 and 1912 respectively. The two works "On the Psychology of the Unconscious" and "The Relations Between the Ego and the Unconscious" were written originally in 1916 and 1917 and subsequently revised a number of times and published finally together in Jung's Collected Works as Volume 7, *Two Essays on Analytical Psychology*. In addition, two smaller essays written in this period are significant statements of Jung's thinking at this period of his work. These are 'The Transcendent Function' (1917) and 'Adaptation, Individuation, and Collectivity' (1916). These works, then, contain Jung's essential metapsychology of the ego as he developed it in this middle part of his career.

Symbols of Transformation (CW 5)

This is the work that Jung wrote in his break with Freud. Although it was meant to dispute Freud's theory of libido, it led to revisions in Freud's theory of consciousness as well. Published in the *Jahrbuch für psychoanalytische und psychopathologische Forschungen* in two parts in 1911 and 1912, *Wandlungen und Symbole der Libido* (literally 'Transformations and Symbols of the Libido') was Jung's own view of the "real nature" of libido. He makes the argument in this work that libido is not "sexual impulse . . . sexual need" (CW 4/251–252) as formulated by Freud in 1905. Jung discards this notion:

> With increasing experience in analytical work . . . I became aware of a gradual change in my concept of libido. In place of the descriptive definition set forth in Freud's *Three Essays*, there gradually grew up a genetic definition of the libido, which rendered it possible for me to replace the expression 'psychic energy' by the term 'libido'.
>
> (CW 4/278)

Before I venture further into Jung's revision of the libido theory, I would like to comment first on Jung's formulation of Freud's libido theory. Glover (1950) in his criticism of Jung felt that Jung "had never really grasped Freud's concept of libido and that he continued to equate it with the energy of adult sexual instincts" (p. 57). Jung does indeed describe Freud's theory, referring in particular to *Three Essays on the Theory of Sexuality*, as overly focused on the sexual instinct and characterizing libido as an impulse which functions according to energic principles (CW 4/251–255, for example). In the first edition of *Symbols of Transformation* Jung allows that Freud recognized a wider application for the concept of libido (CW 5/219) but that due to his own researches into Dementia Praecox, he felt justified in disputing Freud. Jung wrote, for example, "the sexual definition of [libido] did not permit me to understand those disturbances of function [in paranoic psychology]" (CW 5/222). Here Jung was asserting that Freud's theory of libido could explain neurosis but could not account for paranoid phenomena such as delusions. A theory of libido, for Jung, needed to account for all psychical phenomena, not just neurosis. For Jung, then, Freud's theory of libido was limited rather than outright wrong.

I would disagree with Glover's assessment of Jung. In my reading of his works, Jung, in his critique of Freud's theory, did not characterize libido as adult or child or any other type of personal sexual energy. His point, rather, was that focusing on the sexuality aspect of libido was limiting. His emphasis in *Symbols of Transformation* was on the dynamic of the libido; its movement and evolution in the psyche and how much further one's understanding becomes when one lets go of the exclusive sexual definition. Jung rejected Freud's formulation of libido less because of its sexual nature and more because it was an inadequate (to him) theory.

Libido theory

Jung concentrates his essential revisions of libido theory in the first three chapters of Part 2 of his work: 'Aspects of the Libido', 'The Conception and the Genetic Theory of Libido', and 'The Transformation of the Libido'. He begins by making the point that libido is to be understood in its widest sense, quoting classical literature to support this assertion (CW 5/212–218). It is understood as 'to wish', or 'to will', as well as possessing connotations of sexual desire. Psychoanalysis, according to Jung, has given libido the connotation of mental energy in the same sense of physical energy, putting it in the energic realm (CW 5/218). Jung wants to take the whole concept of libido out of the energic realm, however, by expanding its definition.

Jung thus begins to build up his argument that libido is to be understood as a creative continuous life impulse. This is in keeping with *Naturphilosophie*. First, he points out that in Dementia Praecox there is a loss of the reality function. If repression of sexual libido were to account for this disorder (the hypothesis of neurosis being that repression of sexual libido accounts for the neurotic symptoms), then the repression of sexual libido in psychosis would lead to the psychotic symptom – loss of reality. In other words, reality would be a characteristic of sexual libido. This, for Jung, is the flaw in the theory. He asserts,

> The sexual character of this [Dementia Praecox] must be disputed absolutely, for reality is not understood to be a sexual function.
>
> (CW 5/221)

Jung next proposes that there are impulses in the psyche that are not of a sexual nature, indeed the greater part of the impulses therein are nonsexual (CW 5/222). There is instead only a "continuous life impulse, a will to live which will attain the creation of the whole species through the preservation of the individual" (CW 5/223). This concept of libido then "coincides with the idea of Will in Schopenhauer" ('will' as a thing-in-itself and not its phenomenal manifestation), but also, "to a conception of the will in general" (CW 5/223). Jung goes further, however, and associates this concept of libido with even the "cosmogonic" [world-creating] principle, such as Eros in Plato and Hesiod, and Kâma in India. Libido, in other words, is the "creative primal principle" (CW 5/223), the basic force of life development in mankind. Even more, as he would elaborate at this point later in his 1952 revision, this creative primal principle is "purposive" (1952, CW 5/182).

Jung then discusses the nature of this creative primal principle and thus begins to describe the mechanisms of the psyche in this revision of depth psychology. Comparing it to the "world soul" of neo-Platonic philosophy, he characterizes it as having "the tendency towards a divided existence and toward divisibility, the *sine qua non* of all change, creation, and procreation" (CW 5/223). In the 1952 revision, Jung, in another context, goes further and makes the point that splitting, this tendency to divide, is "connected to consciousness and the process of becoming conscious" (1952, CW 5/226). Thus, although the creative primal principle exists as a unity, it has the tendency, an innate disposition, to divide.

This point in Jung's argument, then, brings up the ultimate aim of purposiveness as well as the mechanisms toward this end. There is a unitary primal energy in the psyche that has a tendency to split or divide. This mechanism of splitting is purposive in that it serves the process of creating consciousness.

Jung builds his case that the reality function as adaptation arises from this creative primal principle. The genetic viewpoint, that is, the idea of a primal creative principle called libido, assumes a primal unity in the psyche, according to Jung, from which instincts issue (CW 5/230). Part of this libido, this creative primal principle is available for sexual instinct, but a substantial amount is also available for "the function of reality". By reality function, Jung means adaptation, and he makes this clear in his 1952 revision:

> The fact that an archaic world of fantasy takes the place of reality in schizophrenia proves nothing about the nature of the reality function as such. . . . A loss of the latest acquisitions of the reality function (or adaptation) must of necessity be replaced, if at all, by an earlier mode of adaptation.
>
> (1952, CW 5/200)

I want to focus here on the general dynamic mechanisms he is introducing in his argument. As I said, Jung has introduced the concept of a 'primal unity' in the psyche, which has the innate tendency to split or divide. He then proposes, in his argument, two contradictory forces in the psyche as a mechanism of change: an immediate sexual libido and a resistance that opposes sexuality (sexual libido was never eliminated in Jung's theory and here he integrates it). Libido is thus transformed by the dynamic interaction of these two forces.

In this argument, Jung is introducing a theme that would dominate his theory henceforth: the advance and retreat of libido with the goal of renewal and redemption. The ego develops by first retreating to the unconscious, opening itself up to unconscious energy. This is the Nietzschean idea of renewal through death and rebirth. Renewal occurs because of the basic assumption in the symbolic paradigm of the unconscious as a source of creative life.

What is the nature of these two libidinal energies and their interaction? What is the purpose or goal of this transformation? In a lengthy discussion of primitive fertility rituals, the Australian Watschandi tribe in particular, Jung illustrates his point that there is a force in the psyche that resists sexual libido and leads psychic energy into human development in the form of discoveries beneficial for society. He asks the question first, why do primitives transfer the libido of the sexual act into ritual activity when doing so requires more effort and is impractical and much less amusing (CW 5/249)? Jung concludes,

> It is hardly possible but that a certain compulsion conducts the energy away from the original object and real purpose, inducing the production of surrogates. . . . This compulsion [. . .] removes a certain amount of libido from the real sexual activity, and creates a symbolic and practically valid substitute for what is lost.
>
> (CW 5/249)

The argument so far has thus not strayed from Freud's principle of sublimation. But Jung has another point to make. He asks, "Whence comes this compulsion?" (CW 5/249). It is this opposing force mentioned earlier. Jung writes,

> It is a question of an internal resistance; will opposes will; libido opposes libido; since a psychological resistance as an energic phenomenon corresponds to a certain amount of libido. The psychological compulsion for the transformation of the libido is based on an original division of the will.
>
> (CW 5/249)

Therefore, Jung is suggesting a division in the psyche between two forces; one represented by sexual libido, the other by a force directed toward substitution and symbolization. Whereas Freud saw the reality principle, the encounter with the world's limitations and realities, as forcing substitution and symbolization of the libido, Jung sees this occurring through an equal counter-force in the psyche itself.

Symbolization occurs because the psychic energy thus removed from the sexual act does not regressively flow toward the parents because of the incest taboo. The libido is pushed back to the presexual stage, desexualized because of the incest taboo, and reaches a level of "countless possibilities of application" (CW 5/250). In the case of fertility rituals, for example, Jung describes the regressed libido filling ancient symbols of agriculture, leading to a new valuation of the earth as nourishing mother. In the case of the discovery of fire according to Jung, the regressed libido meets the rhythmic pattern of boring of infancy, leading to the rhythmic rubbing of sticks together to produce fire.

In other words, psychic energy (libido) fills and activates the earlier presexual and historically primal images that exist in the psyche. These in turn are employed to further societal development.

If the nature of the interaction between these two forces in the psyche is oppositional or conflictual, and the goal is development of the individual and society, then the question remains, what are the mechanisms that Jung has identified thus far to bring about this change? One mechanism already described, propensity to splitting, is an inherent characteristic of the libido itself. As a primal unity, libido nevertheless follows a path of development. Jung offers the following interpretation and explanation, after quoting a passage from the Hindu Brihadâranyaka-Upanishad,

> We meet here a peculiar myth of creation which requires a psychological interpretation. In the beginning the libido was undifferentiated and bisexual; this was followed by differentiation into a male and female component. From then on man knows what he is. . . .
>
> (CW 5/252)

Citing numerous other examples of myth in *Symbols of Transformation* as well as the Miller fantasies, Jung makes essentially the same point over and over; there is a unitary, undifferentiated force in the psyche which is characteristic of the unconscious itself. Opposing this unitary force is a force toward separation from the unconscious, toward consciousness. It is libido directed toward development that is represented by the symbol of the hero. This force then is the element in the psyche which facilitates/supports/enables development. Facility toward separation and differentiation, then, are the mechanisms in this second force analogous to the facility to split seen in primal unity.

Jung describes this moment of separation of conscious and unconscious: "The moment of the rise of consciousness, the separation of subject and object is a birth" (CW 5/514). And here, for example, Jung connects the process of adaptation and consciousness with differentiation: "We have the appropriate tendency always to recognize only the difference in things. This is demanded by the psychological adaptation which, without the most minute differentiation of the impressions, would be absolutely impossible" (CW

5/290). He associates undifferentiation with unconsciousness and any development of this state with actions by individual conscious differentiation:

> We know that, although individuals are widely separated by the differences in the contents of their consciousness, they are closely alike in their unconscious psychology. [. . .] Difference first arises from individualization. [. . .] The very evident uniformity of the unconscious mechanism serves as a psychological foundation for these philosophic views. The unconscious contains the differentiated remnants of the earlier psychological functions overcome by the individual differentiation.
>
> (CW 5/289)

Jung was not interested in exploring this function of differentiation in consciousness because he felt the contents of consciousness were too variable and individual. He was much more interested in exploring the contents of the unconscious:

> The individual content of consciousness is, therefore, the most unfavorable object imaginable for psychology, because it has veiled the universally valid until it has become unrecognizable. The essence of consciousness is the process of adaptation, which takes place in the minutest details. On the other hand, the unconscious is the generally diffused, which not only binds the individuals among themselves to the race, but also unites them backwards with the peoples of the past and their psychology. Thus the unconscious, surpassing the individual in its generality, is, in the first place, the object of a true psychology, which claims not to be psychophysical.
>
> (CW 5/290)

The first edition of *Symbols of Transformation*, therefore, was not to offer a deeper exploration of the conscious functions, merely characterizing them as aspects of the individual and uninteresting. That exploration would have to wait until Jung's next major work, *Psychological Types*. The questions left open were: what is the nature of consciousness as part of a dynamic process? What is the role of the subject, the personal self, in this process, that is, the individual, the ego?

Psychological Types (CW 6)

Written in the period 1913 to 1917 and published in 1921, *Psychological Types* arose out of Jung's need to understand the differences in type between the psychological theories of Freud and Adler (Jung, 1983a, p. 233). It is Jung's main work devoted to the 'organization and delimitation' of conscious processes in concert with the unconscious processes. In this work, then, Jung begins to define for the first time specific structural and psychodynamic characteristics of the ego and the individual and how these entities emerge or evolve out of the dynamic interaction of the opposing libido tendencies.

In this work Jung describes this dynamic process between the two libido tendencies he identified in the *Symbols of Transformation* as (1) a force directed toward the unconscious which he calls introversion and (2) an opposing force directed toward consciousness which he calls extraversion. He describes two innate psychical mechanisms – compensation/enantiodromia and the Transcendent Function – which, through their actions, make the transition from one conscious attitude to another possible. He also begins to formulate the ego as a dynamic function rather than a subjective state and as an entity that acts in opposition to the unconscious to create the individual.

Before I go further into exploring this particular work, I want to discuss the terms ego, self, and individual. These are all names for describing aspects of the subjective sense of oneself and have, especially for readers with a background in psychology, specific connotations. The ego up to this point in Jung's writings has been defined as the center of consciousness but has also been used rather loosely to describe the subject as opposed to the object or the other. In *Psychological Types*, however, Jung distinguishes between the ego and the individual. The ego remains the center of consciousness but is now further understood as a collective entity that carries the subject's collective sense of selfhood, identity, and will. In the dynamic encounter of the ego with the unconscious, however, a more personal, more individualized focus of subjective experience, identity, and will develops. This new entity Jung calls the individual, and this dynamic process of encounter and development is called by Jung individuation (CW 6/755–762). As described in Chapter 1, in order to distinguish the entity that is a product of individuation from the common use of the term 'individual', I will italicize the former term as *individual* and leave the latter as is.

Jung makes use of the term 'self' for the first time in *Psychological Types* to mean a psychical entity distinct from the ego but there are instances, confusingly, when it is used as the equivalent of ego or as an everyday word such as 'me'. Again, as described in Chapter 1, therefore, when Jung uses the word self in its everyday usage – in the sense of the reflexive pronoun 'myself', for example – I will leave it as it is. In the instances when he is referring to this new psychical entity, I will capitalize the term as 'Self'. When he is using it as the equivalent of the term 'ego', I will indicate that ego is meant.

The two libido tendencies

Jung, in *Psychological Types*, has arrived at a point where he now formally names the two libido tendencies: introversion and extroversion. They are, for him, a psychodynamic process of energy exchange, at times directed outwardly toward the world of objects, and at other times directed inwardly toward the subject:

> In general one could say that the introverted standpoint is one which sets the ego and the subjective psychological process above the subject and the objective processes, or at any rate seeks to hold its ground against the object. This attitude, therefore, gives the subject a higher value than the object, and the object accordingly has a lower value. (CW 6/5)

> The extraverted standpoint, on the contrary, subordinates the subject to the object, so that the object has the higher value. In this case the subject is of secondary importance, the subjective process appearing at times as no more than a disturbing or superfluous appendage of objective events. (CW 6/5)

> These contrary attitudes are in themselves no more than correlative mechanisms: a diastolic going out and seizing of the object, and a systolic concentration and detachment of energy from the object seized. (CW 6/6)

Jung is very clear in his view that these orientations – inward toward the subject or outward toward the object – are dealing with two equal and complementary realities. Here one can see especially the influence of *Naturphilosophie*: whereas in Freud's energic/materialistic paradigm, the reality of the outer world compels the individual to modify or manage the demands of the inner world, in Jung's new paradigm, the individual is caught between two realities and must adapt to both:

> The peculiar reality of unconscious contents, therefore, gives us the same right to describe them as objects as the things of the outside world. Now just as the persona, being a function of relationship, is always conditioned by the external object and is anchored as much in it as the subject, so the soul, as a function of relationship to the inner object, is represented by that object; hence she is always distinct from the subject in one sense and is actually perceived as something different. Consequently, she appears to Prometheus [in Spitteler's poem] as something quite separate from his individual ego. In the same way as a man who surrenders entirely to the outside world still has the world as an object distinct from himself, the unconscious world of images behaves as an object distinct from the subject even when a man surrenders to it completely. And, just as the unconscious world of mythological images speaks indirectly, through the experience of external things, to the man who surrenders wholly to the outside world, so the real world and its demands find their

> way indirectly to the man who has surrendered wholly to the soul; for no man can escape both realities. If he is intent only on the outer reality, he must live his myth; if he is turned only toward the inner reality, he must dream his outer so-called real life.
>
> (CW 6/280)

We see also in the preceding quote the essence of the system Jung is building up. There is a division between two areas of the psyche – the conscious and unconscious – which represent Jung's topographical model. These two areas are equal realities, both demanding a form of relationship to the individual. The function of relationship to the outer world, the world of consciousness and objects and outer reality, is the persona. The function of relationship to the inner world, the world of the unconscious and subjective experience (affectivity) and mythological reality, is the soul. Jung refers to 'man's' experience and 'man's surrender' to these two realms, leaving open the question about what part of the psychic structure is he is referring to, if not the persona or soul. If the persona and the soul are functions (albeit functions of relationship), then what central element of the psychic structure are they functioning for?

Jung answers this question is his usual circuitous fashion. He builds up the argument, scattered really through all his analyses of various type problems in medieval and classical thought presented in this work, that there are two psychical entities or structures associated with the subject, the experiencing conscious person. The first is the ego; a psychodynamic function of consciousness. The second is the *individual*; the subjective experience of oneself which arises out of a specific developmental process. These two concepts then, ego and *individual*, take the psychical system out of a typographical model and into a structural-dynamic model. This psychodynamic model, however, is not the straightforward energy model of Freud. Part of Jung's innovation was to work out the concept of the *individual* as the developmental achievement of individuation. It is the vehicle of purpose in his purposive system. The ego, as part of its qualities, becomes the dynamic function for the creation of this entity.

I shall address each of these in turn in terms of their characteristics, development, and psychodynamic function. After this I will discuss the concept of the *individual* introduced in *Psychological Types*.

The ego

Jung gives the following definition of the ego in a chapter he added at the end of *Psychological Types:*

> By ego I understand a complex of ideas which constitutes the center of my field of consciousness and appears to possess a high degree of

> continuity and identity. Hence I also speak of an ego-complex. The ego-complex is as much a content as a condition of consciousness, for a psychic element is conscious to me only as far as it is related to my ego-complex. But inasmuch as the ego is only the center of my field of consciousness, it is not identical with the totality of my psyche, being one complex among other complexes. I therefore distinguish between the ego and the [S]elf, since the ego is only the subject of my consciousness, while the [S]elf is the subject of my total psyche, which also includes the unconscious. In this sense the [S]elf would be an ideal entity which embraces the ego.
>
> (CW 6/706)

Jung discusses the psychological theories of Freud and Adler (CW 6/88–91), defining Freud's as oriented toward the instincts, while Adler's embodied the opposing standpoint, Ego Psychology. In describing Adler then, Jung reveals a number of his assumptions and characterizations about the ego. For him, ego and instinct form a pair of opposites, the ego "owes its existence to the *principium individuationis*, i.e., to individual differentiation" from the collective, and from the biological realm. By following Adler's conception, the ego is also associated with "superiority" and power. With this formulation Jung is equating the ego with a subjective and individual sense of self, a self detached from its instinctual roots. In his definition quoted earlier, Jung also associates the ego with feelings of continuity and identity, two subjective experiences that construct one's sense of self.

Yet by referring to the ego-complex as the basis for this assertion, Jung implies the opposite, because the ego-complex for him, as discussed in the previous chapters, refers to the neurological basis of the ego as the center of consciousness and is a biological entity. The neurologically derived definition of ego concentrates on conscious and unconscious functions of perception and defense. At the same time he ascribes individual characteristics to an entity that is transpersonal and collective. As was discussed in previously, this contradiction points out Jung's associating subjective as well as structural qualities to the ego.

Because of these contradictions, it is not clear if Jung intended to view the subjective sense of self in the ego concept as part of its fundamental attributes. Is the ego a psychodynamic function (the structural element) separate from the subjective sense of self, or do these two elements exist in an undifferentiated state only initially and are meant to separate later through a process of development? I ask this because the *individual* concept Jung presents in *Psychological Types* suggests that there is a process of development out of a collective and instinctual (and rather unconscious) state, through individuation, toward a subjective conscious sense of self that is separate from the ego. So Jung is inconsistent when he describes the ego as owing its existence to the *principium individuationis* but at the same time proposing and describing another entity, the *individual*, which is then the result of the *principium individuationis.*

We have to presume Jung meant what he said however, and that there is therefore a process of development for both entities contained in the *principium individuationis*. I would suggest that ego development and *individual* development are driven by this same principle (Jung's 'creative primal energy') but that this development is sequential rather than simultaneous. In other words, the development of the ego precedes the development of the *individual*, and indeed it is even necessary for a stable and unified ego to exist before development of the *individual* is possible.

CHARACTERISTICS OF THE EGO

In *Psychological Types*, Jung does begin to describe, or at least imply, three main characteristics of the ego. First, it is conscious, second it is collective, and third, it is a dynamic function. I will address each of these three characteristics in turn:

EGO AND CONSCIOUSNESS

Jung defines the ego as the center of consciousness (CW 6/706). He states, "a psychic element is conscious to me in so far as it related to my ego complex". What is conscious is defined then as what is perceived by the ego (CW 6/700), all else remains unconscious. This is what is meant by the metaphor of the ego as a light shining in the darkness, illuminating only that which it touches. This element of the ego, that it is the center of consciousness, seems to be Jung's most emphatic statement about the ego and upon which his whole definition of the ego depends.

Consciousness for Jung at this point in his writings is defined, as I have pointed out, in a rather circular way as that which is perceived by the ego or what the ego is aware of. Consciousness is a process or activity "which maintains the relation of psychic contents to the ego" (CW 6/700). So if 'something' is perceived by the ego, it is considered conscious, and if it is conscious, then it is because the ego is aware of it.

The problem with defining ego-consciousness by ego perception and ego awareness in this way is that it is far too limiting a definition. As Wilhelm Wundt showed in his experiments, people can perceive all manner of things and react to them despite not holding it all in their immediate awareness (as every driver knows for example). Also, by tying perception and awareness closely together, there is a danger of making awareness dependent on the physical senses or rational thought. Awareness, and consciousness, can emerge out of one's own experience of life in the form of an emotion or attitude, for example, and not as a thought or insight perceived with the mind's eye.

Despite this, it may be that Jung's definition is open enough to include all these. The problem ultimately, as I have stated, is that he uses a circular argument by defining the ego as the center of consciousness and consciousness as what is related to the ego. In the end, it goes back to what he meant by 'related', that is, *bezogen*, the German word filled with levels of emotional meaning that figures greatly in his theory. The word *bezogen*, as I have described earlier, has the connotation of emotional involvement and attachment. Jung in fact refers to 'relatedness' as "proneness to affect" (CW 6/138). There is the implication, then, that despite the narrowness of perception and awareness as ego characteristics, there is further or deeper emotional involvement with the psychic content.

Another aspect of consciousness as it relates to the ego is its discrimination capability. Jung wrote,

> The whole essence of consciousness is discrimination, distinguishing ego from non-ego, subject from object, positive from negative, and so forth. The separation into pairs of opposites is entirely due to conscious differentiation; only consciousness can recognize the suitable and distinguish it from the unsuitable and worthless.
>
> (CW 6/179)

It is not explicit that the ego is the agent for discrimination, but since the ego is the center of consciousness according to Jung, it is likely that is his intention.

Discrimination as it is described earlier also implies valuation in addition to reality testing. Distinguishing what is suitable or valuable versus what is unsuitable and worthless has a different brief from distinguishing subject from object. This function of valuation is associated with one's typology, according to Jung, since psychological types operate according to the path of libido (CW 6/138, 481).

There are a number of problems with Jung's emphasis on discrimination and its correlate separation. In Jung's theory, these actions are the essence of consciousness as characteristics but also essential for development of consciousness itself. Jarrett (1988) has pointed out that discrimination, or differentiation, is only one possible avenue for consciousness to develop. Discrimination relies too heavily on a Logos, or thinking, attitude, characteristic of Jung himself. Jarrett offers the example of Eros, the function of making connections rather that separating, as another path to consciousness. He wrote, "Jung's exceptionally powerful Logos led him to exaggerate the importance of discriminative, abstract, divergent, oppositional – even polarizing – understanding, and to underestimate the powers of Eros to join what has been put asunder" (Jarrett, 1988, p. 355). He makes the point that opposites, that is, positive versus negative qualities, are oppositional in perhaps one aspect but at the same time similar in other aspects (for example, the North and South Pole being experientially the same despite being at opposite ends of Earth). It appears, then, that Jung understands differentiation in a rather undifferentiated way, at least at this point in his theory.

Another characteristic of the ego and consciousness that Jung describes is the ego quality of continuity and identity (see the previous ego definition). Here he is touching upon subjective experience: consciousness and ego as the center of consciousness as a continuous experience. This recalls James' formulation of "the personal nature of consciousness", a consciousness that is a stream rather than dissociated moments and one that is experienced continuously as one's own. Jung would be quite familiar with James' formulation of the 'me' versus the 'I' : the "me" is the inner subjective state whose nucleus is physical experience, whereas the "I" is more the observing thought which reflects and possesses the quality of continuity. The ego for Jung possesses both "me" and "I" qualities. It is based on physical and emotional experience (through the ego-complex) but also is reflective and continuous.

The form of libido, that is, introversion or extraversion, shapes continuity of consciousness. The introverted ego, that is, the libido directed inward, focuses the person on his own affects. Conversely, the extraverted ego, that is, the libido directed outward to the object, fills the person with the relationship to the other. As Jung wrote,

> For only with the introvert is the 'person' exclusively the ego; with the extravert it lies in his affectivity and not in the affected ego. His ego is, as it were, of less importance than his affectivity, i.e. his relatedness. . . . The ego is not 'eternally constant', least of all in the extravert, who pays little attention to it. For the introvert, on the other hand, it has too much importance. . . .
>
> (CW 6/138)

Jung is implying, then, that the ego (and by extension consciousness) is an instrument of continuity as far as the libido turns inward to one's own emotional life. This suggests a bias of Jung's toward the introverted life.

EGO AS A COLLECTIVE STRUCTURE

Jung would make the argument in 1950 that the ego was an archetype and collective in its nature (Vol 9ii). It is possible to make a case, however, that Jung in 1921, as he wrote *Psychological Types*, also viewed the ego as a collective structure in its capacity as a function, although his conclusions were more tentative and contradictory. Jung wrote,

> For whereas the ego has a relative constancy, its relatedness, or proneness to affect, is variable. [. . .] And as a matter of fact the one side of it is the conscious ego-function, while the other side is the ego's relation

> to the collective. Both determinants are inherent in human psychology. But the various types will each see these basic facts in a different light. For the introvert the idea of the ego is the continuous and dominant note of consciousness, and its antithesis for him is relatedness or proneness to affect. For the extravert, on the contrary, the accent lies more on the continuity of his relation to the object and less on the idea of the ego.
> (CW 6/138)

'Collective' for Jung means qualities that apply not simply to the individual but to groups of people or even the whole of mankind (CW 6/692). There can be collective functions in addition to collective contents (CW 6/692), such as thinking, feeling, sensation, and intuition: all ego functions, what "constitut[e], in their totality, the subject" (Jung, 1990, p. 122).

Thus in the preceding quote, Jung is saying a number of things about the collective nature of the ego. First, there are two directions or tendencies, according to the libido direction, for the ego's actions. Both these tendencies are collective, that is, non-personal; to the extent they represent ego function, "determinants . . . inherent in human psychology".

Next, Jung describes the introverted ego as directed toward the conscious ego function and the extraverted ego directed toward the collective. What is Jung saying about the ego with such a conclusion? By using texts from Schiller, Jung concludes 'conscious ego function' and 'the ego's relation to the collective' are two sides of a polarity: the person versus his affect. In other words, he describes the ego that perceives and experiences itself versus the ego that is emotionally connected and related (*bezogen*) to the other. The former is an "abstracting, self-contained attitude" (CW 6/139) while the latter is the "affectivity" (CW 6/138). These two sides of the ego are also the two sides of any complex in general; the image (in this case the person himself) and the affect (one's own). One side is the ego as it experiences itself through its emotions, but also as it perceives itself as separate.

EGO AS A PSYCHODYNAMIC FUNCTION

This is the basic principle behind the typology concept. Typology according to Jung is a form of interaction with the world of objects or the inner 'subjective' world. The four types (thinking, feeling, sensation, intuition) are attitudes, that is, "predisposition[s] of the sensory or motor centers to react to a particular stimulus or constant impulse" (CW 6/687), "a readiness of the psyche to act or react in a certain way" (CW 6/687), as well as "[a]n a priori orientation" whether conscious or not, which will determine action or reaction, as well as active apperception (CW 6/687). Jung relates attitude to Wundt's concept of apperception, with the difference that Wundt's concept represents an essentially broad unified process, while Jung associates typology with differentiation.

One's typology, then, one's attitude, is associated with a subjective sense of self in so far as it is the conscious perception and orientation toward one's world. For example, the purely feeling type (in theory, at least, for such a one-sided type would hardly exist) perceives and is oriented toward the world according to its emotional value, without consideration of its objective reality. This stance toward the world would be a subjective experience of the world and therefore color one's perception of oneself. But that perception remains nevertheless an autonomous function so long as it is fused with subjective experience. Jung makes the point that as a person develops through individuation (develops a conscious realization of one's individual needs, tasks, duties, responsibilities, etc.; see for example Jung's letter to Henry Murray, 2 Jul 1948), the ego as a psychodynamic function and the subjective sense of self separate, making the sense of self less dependent on autonomous (or unconscious) perception and orientation and influenced by mass psychology and more differentiated and self-directed. That is the meaning of the following passage:

> Under normal conditions [. . .] energy must be artificially supplied to the unconscious symbol in order to increase its value and bring it to consciousness. This comes about (and here we return to the idea of differentiation provoked by Schiller) through a differentiation of the self from the opposites [as in typology for example]. This differentiation amounts to a detachment of libido from both sides, in so far as the libido is disposable. For the libido invested in the instincts is only in part freely disposable, just so far in fact as the power of the will extends. This is represented by the amount of energy which is at the 'free' disposal of the ego. The will then has the self as a possible aim. . . .
>
> (CW 6/183)

The theory of typology has received its share of criticism (Jarrett, 1988; Marshall, 1968; Samuels, 1985, for example), very often valid. It would lead too far afield, however, to explore all of its particulars. What is relevant, though, are the implications regarding energy in the preceding quote and what this means for the ego as a psychodynamic function separating from the subjective sense of self.

Jung created a new world, in a sense, in his revision of Freud's theory. Whereas Freud emphasized the ideal of reason (a quality he associated with the ego), establishing "a dictatorship in the mental life of man" (Freud, SE 22, p. 208), Jung saw much more a collaboration between the conscious and unconscious realms of the mind. The basic premise of Jung's system is the totality of the psyche: in its dynamic process, the psyche uses the two instruments of consciousness and unconsciousness. The ego, as the center of consciousness, interacts with the unconscious, as it is manifested and experienced in the inner world in dreams or fantasy, or in the outer world in projection. This interaction, the psychodynamic process of the psyche, is characterized by mutual relatedness.

Mutual relatedness (also called Eros, CW 11/621) is a psychodynamic concept Jung came to describe explicitly only in his later work and this concept will be explored in the next chapter in greater detail. However, in this middle period of Jung's work, Jung is beginning to articulate a theory of psyche with this concept of psychodynamic interaction implicit. Freud was right, he would argue, to ground his psychological theory in sexuality, but it is a one-sided view of sexuality grounded in a "materialistic epoch" which fails to see that libido is more than sexual energy; it is "a creative world-principle" which is "a projected perception of the living essence in man himself" (CW 6/337). The basic psychodynamic process in man is essentially and autonomously creative. This is the basic principle of Jung's Eros concept.

The ego as center of consciousness acts as the counterpoint to the unconscious psyche, but Jung makes the point that the ego is not the opposite of the Self, for the Self embraces the ego too. The ego is an exponent of the self according to Jung (CW 11/391); it is a representation of the Self in the conscious sphere and lacks individuality just as the Self lacks the quality of individuality. The polarity ego–Self is therefore misleading, for the Self in that context would be the center of the field of unconsciousness. The polar opposite for the Self as the totality of the psyche would be the *individual* – the totality of one person separated from collectivity. Therefore one would speak more accurately of the *individual*–Self axis rather than the ego–Self axis.

The development of the ego

There is no discussion of ego development in *Psychological Types*, and Jung mentions the idea of ego development only once in passing (CW 6/623). Jung nevertheless makes a number of assumptions that offer a possible framework for a theory of ego development at this stage.

First, he assumes there is a structure in the psyche prior to ego development. He wrote,

> The introverted attitude is normally oriented by the psychic structure, which is in principle hereditary and inborn in the subject. This must not be assumed, however, to be simply identical with the subjects ego [. . .], it is rather the psychic structure of the subject prior to any ego-development.
>
> (CW 6/623)

There is the assumption then that this psychic structure is the foundation for later development of the subject, that is, the *individual*.

He defines the 'psychic structure' as the collective unconscious (CW 6/624) of which "the inborn mode of acting", that is, the behavioral manifestation, is instinct, while the "inborn mode of psychic apprehension" is the archetype (CW 6/624). The entity, which encompasses the conscious as well as the unconscious psychic structures, is the [S]elf (CW 6/623–624). The ego is assumed by implication, then, to be derived from the [S]elf and is an aspect or part of the [S]elf (CW 6/623–624). A more thorough theory of ego development, however, would only emerge in subsequent works.

The individual

In *Psychological Types*, Jung introduces the concept of the *individual* as an entity separate from the ego or the Self. As discussed above, this entity has its own developmental sequence and process, as well as its own characteristics and structure. A diagram from Jung's 1925 seminar (Jung, 1990, p. 129) illustrates where he places the individual in the overall psychical scheme (see Figure 4.1).

In this scheme, the ego is the center of consciousness, and the shadow, as the repressed aspects of the conscious personality, is the center of the

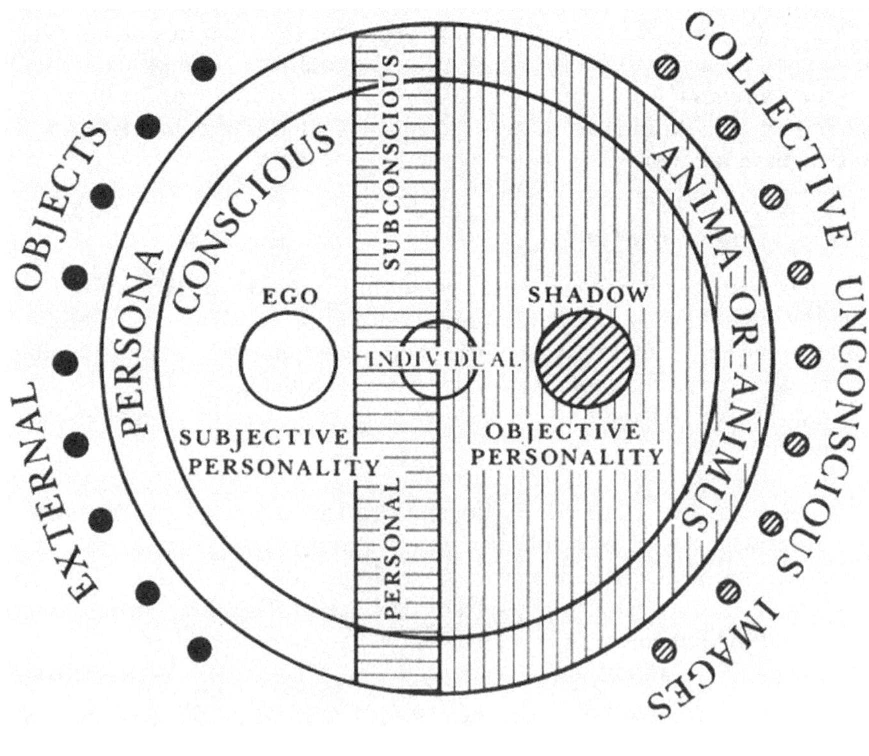

Figure 4.1 The Psychic Structure

personal unconscious. Straddling the two psychical areas of consciousness (or personal subconscious) and the personal unconscious is the *individual*. It is noteworthy that the *individual* is not identical with the ego (or the Self) but rather, occupies a place somewhere in between. Thus one can see Jung is building up a further complexity of psychical regions in his topographical theory.

Jung defines the *individual* in *Psychological Types* this way:

> The psychological individual is characterized by a particular and in some respects unique psychology. The particular nature of the individual psyche appears less in its elements than in its complex formulations. The psychological individual, or his individuality, has an a priori unconscious existence, but exists consciously only so far as a consciousness of his particular nature is present, i.e., so far as there exists a conscious distinction from other individuals. The psychic individuality is given *a priori* as a correlate of the physical individuality, although, as observed, it is first unconscious. A conscious process of differentiation, or individuation, is needed to bring the individuality to consciousness, i.e., to raise it out of the state of identity, with the object. The identity of the individuality with the object is synonymous with its unconsciousness. If the individual is unconscious, there is no psychological individual but merely a collective psychology of consciousness. The unconscious individuality is then projected on the object, and the object, in consequence, possesses too great a value and acts as too powerful a determinant.
>
> (CW 6/755)

Jung is describing three characteristics of the *individual* in this definition. First, it has its origins a priori in the physical, that is, biological and instinctual, unconscious realm. Second, it is the product of a developmental process called individuation. And third, it does not have the quality of collective psychology, but rather, is the expression of a "unique psychology". I will address each of these three topics in turn.

A priori origins

Jung takes as a basic assumption that there is an a priori existence of the *individual* in the psyche; hence his statement presented earlier, "The psychological individual, or his individuality, has an a priori unconscious existence". There is of course no way of assessing this in any objective or scientific way, though he bases this assumption on the fact that the potential for individuality in the psychical realm is "a correlate of the physical individuality". In other words, because we are all alike as human beings physically but there are nevertheless individual differences that distinguish each from the other, it must follow that the same is true in the psychical realm.

What Jung assumes, therefore, is an inborn developmental process waiting for the maturational forces and environmental climate to bring forth. The background assumption for this action is in accordance with Materialist principles but also within the symbolic paradigm. Materialism presents growth and development as an autonomous innate characteristic of physical being. In the symbolic paradigm, however, the growth of the *individual* is required because the relationship to the inner world must be established.

Individuation as a developmental process

Jung proposing existence a priori of the *individual* is not declaring, in a kind of sentimental way, that we are all originally special and unique. Rather, the *individual*, as described by Jung, is a central element in the basic mental structure, which arises from a particular developmental process in the psyche. By asserting this a priori existence, Jung is assuming a potential for a unique, non-collective existence. He is also proposing that this personal experience, this existence, is not the same experience or existence of the ego. The *individual*, in other words, is a third position built up out of dynamic relatedness of the ego and the unconscious.

It is an entity that develops through and out of the interaction of the ego and the unconscious. Jung wrote, for example, in interpreting Schiller on instincts and mind:

> Here, it seems to me, Schiller has put his finger on something very important, namely, the possibility of separating out an individual nucleus, which can be at one time the subject and at another the object of the opposing functions, though always remaining distinguishable from them.
>
> (CW 6/174)

The danger, according to Jung, is that "the individuality (as we might call the 'individual nucleus' for short) fails to differentiate itself from the opposites, it becomes identical with them and is inwardly torn asunder, so that a state of agonizing disunion arises" (CW 6/175). As long as an *individual* entity exists in the psychic structure, there is stability and harmony in the personality, but this aspect of the personality can become identified ("identical") with the ego or the unconscious. In identification with the ego there is a falling into mass psychology, in identification with the unconscious there is a falling into collective instinctual behavior.

It is an entity that stands outside the interaction of the ego and the unconscious. As Jung wrote in 1916 in an early version of his essay 'The Structure of the Unconscious':

> The individual stands . . . between the conscious part of the collective psyche and the unconscious part. He is the reflecting surface in which

> the world of consciousness can perceive its own unconscious, historical image, . . . the individual would be a point of intersection or a dividing line, neither conscious nor unconscious, but a bit of both.
>
> (CW 7/507)

And again later in a revision of this same essay, he wrote in 1926:

> It may not be immediately apparent what is meant by a 'mid-point of the personality'. . . . If we picture the conscious mind, with the ego as its center, as being opposed to the unconscious, and if we now add to our mental picture the process of assimilating the unconscious, we can think of this assimilation as a kind of approximation of conscious and unconscious, where the center of the personality no longer coincides with the ego, but with a point midway between the conscious and unconscious. This would be the point of a new equilibrium, a new centering of personality, a virtual center, which, on account of its focal position between conscious and unconscious ensures for the personality a new and more solid foundation.
>
> (CW 7/365)

Expression of the unique individual

In Jung's definition of the *individual*, he states, "If the individual is unconscious, there is no psychological individual but merely a collective psychology of consciousness" (CW 6/755). This emphasizes the difference between the ego (in its capacity as the center of consciousness) and the *individual* (the expression and experience of one's unique self). In essence, the definition of the *individual* is this quality of non-collectivity, and this is why it is a separate psychic entity from the ego.

Jung is less clear, however, when he describes the mental experiences of the experiencing ego and the *individual*, for these two entities are used or implied interchangeably. The *individual* is a subjective inner experience that exists only as far as there exists consciousness of distinctness from others (CW 6/755). The ego, on the other hand, is defined by Jung by its structural function, but is used as a term to describe personal experience.

Two Essays on Analytical Psychology (CW 7)

Volume 7 of Jung's Collected Works is a set of two essays written between 1912 and 1916 and revised a number of times until their present form in 1943. They are considered a turning point in the history of analytical psychology because these two essays represent the foundation for all Jung's subsequent theoretical work developed after his break with Freud (CW 7, p. v).

The period from 1912 to 1943, with two devastating wars, was a time of immense upheaval in Europe. For Jung, the time was also one of personal and professional turmoil: he severed his ties with the psychoanalytical movement, resigning all his associated posts as well as his position at the University of Zürich. He suffered what he described as a breakdown: what Carl Meier categorized, "phenomenologically . . . as a schizophrenic episode" (unpublished interview cited in Hayman, 1999, p. 175).

In this period of breakdown, Jung rejected scientific activity but instead began to explore the 'revelations' of the unconscious. He kept a journal that became the Red Book. In this he wrote of and drew his dreams and waking visions in an attempt to look at these objectively.

This period of inner upheaval was balanced by outer responsibility (for example, he had a growing family to support, patients to see, and military service to fulfill) and the intellectual work of organizing and understanding the products of the unconscious he observed in himself. This "creative illness" (Ellenberger), alongside the psychological material produced by his patients, was in a sense the psychological data he would interpret to produce his new theories.

I want to make the point, however, that although he began to look at and understand his personal and professional material in a new way, Jung retained – intentionally in many cases – assumptions about the basic character of energy that remained in the energic/materialistic tradition. These assumptions were then part of the basic concepts that made up his new revised psychological theory. For example, in the *Two Essays*, Jung describes the transformation of libido through the action of the symbol by introducing the concept of the Transcendent Function. The Transcendent Function is a "natural process by which the opposites are united . . ." (CW 7/121). Opposing psychic energies, a conflict between conscious attitude and unconscious imperative for example, are 'reconciled' through the emergence of a third entity, the symbol. This symbol then becomes a dynamic factor when it is experienced and understood (what 'experienced and understood' means will be elaborated later). The concept of a reconciling creation arising out of the conscious confrontation of opposing psychic energies is part of the essence of the symbolic paradigm. But the basic premise that the psyche follows the principles of conservation of energy (CW 7/106–108) and therefore psychic energy moves in certain ways between energy gradients is frank energic paradigm.

Jung, in these two essays then, is creating a synthesis of energy concepts based, on the one hand, on scientific principles (the energic paradigm) and on the other hand, on metaphysical concepts (the symbolic paradigm). It is self-evident to Jung, for example, that psychic energy seeks harmony between conscious and unconscious attitudes: this is the principle behind the mechanism of enantiodromia. Jung attributes to this concept the principle of the conservation of energy. He takes the materialist argument, that the mind follows the rules of physical nature, in order to understand the psychic phenomena he observed and experienced. In 1946 he acknowledges the inherent difficulties with this viewpoint:

> [I]n spite of the nonmeasurability of psychic processes, the perceptible changes effected by the psyche cannot possibly be understood except as a phenomenon of energy. This places the psychologist in a situation which is highly repugnant to the physicist: the psychologist also talks of energy although he has nothing measurable to manipulate, besides which the concept of energy is a strictly defined mathematical quantity which cannot be applied to anything psychic. . . . If psychology nevertheless insists on employing its own concept of energy for the purpose of expressing the activity . . . of the psyche, it is not of course being used as a mathematical formula, but only as its analogy.
>
> (CW8/441)

In this period of Jung's work, he is doing two things relevant to the study of the ego concept: first, he is proposing a new form of confrontation of opposite energies. Rather than the conflictual energic paradigm in which psychic energy (libido) is an instinctual force seeking its satisfaction (this is Jung's interpretation of Freud which was also Jung's starting point), Jung proposes a model in which psychic conflict is inherently a creative impulse. In this creative conflict, a conflict of conscious attitude versus unconscious impulse or imperative, the ego (as center of consciousness) and the unconscious act collaboratively to effect a transformation. This means relationship is the medium of change. It also means relationship (and relatedness) is the basic organizing principle of the psyche: this is the true meaning of his theory of the opposites.

This leads to the second point about the ego. If the nature of the psyche is based on relatedness, then the ego is the central and indispensable partner to the unconscious. In other words, the ego as the center of consciousness

1. Must actively participate in the confrontation with the unconscious; it has the responsibility to experience, receive, and understand the opposing unconscious entity.
2. Must realize its 'wholeness', that is, expand its view of itself and the world.

Therefore, the ego has two roles to play. The first is the structural role as 'gatekeeper' of the conscious attitude. Unacceptable attitudes are repressed or projected (and thus build up into the shadow) or are allowed in through awareness and acceptance. These gatekeeper functions are not necessarily conscious. But also the ego has an experiential role: to open oneself emotionally to the experience of the unconscious, the symbol.

'On the Psychology of the Unconscious' (1943)

This is the first essay in Volume 7 of Jung's Collected Works. It evolved from an essay written in 1912 called 'New Paths in Psychology' and was revised in 1916 (published in 1917) as 'Psychology of Unconscious Processes'. This second version was revised again in 1926, and then thoroughly rewritten in 1943 to its present form. Certain concepts are present in all versions but were expanded over time, while other concepts are progressively introduced. Two key concepts introduced or explored in this essay relevant for the study of ego are the 'Transcendent Function' and 'enantiodromia'. I will discuss each of these in turn.

The Transcendent Function

In essence, the Transcendent Function (TF) is the union of conscious and unconscious contents. Jung described the process this way:

> The process of coming to terms with the unconscious is a true labor, a work which involves both action and suffering. It has been named the 'transcendent function' because it represents a function based on real and 'imaginary', or rational and irrational, data, thus bridging the yawning gulf between conscious and unconscious. It is a natural process, a manifestation of the energy that springs from the tension of opposites.
>
> (CW 7/121)

He describes this function as non-metaphysical in earlier writings; in 1916, he likens it to a mathematical operation. In the last phase of his life, however, Jung sees a much more spiritual aspect in the TF. In 1954 he said:

> This function progressively unites the opposites. Psychotherapy makes use of it to heal neurotic dissociations, but this function had already served as the basis of Hermetic philosophy for seventeen centuries. Besides this, it is a natural and spontaneous phenomenon, part of the process of individuation. Psychology has no proof that this process does not unfold itself at the instigation of God's will.
>
> (CW 18/1555)

Again, this is what Jung had to say in 1958: "The transcendent function . . . is the discursive co-operation of conscious and unconscious factors or, in theological language, of reason and grace" (CW 10/855).

Jung wrote that the TF "arises from the union of conscious and unconscious contents" (CW 8/131). It is not used in a 'mysterious' or 'metaphysical' sense, but rather is "comparable in its way to a mathematical function" (I assume that when Jung compares the Transcendent Function to a mathematical function, he is referring to a mathematical formula that describes a binary relationship between two variable quantities: for example, $x = n + y$).

Jung stresses that the TF is a natural process; it results from a failure of adaptation, a demand for a new attitude/adaptation. Adaptation, according to Jung, is never definitive, but rather for the moment.

In describing the characteristics of this function, Jung emphasized the participation of both the ego and the unconscious. He wrote, "The process of coming to terms with the unconscious is a true labor, a work which involves both action and suffering. It has been named the 'transcendent function' because it represents a function based on real and 'imaginary', or rational and irrational, data, thus bridging the yawning gulf between conscious and unconscious. It is a natural process, a manifestation of the energy that springs from the tension of opposites" (CW 7/121).

What are the dynamic principles of the Transcendent Function? In other words, how does the union of opposites occur in the structure of the psyche?

FIRST PRINCIPLE

The TF is the energetic aspect of the symbol. The unconscious has an essentially compensatory or complementary relationship to consciousness. There is an inherent conflict, according to Jung, between consciousness, which is concerned with collective adaptation, and the unconscious, which is concerned with individuation (CW 18/1084–1106). The symbol, in Jung's formulation, is the bridge between the conscious adaptation, that is, one's reality, and what is unconscious, that is, what one does not know or feel or understand. Having defined a symbol as derived from the conscious encounter with archaic, that is, non-personal, layers of the unconscious (CW 6/402), Jung would then describe the mechanisms of this encounter in his account of the TF. First "consciousness puts its media of expression at the disposal of the unconscious content" (CW 8/178). Then, "the second and more important stage of the procedure, the bringing together of the opposites for the production of a third: the transcendent function" (CW 8/181). The TF, in other words, is the mechanism of bridging the conscious and unconscious contents, which is represented at the psychic level as the symbol, at the experiential level as a change in attitude.

SECOND PRINCIPLE

The TF requires an active, strong and stable ego: Jung makes this point several times in his essay on the TF. He wrote,

> Once the unconscious content has been given form and the meaning of the formulation is understood, the question arises as to how the ego will

> relate to this position, and how the ego and the unconscious are to come to terms. . . . At this stage it is no longer the unconscious that takes the lead, but the ego.
>
> (CW 8/181)

Again: "The position of the ego must be maintained as being of equal value to the counter-position of the unconscious, and *vice versa*" (CW 8/183). And again: "In coming to terms with the unconscious, not only is the standpoint of the ego justified, but the unconscious is granted the same authority. The *ego takes the lead* [emphasis added], but the unconscious must be allowed to have its say too . . ." (CW 8/185). Jung would also prescribe, when one is faced with visual products of the unconscious, that "the ego must seize the initiative and ask: How am I affected by this sign?" (CW 8/188). There is one huge assumption here. There is implied in these passages an ability on the ego's part to observe itself in this encounter: in other words, that there an objective cognition of the process in addition to participation with all one's affect (CW 8/183).

This raises the question of how this mechanism can proceed at all if the ego is weak or immature in terms of normal development (in children for example) or because of regression or neurosis or trauma (in adults). How can the ego take the lead or observe itself if it is weak or fragmented? Moore (1975) addresses exactly this question in her article 'The Transcendent Function and the Forming Ego'. She makes the point that although the ego participates in the TF, it can only do so with the psychic functions that have evolved up to that point. Without the ability to observe the conscious–unconscious encounter, for example, the ego will fall into either the conscious or the unconscious perceptions. Before there is objective cognition (i.e. an observing ego capacity) the ego, according to Moore, experiences the encounter with the unconscious as a threat to its continuity and begins simultaneously to 'deintegrate' (in the Fordham sense of experiencing oneself and the world in fragments), to build boundaries around itself as a defense against the unconscious, but at the same time also attempt to relate to the unconscious (Moore, 1975, p. 171).

One needs to examine these preceding scenarios separately in children and in adults. The developing ego in the child has the potential maturational capacity for self–other relatedness and integration, as infant and early childhood research informs us. The adult with ego weakness, however, is in a more defensively structured relationship to the realm of the other, which includes the unconscious. A child would therefore, in theory, proceed in development as described earlier. For the child there would be a natural tendency to experience the separateness of the other, because of frustration or mutual relatedness, and thus begin to experience his or her own being in a self-observing way. The regressed or neurotic adult with a weak ego, according to Moore, would have built up defenses to prevent either the experience of separateness or the experience of closeness and mutuality since both represent devastating existential states for the wounded ego.

Symbol formation in adults with weak ego structure is limited or impaired because of this lack of the observing third position. Moore wrote, "When the ego boundaries are slight [in the adult] symbolic experience is an equation between the inner and the outer contents, without a sense of 'as-if'" (1975, p. 170). This lack of the sense of 'as-if' prevents the ego from experiencing a symbol as a representation of something as yet unknown (as per Jung's definition) but instead the symbol is experienced as an equivalence of inner and outer (Milner, 1952; Segal, 1950; cited by Moore, 1975). In other words, the symbolic image is experienced concretely rather than imaginally. As an example of this phenomenon, I think of my clients who self-mutilate: the sadistic inner figure coupled with a self-loathing ego experience leads to concrete self-injury.

Enantiodromia

This is a term Jung took from the philosopher Heraclitus, and it means 'running counter too' or the idea that everything eventually turns into its opposite. But it has a deeper implication when used by Jung. He quotes Stobaeus paraphrasing Heraclitus in his definition in Volume 6: "Fate is the logical product of enantiodromia, creator of all things". Jung sees enantiodromia as an unseen cosmic truth, an ultimate background force that acts in the psyche as one of the principles of psychic energy.

It is different from compensation by degree: compensation is the action of the unconscious to balance the conscious attitude. If one has acted too much in a thinking way, for example, then the dream from the unconscious will bring up the feeling aspect. Jung emphasizes that compensation is the psyche balancing itself, 'tweaking' that goes on like background noise, an unconscious process we might not notice except for example to feel a bit different when you wake up.

Enantiodromia, on the other hand, occurs when there is a powerful one-sidedness. The conscious attitude has resisted the psyche's attempts at balancing and has now taken an extreme position vis à vis the unconscious. We could say that compensation and enantiodromia are part of this same energic principle: "every psychic development, whether individual or collective, possesses an optimum which, when exceeded, produces an enantiodromia, that is, turns into its opposite" (CW 13/294).

Jung's formulation implies that there is a background, or inner, sense of what needs balancing, what is too one-sided. It is not a sense based on physical laws like the body failing when it has for example exceeded a critical temperature, but rather, one could say, a soul sense. We each carry in us an unconscious sense of what is too one-sided, even though consciously we might be sliding right toward it and defend against any actions of the psyche to put us back in balance.

This idea, that there is a background of natural wisdom in our psyche, is what I mean when I say Jung over his lifetime evolved away from the materialist model of psychic energy to a more spiritual perspective.

The psychic mechanism of compensation/enantiodromia then is characterized by the following assumptions:

Everything contains its opposite, but not a rational opposite. These are not opposites chosen by the physical world, although Jung used opposites like hot/cold, wet/dry as examples. In the psyche the opposites are part of a symbolic process and therefore contain a feeling value; the opposites are therefore qualitative rather than quantitative. The connection of one thing to its opposite is heart-centered rather than a cognitive or physical connection (CW 12/108).

For Jung, the conscious standpoint, or ego, concerns being and feeling, an emotional orientation or center rather than a cognitive standpoint. Only a 'heart'-centered conscious attitude can relate to the unconscious. Without emotional investment in the process, it is just an intellectual exercise and the ego is not fully engaged. The assumption made by Jung about this process from evidence from the psyche is that the heart-centered conscious attitude has more value in terms of individuation. And this again brings up this idea of something beyond empirically demonstrable physical reality acting in the background.

There is always a movement back toward the opposite, which is directed by this innate sense in the psyche of incompleteness of the conscious attitude. Jung wrote,

> The tendency to separate the opposites as much as possible and to strive for singleness of meaning is absolutely necessary for clarity of consciousness, since discrimination is of the essence. [Discrimination is an ego function.] But when the separation is carried so far that the complementary opposite is lost sight of, and the blackness of the whiteness, the evil of the good, the depths of the heights, and so on, is no longer seen, the result is one-sidedness, which is then compensated from the unconscious without our help. The counterbalancing is even done against our will, which in consequence must become more and more fanatical until it brings about a catastrophic enantiodromia.
>
> (CW 14/470)

Jung comes back again and again in his writings to the point that the unconscious does not orchestrate this movement back and forth; it reacts to the conscious attitude. The ego has a fundamental role in this movement inherent in the psychic system. *The ego must take a stand first before there can be a reaction from the unconscious*, whether compensation or enantiodromia. When the ego refuses to abandon its conscious attitude, then the result is a neurosis. The neurosis is related to the failure of the individual to adapt to the demands of the inner world to grasp the opposing perspective.

A common misconception in Jungian psychology is the idea that the Self (the archetypal concept) directs the ego. For example, a Zürich analyst from the original group around Jung told me it was common in the early days for students to look to a dream for guidance in making ordinary decisions such as whether to accept a dinner invitation or not. This attitude was contrary to Jung's insistence that the ego must take the lead in life's decision-making for only then can the unconscious react. When the ego abandons its directive role, consciousness is in danger of being overwhelmed by the unconscious, leading to inflation or a potential psychosis. Jung wrote, for example, that the Self is only helpful when the individual is conscious (Jung, 1976, p. 464). Samuels (1983) makes a similar point that the Self has been overvalued by Jungians in the past and has begun a process of relativization by post-Jungians.

Life consists of this continual movement. Jung emphasized that life itself can be characterized by change. He said in the Nietzsche seminars, for example,

> [life] is always undoing itself, always creating a new day, a new generation. . . . It must follow the law of enantiodromia: there must be destruction and creation, or it would not be at all. A thing that is absolutely static has no existence. It must be in a process or it would never even be perceived.
>
> (1984, p. 1214)

In a sense, this swinging of the pendulum is the core of adaptation. It is never completed, there is always a new inner or outer world to meet and the old structures have to die in order for new ones to emerge. This is why failure to respond to this imperative of life's movement by the conscious ego, brings about neurosis – neurosis in this model is a form of stasis.

Enantiodromia does not lead to the union of opposites. Jung gave a talk in 1958 about religious belief, and he was asked the following question: "You stress the principle of the opposites and the importance of their union. You also write of enantiodromia in relation to the opposites but this would never produce a condition of stability, which could lead to a union of opposites. So is there a contradiction in what you say about opposites?"

Jung answers: "'Enantiodromia' describes a certain psychological fact, i.e., I use it as a psychological concept. Of course it does not lead to a union of opposites, has – as a matter of fact – nothing to do with it. I see no contradiction anywhere".

The questioner persists: "If the principle of enantiodromia, a perpetual swinging of the pendulum, is always present would we not have a condition in which there would be no sense of responsibility, but one of amorality and meaninglessness?"

Jung replies: "Naturally life would be quite meaningless if the enantiodromia of psychological states kept on forever. But such an assumption would be arbitrary and foolish" (CW 18/1596–1598).

The mechanism of enantiodromia can only lead to individuation in concert with the mechanism of the TF: the former driving the conscious realization of conflict, the latter bringing reconciliation.

Ego functions differentiate according to the principles of adaptation. Certain functions are repressed according to demands of outer world circumstances: for example, the feeling function is repressed or encouraged according to the value of emotional responses in one's group; its repression may represent a defensive/protective response to a climate hostile to emotional responses. Those functions repressed are then subject to retrieval through enantiodromia.

Jung makes the case in Volume 6 for the role of types in adaptation. He said that initially we contain all the types as potential, but in childhood certain types dominate to adapt to the outer world (family, community, etc.). This sets up then an opposition or a 'one-sidedness':

> A one-sided attitude leaves a deficiency in the adaptive performance which accumulates during the course of life, and sooner or later this will produce a disturbance of adaptation that drives the subject towards some kind of compensation. But the compensation can be obtained only by means of an amputation (sacrifice) of the hitherto one-sided attitude. . . . The adaptive deficiency, which is the *causa efficiens* of the process of conversion, is subjectively felt as a vague sense of dissatisfaction.
>
> (CW 6/28)

In other words, the first adaptation made is to collective consciousness, and in this process of adapting, certain ego functions are repressed. We all have these four functions, but the dominant ones we express in our personality are shaped first through adaptation.

Jung also contrasts the qualities of the functions we take as our main function to what is repressed:

> On account of its relative repression, the inferior function is only partly attached to consciousness; its other part is attached to the unconscious. The differentiated function is the most fully adapted to external reality; it is essentially the reality function.
>
> (CW 6/171)

What is not adapted to causes energy to flow to the opposite. Jung wrote,

> When the libido invested in a particular function cannot be equilibrated by the exercise of the function, it accumulates until it attains a value which exceeds that of the neighboring functional system. Then a process of equilibrium begins, because a potential is present. The energy flows over, as it were, into another system. When, therefore, adaptation to the

inside is not achieved, the libido intended for that purpose accumulates until it begins to flow out of the system of inner adaptation into the system of outer adaptation, with the result that characteristics belonging to inner adaptation are carried over into outer – that is to say, fantasies intervene in the relation to the real world.

(CW18/1090)

'The Relations Between the Ego and the Unconscious' (1935)

This work began as an essay written in 1916 in French originally entitled 'The Structure of the Unconscious'. This went through various versions and was finally revised in 1928 and given its present name. Although entitled 'The Relations Between the Ego and the Unconscious', it would be more accurately entitled 'Effects of the Unconscious on the Ego', so much is it skewed toward exploring the nature and actions of the unconscious. In 1916 Jung was emerging from his period of "disorientation" and "confusion" after his break with Freud, and was focusing his professional energy on understanding the psychic forces and images he had experienced. Eisold (2002) suggests another factor for Jung's emphasis on the unconscious at this point. Jung had just broken from the dictative cabal-like psychoanalytic movement of Freud and his followers and sought instead to focus on "exploration of myths and religions, on education in occult traditions of symbolism, and on articulating the notion of spiritual development" (p. 507) rather than building up another organization with all the attendant politics.

There are several themes developed in this essay that build on what was introduced previously. The mechanisms of the TF and enantiodromia are examined in greater detail and implications for therapy are discussed.

The TF and enantiodromia are seen in the wider context of individuation as innate and autonomous processes:

1 "[T]he unconscious is never quiescent in the sense of being inactive, but is ceaselessly engaged in grouping and regrouping contents. This activity should be thought of as completely autonomous in pathological cases; normally it is coordinated with the conscious mind in a compensatory relationship" (CW 7/204).
2 "It would be wrong to leave the matter as it stands without at the same time recognizing that there is, after all, something individual in the particular choice and delineation of the persona, and that despite the exclusive identity of the ego-consciousness with the persona the unconscious self, one's real individuality, is always present and makes itself felt indirectly if not directly. Although the ego-consciousness is at first identical with the persona [. . .] yet the unconscious self can never be repressed to the point of extinction. Its influence is chiefly manifest in

the special nature of the contrasting and compensating contents of the unconscious" (CW 7/ 247).

3 "I regard the loss of balance as purposive, since it replaces a defective consciousness by the automatic and instinctive activity of the unconscious, which is aiming all the time at the creation of a new balance and will moreover achieve this aim, provided that the conscious mind is capable of assimilating the contents produced by the unconscious, i.e., of understanding and digesting them" (CW 7/ 253).

4 "So far as our present experience goes, we can lay it down that the unconscious processes stand in a compensatory relation to the conscious mind. I expressly use the word 'compensatory' and not the word 'opposed' because conscious and unconscious are not necessarily in opposition to one another, but complement one another to form a totality, which is the [S]elf" (CW 7/ 274).

These above passages reinforce the central argument that the totality of the psyche, that is, the conscious and unconscious elements together, work in concert through the mechanisms of the TF and enantiodromia to bring about the development of the individual. Jung uses the term 'self' here in an ambiguous way, implying or stating in quote numbers 2 and 4, for example, that the self is the totality of the individual (as also noted in a different context by Redfearn, 1983) yet also as a kind of primary force related to the mechanisms of compensation in the unconscious. The unconscious is also characterized as a force, 'automatic and instinctive', but is not yet an organizing entity. Jung is not using the concept of self to refer to a kind of cosmic unity or as the organizing principle itself, and instead refers to the 'unconscious' as the interactive partner with consciousness.

5 "The unconscious processes that compensate the conscious ego contain all those elements that are necessary for the self-regulation of the psyche as a whole. [. . .] [T]he more we become conscious of ourselves through self-knowledge, and act accordingly, the more the layer of the personal unconscious that is superimposed on the collective unconscious will be diminished. In this way there arises a consciousness which is no longer imprisoned in the petty, oversensitive, personal world of the ego, but participates freely in the wider world of objective interests. This widened consciousness is no longer that touchy, egotistical bundle of personal wishes, fears, hopes, and ambitions which always has to be compensated or corrected by unconscious counter-tendencies; instead, it is a function of relationship to the world of objects, bringing the 'Individuum' [original text] into absolute, binding, and indissoluble communion with the world at large" (CW 7/275).

This passage is the quintessence of what Jung is saying about the ego, consciousness and the individual is this middle period of his work.

> He is making three statements here: first, *the ego is not equivalent with consciousness*; indeed he proposes a process whereby the ego separates from an ego-consciousness 'imprisonment' and the '*individuum*' (the *individual* concept) takes its place. Second, the *individual* is a new entity that has, in contrast to the 'egotistical' ego, the capacity for relatedness ("absolute, binding, and indissoluble communion with the world at large"). Third, the goal of this process, individuation, is not only self-knowledge or consciousness, *but also more importantly, relatedness*. This relatedness, however, is not on a personal level only, because it develops as the personal level is transcended and the wider collective level is reached.

In this essay, then, the deeper assumption about the ego is that it is a limited entity: it has no capacity to relate to others or to the unconscious. As long as consciousness is dominated by the ego, it is incomplete, and even more, incapable of seeing a wider perspective than itself. This is Jung at his most derogatory regarding the ego, possibly because he has begun to (over)value the unconscious.

The psychological entity *individual* is again emphasized in this essay. Here Jung stresses the aspect of relatedness, which is not, to him, a characteristic of the ego. Jung implies a kind of linear development: the ego lets go of self-absorption through self-knowledge (which strikes me as potentially a complete exercise in self-absorption), and it connects more and more to the Other, the world of inner or outer objects. This theoretical construction, it seems to me, ignores the possibility that an individual can be self-absorbed and, in addition, related at varying times.

Another deeper assumption: the ego is bad and the *individual* is good, because the *individual* relates to the Other, while the ego is related only to itself. Jung is clearly moving toward an attitude that favors the unconscious and the collective over the personal and the 'imprisoned' consciousness.

This valuation of the unconscious over consciousness (the opposite attitude from psychoanalysis) is an attitude that can best be understood as reflecting the tenets of *Naturphilosophie*: that nature is a font of wisdom. This is evidence that his writings are becoming dominated by the symbolic paradigm. This emphasis on the unconscious would lead, in the third phase of Jung's work, to a 'glorification' of the Self (CW 9ii/70) as the Self acquired the qualities of a 'divine' entity rather than a dynamic force. As a dynamic force, it still retained aspects of a materialist framework. (This process will be explored further in the next chapter.)

As the individual gains greater awareness and access to the unconscious field through mechanisms of individuation, there is an expansion or strengthening of unconscious autonomous processes as well; in Jung's theory the most relevant here being enantiodromia. This drives the ego and field of consciousness to expanded self-awareness leading to an expansion of self. The ego becomes an instrument of this process.

One problem with this schema is the question of what happens to the ego as the *individual* develops. Does the ego continue to function as a counterpoint to the unconscious so that the *individual* may remain the middle point? Or is the ego assimilated into the *individual*? Jung implies in his writings that part of the ego remains unassimilated to function as a dynamic structure, while another part becomes the subjective self. The ego, as the aspect of personal and self-experience, loses its "petty, personal" world view, and experiences itself connected to others, open to others, and influential to others. (The term 'others' refers not just to other individuals but also to the energies of the unconscious, which are personified by Jung as archetypes).

Key ego concepts of this period

Ego development

After his first formulation of a developmental theory in 1913, Jung would write again in 1930 a more elaborate examination of development in general and ego development in particular. In a series for one of the local Zürich newspapers (CW 8/749–795), Jung addressed the problem of the stages of life. What he formulated in this essay, as his theory of life stages and development, would remain essentially unaltered in the rest of his work. All his other work in this regard was a repetition of the points he makes here.

The essay 'Stages of Life' begins with the assumption that what grows and develops throughout the life of the individual is consciousness (CW 8/750). This is noteworthy first because at the time other psychologists were emphasizing the growth and development of other attributes in theories of development. Piaget, for example, looked at the development of cognitive ability, while Freud, in his work on ego development at about the same time, was focusing on the development of ego structure. Second, the idea of development as a lifelong process was unique to Jung. Samuels (1985) notes the acknowledgment to Jung for his original work in this area by other, more recent, researchers in the field of adult development (the work of Erik Erikson is notable in this regard). It is possible, however, that the idea of adult development and research into this topic was resisted for so long by more mainstream psychologists and psychoanalysts precisely because it was a part of Jung's theory, and this resistance reflected a more general rejection of Jung rather than of the idea itself (Eisold, 2002).

The next assumption Jung makes regarding development is the stance he has taken toward the structure of the psyche as a whole: that there is a basic tension between competing demands on the ego. In the initial phases of life, these demands are from external sources and are dealt with through instinctual action. (For example, an infant has a certain number of responses to a variety of environmental frustrations that are instinctual and present at birth or soon after: i.e. crying, turning away, and general agitation.) It is only when there are competing inner demands that the possibility of consciousness arises. By this Jung meant a kind of approach–approach dilemma: for example, an inner wish to be a good boy versus an inner urge to do something fun but nevertheless prohibited. The child then would experience both these wishes as incompatible and need to reconcile the competing demands.

Before this point, however, there needs to be a focus or center of perception and conscious awareness that can experience the tension or conflict of competing inner demands. That center is the ego. Jung therefore describes his *first stage of development as ego creation.*

Out of the "mere connection", that is, perception, between two or more psychic contents (such as mental images or emotions) an initial consciousness is formed that is sporadic and consists of "islands of consciousness" (CW 8/755). These islands contain memories associated with subjective experience and are perceived only slowly as an 'I'. Jung said this is why young children at first speak of themselves objectively in the third person. (Although this is in fact not what young children do according to linguistic research by Charney [1980] and others; the child uses first and second person pronouns first, and only later uses the third person.)

By the continued association of these "islands of consciousness" a focus forms, the ego-complex, which, as it acquires its own energy, gives the experience to the child of subjectivity and 'I'-ness. *This constitutes the second stage of development* of consciousness. In this period, according to Jung, the continuity of memories begins. This idea is similar to James' (1890) concept of stream of consciousness.

Jung, in his formulation, therefore, associates the continuity of memories with the establishment of an experiencing, that is, subjective, ego. Stern (1985), in looking at the issue of memory and self, makes a similar point that a sense of a core self requires a continuity of memory. He highlights the distinction, however, among different types of memory – motor memory versus perceptual memory versus affect memory – not all of which are conscious. The kind of conscious continuity-of-memory Jung seems to be referring to is perhaps more associated with what is called episodic memory by Stern and others: the memory for real-life experiences occurring in real time (i.e. what I ate for dinner yesterday, how I felt reading the newspaper this morning). Stern, citing numerous sources (p. 95), describes this type of memory as occurring in discrete units, which are then collated over time and through repeated experiences (of actions or perceptions or emotions) to provide the basis of generalized or prototypic memories. These generalized memories form a personal narrative, a kind of personal myth, that is then a component of the core self. The ego-complex at Jung's second stage of consciousness development may thus correspond to these aspects of Stern's core self.

The third stage of the development of consciousness occurs, according to Jung, with the advent of puberty:

> Psychic birth, and with it the conscious differentiation from the parents, normally takes place only in puberty, with the eruption of sexuality. The

> physiological change is attended by a psychic revolution. For the various bodily manifestations give such an emphasis to the ego that it often asserts itself without stint or moderation. This is sometimes called the unbearable age.
>
> (CW 8/756)

In addition to more or less equating the ego with being unbearable in this stage, Jung places great emphasis on the role of sexuality in effecting change in the psyche – the sexual instinct creates a conflict, a "problem" according to Jung, between the physical urges and the ego (CW 8/757). (Presumably because frank expression of one's sexual urges clashes with the persona-adapted aspect of the ego.) It is this area of conflict and its resolution, then, between instincts and ego, which will prompt the lifelong development of consciousness. The conflict begins in puberty between the sexual instinct and the ego, but over time the counter-pole to the ego becomes the whole instinctual world, by which Jung, as we have seen, means the unconscious. Therefore, youth (which Jung extends in his developmental model to about age 40) is the period of life in which the ego must assert itself over these unconscious urges in order to build up one's outer life (CW 8/760).

This leads to Jung's larger point about the first half of life and the second half of life. Using the metaphor of the sun rising, reaching its zenith, and then setting, Jung sees differing tasks for the two halves of life:

> We cannot live the afternoon of life according to the program of life's morning, for what was great in the morning will be little at evening, and what in the morning was true will at evening have become a lie.
>
> (CW 8/784)

The first half of life is meant to be a time of building up and living one's outer life, and the second half of life is a reversal and a turning inward. Part of this reversal involves developing one's contra-sexual personality: men developing their feminine side, and women, their masculine.

Jung's theory of adult development has been praised, as was noted earlier. Levinson (1978) wrote, for example, "In our view, the person who can justly be considered the father of the modern study of adult development is Carl G. Jung" (p. 4). Butz (1992), Harker and Solomon (1996), and Sugarman (1986), for example, use or incorporate Jung's developmental theory into their own research into life stage development.

Despite this recognition, however, others have taken a critical view of Jung's first half of life/second half of life theory. Samuels (1985) sees problems in two areas: first, the idea of dividing development into life stages at all and second, the problem of associating trauma and emotional crisis with life stage transitions. Dividing life into stages is problematic because the stages themselves may in fact be derived from certain Western or gender or cultural–historical assumptions or prejudices, and this implies that failure to achieve these stages is a failure to fulfill certain arbitrary expectations. For example, it was not so long ago in Western culture that women who did not marry were considered failures. Also, Jung is quite explicit in condemning youths who look into their own inner world – "For a young person it is a sin to be preoccupied with himself, for the aging it is a duty" (CW 8/785) – yet this is a quite arbitrary and unrealistic expectation. It assumes that one even has a choice in such matters. For the phenomenologist Jung, it is extraordinary that he did not see it is frequent and normal for young and old alike to have a mixture of both these tendencies.

As Samuels notes, there is still the issue of what is lost when one thinks in terms of linear progression and development. Many Jungian analysts use the metaphor of the spiral to describe the pattern of development in which issues are re-met at numerous points in life and adapted or abandoned to new circumstances. In a model of development based on linear progression, issues are instead met and 'dealt with' and then left behind. As Levinson's (1978, 1996) research shows, the spiral model is closer to what is experienced in reality. Surprisingly the whole area of life stage development has been largely left to non-Jungians to research empirically, considering its status as 'canon' in Jungian theory.

Samuels also highlights the problem of seeing trauma and crisis in life stage transitions. He is convinced, as are several others (Hayman, Atwood & Stolorow, Ellenberger) that this reflects the personal situation of Jung at the time he was 40 years old and had a crisis. (Jung was not unique in this regard. It is revealing to note that Erik Erikson [1950] emphasizes the search for identity in his own theory of adult life stages just as he spent a lifetime never sure who his biological father, or even what his own true surname, was [Friedman, 1999]).

Levinson's research in this area found that crises at stages of life transition are more consistently seen in men, whereas for women the picture is less straightforward. Women tend to have more complex or multifaceted stages than men corresponding to their more complex and conflicting roles in modern Western society. In any case, Jung does not address the topic of life stage development in women in this essay. Again, there is a need for much more empirical research in this area.

Levinson also makes the point in his research that 'crisis' is a term that covers a range of experiences; there are those for whom life transitions are a time of major traumatic upheaval, but for others there is more a sense of adjusting or expanding ones established life structure. These changes in life structure are not initiated solely by inner imperatives as Jung implies, but arise just as well from outer-world realities that bring about a crisis such as childbirth, illness, or economic downturns.

Jung's data regarding ego development was, like Freud's, extrapolated from his work with adults (and not through extensive work with children), or from second-hand accounts of children from others, and then finally shaped by his own bias. Hayman relates the story of a luncheon with Emma and C.G. Jung:

> Michael Fordham was having dinner with them and some friends when the conversation settled on children's dreams. Jung launched into a monologue, but Emma, who sometimes said he knew nothing about children, intervened, 'You know very well that you are not interested in people, but your theory of the collective unconscious'.
>
> (Hayman, 1999, p. 233–234)

Fordham adds, in his autobiography, that although Jung lacked the necessary experience to formulate a theory of infant and child development, "[he] had a quick and quite delightful capacity to relate to children" (1993, p. 117).

Finally, in this discussion on development and the ego, I would like to draw attention to the additional transpersonal aspect. Jung begins to make the point in this phase of his life that there is a mutual dependency of the ego and the unconscious that leads to a development of world consciousness rather than personal ego development. In other words, the unconscious, as the instinctual life or the life of the body, needs the ego, the "powerful cohesive force" that binds the components of consciousness together (CW 8/611). This line of thinking would become more prominent in his later work.

Structural concept

In this middle period, Jung modified his theory of the basic structure of the psychic system. Prior to this, Jung saw the ego as an element of the psychic structure that responded to instinctual forces and to reality constraints in keeping with the Freudian model. The ego as a psychic structure had no autonomy. Jung, in this new phase, however, introduces a concept of ego that emphasizes ego autonomy. It is useful to compare these two systems in a diagram (see Figure 4.2).

	1914 Psychoanalytic Model	Jung Model
Paradigm:	Energic	Symbolic
Causal factor:	Psychic determinism	Individuation and mechanisms of
Nature of ego action:	Executive, Reactive	Autonomous, Responsive, Receptive
Ego functions:	Defense, Self-preservation, Reality Principle	Adaptation, Differentiation, Integration, Initiation, Will
Basis of ego–unconscious interaction:	Conflict	Confrontation of Opposites

Figure 4.2 Comparison of Two Systems

Paradigm

The change in paradigm, from the energic to the symbolic, had the effect of changing the role of the ego in the psychic structure. These changes were not simply changes in the function of the ego, but changes that elevated the ego to a much more substantial role in the overall totality of the psyche.

Causal factor

First, the assumption of causality changed. In this period of Jung's work, psychic determinism ceased to be seen as the single motivating dynamic in the psyche. Psychic determinism, as discussed earlier in Chapter 2, is the belief that the law of cause and effect determines all psychical and physical phenomena. This assumption shaped Freud's metapsychology in his early work with Jung; it was in fact a stance Freud never abandoned (see Rangell, 1986, for example).

Jung, in this period of his work, did not completely discard determinism but felt it needed to be balanced by a teleological perspective:

> It would be doing violence to the psyche to consider it from the causal angle alone. One not only can, one *must* envisage it from the standpoint of finality. . . . *In psychology one ought to be as wary of believing absolutely in causality as of an absolute belief in teleology.*
>
> (CW 7/501n, emphasis added)

Indeed, 'causality versus teleology' is a concept that sorts out the psychoanalysts from the analytical psychologists. Glover (1950), for example, skewers Jung for his rejection of determinism (which in fact the preceding quote shows was not the case). Others such as Vacek (1991), but originally and most vehemently Jones (1960), not only reject the concept of teleology, but use this to make their case that Jung is 'mystical' and therefore not to be taken seriously. (Jung's marginalization in the field of depth psychology due to accusations of mysticism is discussed in depth in Eisold, 2002, and Gallant, 1996.)

On the other side, first-generation Jungians (those who worked with Jung most directly) but also others that followed, have misunderstood Jung's attitude toward teleology (finality) versus causality. For example, Jacobi (1962, p. 66) says, "Freud's method is reductive, while Jung's is prospective. Freud treats the material analytically, resolving the present into the past, Jung synthetically, building toward the future from the present situation . . .". In Von Franz (1975), determinism is acknowledged but minimized (p. 87):

> In exactly the same way Jung thought that psychic processes . . . should be described both causally and in respect to their goal or purpose. The psychic healing process can only be understood from the final standpoint,

whereas the causal standpoint is more apt to yield a diagnosis (The latter is in any case not important. . .).

In the debate between both schools it is useful to remember that Jung's concept of individuation is more complex and subtle than its caricature. In this middle period of his work, Jung retains elements of the energic paradigm in the dynamic of the psyche, but he assigns a balancing importance to consciousness in general and to the ego in particular. Whereas the ego in the structural model of Freud is a central station for handling the instinctual forces on the one hand and the pressures of reality on the other, for Jung this role is only one aspect of the ego.

Psychic determinism in the psyche would represent, from a Jungian standpoint, a collective phenomenon. It is characterized by its instinctual basis according to psychoanalytic theory and operates or acts in an autonomous, unconscious way. Like breathing, for example, psychic determinism is capable of being influenced by conscious will, but it is essentially a non-personal aspect of the psychic dynamism.

Individuation, I would argue, is also a collective instinctual psychical mechanism. It is an instinct in the sense that it is an autonomous drive in the psyche and as Jung wrote in 1916, "all basic instincts . . . are collective" (CW 7/462). Its impersonal innateness is part of the argument Jung makes over and over as he builds up his metapsychology: "Individuation is a natural necessity" (CW 6/758); quoting Nietzsche, "so the individual man, in a world of troubles, sits passive and serene, trusting to the *principium individuationis*" (CW 6/876); "Individuation is an ineluctable psychological necessity" (CW 7/462); "Over against the polymorphism of the primitive's instinctual nature there stands the regulating principle of individuation. Multiplicity and inner division are opposed by an integrative unity whose power is as great as that of the instincts" (CW 8/96).

While psychic determinism represents a mono-directional force – psychical events or experiences have an antecedent – the principle of individuation is part of a binary system. Individuation as a psychical mechanism is opposed by the drive toward adaptation and collectivity. The implications of this will be discussed later. However, in developing a dualist system, Jung also developed mechanisms based on this principle.

Just as Hamlet said, "There is more between heaven and earth, Horatio, then is dreamt of in your philosophy", Jung argues there is a reality to the psyche that is not accounted for when using only the laws of physical reality. In this middle period of his work and in the context of the symbolic paradigm, Jung begins to define his own laws of mental functioning. In mechanisms of individuation the ego becomes an equal participant in the overall progression toward the development of consciousness and the individual.

I have discussed two mechanisms Jung describes related to movement of psychic energy. The first is enantiodromia and the second is the Transcendent

Function. These are for Jung basic laws of psychic energy. I would go so far as to call them in the context of Jung's theory *primary mechanisms of individuation* because they are the primary mental processes governing the movement of psychic contents in individuation.

Nature of ego action

The model of ego to this point had been executive and reactive. In Freud's formulation, the ego sits in the middle of the outside world of reality, the inner drive of instincts, and the moral sanctions of the superego.

Jung introduces a level of autonomy to the ego's function in his formulations. Hartmann (1956) and others (Rangell, 1986; Rapaport, 1950, 1958; Waelder, 1960) have examined autonomy in the context of ego function from a psychoanalytic perspective. In their reformulations of Freud's theory, a number of issues were identified. First, the extent the ego's actions are rooted in drives; second, the role or non-role of conflict in ego action; and third, the unconscious decision-making function of the ego.

In his 1935 Tavistock lectures, Jung described what he called endopsychic functions of consciousness: memory, emotions and affects, and a third category he called "subjective components of conscious functions" (CW 18/40). These last functions approach less instinctually derived elements and imply the autonomous aspects of the ego, which involve choice, intention, or free will. Jung said the conscious subjective reaction is accompanied by an acceptance or rejection of a particular thing or situation. The rejected subjective reaction, that is, the personal experience or emotion, forms the shadow-side of the personality.

Jung makes the point that the aspect of the conscious personality with the highest degree of will is the 'superior function': the one of the four functions most developed. The most developed function is presumably less subject to unconscious influence because it is most conscious, while the inferior (least developed) function has the least autonomy. He wrote: "In the center [of the four functions] is the ego, which has a certain amount of energy at its disposal, and that energy is will-power. In the case of the thinking type, that will-power can be directed to thinking" (CW 18/29).

In this formulation, for Jung, will-power is the ego's characteristic most in contrast to unconscious drives. A will so unbound to drive is characteristic of Kantian philosophy. Jung wrote, for example, that the task of the hero is

> firstly the transformation of the daemon from an uncontrolled force of nature into a power that is his to command; secondly the final deliverance of ego-consciousness from the deadly threat of the unconscious in the form of negative parents. The first task signifies the creation of will-power, the second the free use of it.
>
> (CW 5/548)

However, an opposing concept of will derived from Schopenhauer's idea of 'blind will', tends to focus on the autonomy of the will itself, unaffected by conscious motives. Jung wrote, for example, "[t]he motivation of the will must in the first place be regarded as essentially biological" (CW 8/379). Jung accounts for the difference between the two concepts of will by his separation of the psyche into 'regions': spirit and instinct (CW 8/371–380):

> Psyche is essentially conflict between blind instinct and will (freedom of choice). Where instinct predominates, psychoid processes set in which pertain to the sphere of the unconscious as elements incapable of consciousness. The psychoid process is not the unconscious as such, for this has a far greater extension. Apart from the psychoid processes, there are in the unconscious ideas and volitional acts, [emphasis added] hence something akin to conscious processes; but in the instinctual sphere these phenomena retire so far into the background that the term 'psychoid' is probably justified.
>
> (CW 8/380)

The instincts represent a collective autonomous will, whereas the will-power associated with the ego is directed toward freeing the ego from collective power. In this sense it is an extension of the individuation urge. Jung presents the ego's will-power as derived from instinctual will; this reflects the philosophy that the conscious and unconscious realms are in fact a totality called the psyche and therefore share essential forces.

In a conflict-based model such as Jung's, the question of the ego's autonomy in this conflict arises. Rangell (1969) highlights the element of choice in conflict; there are in conflict situations (intra-psychic as well as interpersonal) elements of conscious choice as well as unconscious function. Defense mechanisms represent one form of unconscious resolution, or avoidance, of conflict. Conscious choice in conflict, however, entails first seeing there is a conflict (conscious awareness), differentiating the elements of the conflict, and then choosing or deciding on an ego stance vis à vis the conflict. This process arises routinely in analytical practice: a client, through analysis, becomes aware (conscious) of the conflictual forces in a particular situation and, being conscious of these, is then faced with a moment of decision – even if the decision ultimately is to flee (metaphorically if not literally) from the conflict. The decision-making process, however, remains the clients own.

For Hartmann (1964), autonomous ego functions originate in the ego's "hereditary core" (p. xi): inhibitory functions that form the basis of defenses later. He is implying, as he believed Freud did in a 1937 paper, that the 'inborn' autonomous qualities of the ego derive from the hereditary core of the instincts.

In this respect, Hartmann is very much in line with Jung's thinking. We may then be permitted to speculate that the Kantian free will of the ego is related to the Schopenhauerian 'blind-will' of nature through their shared archetypal core. Jung proposes just this in a later work, that the ego is the "Schopenhauerian mirror" of the Self – deriving its qualities due to its roots in an instinctual/collective ground.

Rangell (1986) also raises the issue of an unconscious decision-making ego function. In contrast to a free-will function, the ego in this concept would be subject to 'psychic determinism': the mind as a "reacting machine" (p. 12). The individual, he proposes, is directed by both ego tendencies – by ego autonomy and free-will, and by an "unconscious problem-solving function" (p. 15). This unconscious problem-solving function is involved in creativity, for example.

Jung sees this kind of creativity as more a spontaneous expression of the unconscious itself, or as a joint unconscious creation through the mechanism of the TF:

1 "The unconscious is best understood if we regard it as a natural organ with its own specific creative energy" (CW 8/702).
2 "From the living fountain of instinct flows everything that is creative; hence the unconscious is not merely conditioned by history, but is the very source of the creative impulse" (CW 8/339).
3 "[I]t is only when the conscious mind confronts the products of the unconscious that a provisional reaction will ensue which determines the subsequent procedure. Practical experience alone can give us a clue. So far as my experience goes, there appear to be two main tendencies. One is the way of creative formulation, the other the way of understanding" (CW 8/172).

The issue of whether creativity is solely an unconscious ego attribute, solely an attribute of the unconscious, or a combination of the ego and the unconscious, depends on one's attitude toward the unconscious itself. Is it separate from the ego, or is the ego capable of interacting with it? Is the unconscious a creative matrix in and of itself, or is it merely the repository of repressed contents? The former attitude reflects the symbolic paradigm and accounts for Jung's formulation of creativity.

In the creative process, according to psychoanalyst Rangell (1986), the ego "permits unconscious drive discharge" (p. 16–17) which is experienced as fantasy. Creativity is then experienced because the ego has lowered the barrier between consciousness and the unconscious. The primary process energy of the id/unconscious is taken by the ego and experienced as uncensored primal material. The ego can abandon its secondary process strictures and 'play' with the primary material. In Jung's formulation of the TF, however, there is an equal contribution from the ego to form the creative product. I believe the two points of view are not incompatible.

This is the essence then of the autonomous ego in Jung's theory: the ego not only perceives and reacts to the unconscious, but it also receives and responds to the unconscious. This implies openness to the unconscious for a mutual process. The ego, therefore, is experientially a partner in a mutual relatedness, but also structurally maintaining a position vis à vis the unconscious.

Ego functions

The ego functions in the psychoanalytic model have been discussed previously. Although less developed, Jung has a stance toward ego defenses. In Jung's model, however, he placed at this stage of his work, special emphasis on adaptation.

Adaptation concept

Jung's adaptation concept evolved in stages. During the first phase of his work, he shared the psychoanalytic views of adaptation. Freud's theory was that the infant and young child was self-absorbed and pleasure seeking; that is, dominated by primary process. By encounters with "the brick wall of reality", according to Freud, the child re-orients himself away from his own instinctual urges and toward external reality. This was the much more mature secondary process. The child adapts to the demands of the outer world. The implicit assumption in this theory is that the demands of the inner world are to be overcome, that they are inherently immature or dangerous and that to remain attentive to the inner world was infantile and self-absorbed.

Jung therefore first formulated neurosis in 1907 as an inability to adapt to outer reality:

> It is in the interest of the normal individual to free himself from any obsessive complex that hinders the proper development of his personality (adaptation to his environment). Time generally takes care of this. . . . But if the complex remains unchanged, which naturally happens only when there is very severe damage to the ego-complex and its functions [i.e. weak ego defenses: no repression, no displacement], then we speak of dementia praecox.
>
> (CW 3/141)

Jung is saying that the failure of the individual to change (free himself from the unconscious) is a failure of adaptation and leads to pathology. He tacitly agrees with Freud's assumption that unconscious urges in the form of individual complexes are pathogenic.

By 1912, as tensions grew, Jung began to assign a different value to the unconscious (the inner world) than Freud. This difference of opinion was reflected in his attitude toward adaptation. He began to value the inner world but was still reluctant to make it equal to the outer world:

> The essence of conscious processes is adaptation, which takes place in a series of personal details. The unconscious, on the other hand, is universal: it not only binds individuals together into a nation or race, but unites them with the men of the past and with their psychology. Thus, by reason of its supra-individual universality [first use of collective unconscious concept], the unconscious is the prime object of any real psychology that claims to be more than psychophysics.
>
> (CW 5/258)

After his break with Freud, Jung continued to shape his own adaptation theory at a time when he personally was going through a crisis demanding new forms of adaptation. In a next formulation in 1914, then, he states that the individual needs to find a way toward a personal philosophy to adapt to his own inner world as a step toward adapting to the outer world.

> Closer study of Schreber's or any other similar case will show that these patients are consumed by a desire to create a new world-system, or what we call a Weltanschauung, often of the most bizarre kind. Their aim is obviously to create a system that will enable them to assimilate unknown psychic phenomena and so adapt themselves to their own world. This is a purely subjective adaptation at first, but is a necessary transition stage on the way to adapting the personality to the world in general. Only, the patient remains stuck in this stage and substitutes his subjective formulation for the real world-which is precisely why he remains ill. I am sure many people will object that psychological adaptation does not come about by first creating a philosophical view of the world, and that it is in itself a sign of morbid disposition even to attempt to adapt oneself by such means.
>
> (CW 3/416–417)

Jung here sees neurosis as staying stuck in the phase of adapting only to one's inner world and not continuing to adapt to the outer world.

Finally, Jung arrives at the position that there needs to be a balance between inner and outer adaptation. Jung understands now the importance of adaptation to one's own inner world. This in the context of the turmoil he was going through at this point in his own life – he was personally falling apart, his relationship with Freud had broken, and he was having visions of a coming catastrophe in Europe. There was an enormous re-ordering going on regarding his view of himself, the world, his values, and his own sense of what we would call the spiritual perspective. He would write in 1914 that a balance between inner and outer is essential or else one's adaptation to the outer world is disturbed:

> 'Mental balance' is no mere figure of speech, for its disturbance is a real disturbance of the balance which-to a far higher degree than has been recognized-actually exists between the conscious and the unconscious contents. What happens is that the normal functioning of the unconscious processes breaks through into the conscious mind in an abnormal manner, and thereby disturbs the adaptation of the individual to his environment.
>
> (CW 3/454)

In this statement then he is beginning to articulate the theory of adaptation he would articulate more fully a few years later. Jung's theory of adaptation is characterized by the following assumptions:

Energetics of adaptation

The basic principle of psychic energy and therefore for adaptation is the principle of opposites. In a kind of zero-sum structure, the gradient of psychical energy, or libido, flows between inner or outer adaptation always seeking equilibrium. Jung wrote in 1916 for example:

> When the libido invested in a particular function cannot be equilibrated by the exercise of the function, it accumulates until it attains a value which exceeds that of the neighboring functional system. Then a process of equilibrium begins, because a potential is present. The energy flows over, as it were, into another system. When, therefore, adaptation to the inside is not achieved, the libido intended for that purpose accumulates until it begins to flow out of the system of inner adaptation into the system of outer adaptation, with the result that characteristics belonging to inner adaptation are carried over into outer – that is to say, fantasies intervene in the relation to the real world.
>
> (CW 18/1090)

Adaptation is required at both inner and outer levels

This view is in contrast to the psychoanalytic view that adaptation is an ego process occurring at 'the brick wall' of external reality. The inner world, and primary process, is considered directional and representational in Freud's view, but adaptation was directed toward fitting into the outer world (Meissner, 2000, p. 161).

Hartmann (1958) also saw adaptation as essentially a process directed toward the outer world. He wrote, for example, "Generally speaking, we call a man well adapted if his productivity, his ability to enjoy life, and his mental equilibrium are undisturbed" (p. 23). Adaptation was wholly a process between the organism and the environment (p. 24); adaptation to the inner world was a non-issue.

In contrast to these viewpoints, Jung stresses in his work *Psychological Types* the reality of two contrasting demands: adaptation to inner reality as well as adaptation to outer reality. In this passage he describes how these two realities will respond if they are ignored:

> The peculiar reality of unconscious contents, therefore, gives us the same right to describe them as objects as the things of the outside world. Now just as the persona, being a function of relationship, is always conditioned by the external object and is anchored as much in it as in the subject, so the soul, as a function of relationship to the inner object, is represented by that object; hence she is always distinct from the subject in one sense and is actually perceived as something different. . . . In the same way as a man who surrenders entirely to the outside world still has the world as an object distinct from himself, the unconscious world of images behaves as an object distinct from the subject even when a man surrenders to it completely. And, just as the unconscious world of mythological images speaks indirectly, through the experience of external things, to the man who surrenders wholly to the outside world, so the real world and its demands find their way directly to the man who has surrendered wholly to the soul; for no man can escape both realities. If he is intent only on the outer reality, he must live his myth; if he is turned only toward the inner reality, he must dream his outer, so-called real life.
> (CW 6/280)

Jung emphasizes here that adaptation must occur according to two 'brick walls of reality'. Reality is not only the outer world and circumstances, as in Freud and Hartmann's system, but also the reality of the inner world. In the preceding passage, Jung is saying regarding these two realities that (1) if the individual is intent only on adapting to outer reality, then as a counter-movement of the adaptation imperative he must live his myth (i.e. the inner reality will go to where the energy is directed in the outer reality), and (2) if the individual is turned only toward inner reality, then the counter-movement will be the dominance of outer life in the inner world ("dreaming one's so-called real life").

An example Jung gives for the situation described in (1) is the transference that arises in analysis. Jung's case examples often revolve around a patient who has neglected to adapt to the inner reality and is excessively adapted to outer reality. In such circumstances there ensues a transference that, according to Jung, is of an archetypal nature. One case he described a number of times in his writings (for example, CW18/634) involved a woman who had a strong father/lover/son transference to Jung. He pursued the meaning of this until she had a dream in which Jung was holding her in his arms, god-like, in a field of corn. After this, he pronounced to her, "I surely am not a god, but your unconscious needs a god. That is a serious and a genuine need. No time before us has fulfilled that need; you are just an intellectual fool, just as much as I am, but we don't know it". He informs us he cured his patient because he "fulfilled the need of the unconscious" (CW 18/634), implying that adaptation to the inner reality was the mutative factor.

Adaptation is a psychological function in individuation as well as collectivity

In 'Adaptation, Individuation, Collectivity', an essay written in 1916 but not published until after Jung's death, Jung wrote out what was for him a rare highly structured schema of his theoretical system. Individuation and collectivity are conceptualized as opposite tendencies in the psyche to which the ego must adapt. Because of the basic assumption of conservation of energy, libido directed to one tendency means a deficit of libido toward the other: "The individual is obliged by the collective demands to purchase his individuality at the cost of an equivalent work for the benefit of society" (CW 18/1099).

Jung saw adaptation occurring on two fronts:

- Adaptation to the outer world – this is adaptation to collectivity.
- Adaptation to the inner world – this is adaptation to individuality.

Individuation and collectivity are opposing demands, and these demands change continually. There is never a final adaptation, only a more or less working adaptation of the moment. Jung said that focusing only on individualistic development

> leads into isolation and death because one's life is no longer connected with the life of mankind. Life in one, single, isolated individual cannot be maintained because the roots are cut off; our roots are in mankind and if we give up the connection we are just like a plant with no roots.
> (1984, p. 790)

So after a time of excessive attention to the unconscious and one's own inner demands, there will be an enantiodromia and the outer world will become overwhelming in its demands for collective adaptation. Or, as was more common with the people Jung describes in his writings, the adaptation to the collective is excessive, and there is a demand from the unconscious for adaptation to the inner world: individuation.

Jung makes the case in CW 6 for the role of types in adaptation. He said that initially we contain all the types as potential, but in childhood certain types dominate to adapt to the outer world (family, clan, etc.). This sets up then an opposition or one-sidedness.

> A one-sided attitude leaves a deficiency in the adaptive performance which accumulates during the course of life, and sooner or later this will produce a disturbance of adaptation that drives the subject towards some kind of compensation. But the compensation can be obtained only by means of an amputation (sacrifice) of the hitherto one-sided attitude. . . . The adaptive deficiency, which is the *causa efficiens* of the process of conversion, is subjectively felt as a vague sense of dissatisfaction.
>
> (CW 6/28)

In other words, the first adaptation made is to collective consciousness, and in this process of adapting, certain ego functions are repressed. We all have these four functions, but the dominant ones we express in our personality are shaped first through adaptation.

Jung also contrasts the qualities of the functions we take as our main function to what is repressed:

> On account of its relative repression, the inferior function is only partly attached to consciousness; its other part is attached to the unconscious. The differentiated function is the most fully adapted to external reality; it is essentially the reality function.
>
> (CW 6/171)

The 'reclaiming' of these repressed functions is part of the work of adaptation to inner reality, i.e. individuation.

A defense concept

Jung does not make defense a center of his theory in the manner Freud made repression a focus, or Anna Freud focused on the whole issue of defenses. For the Freuds, repression was one of the basic dynamic forces in the psyche. For Jung, however, repression and other defenses were aspects of the larger dynamic process between the ego and the unconscious as these two opposing forces strove toward greater consciousness and relatedness.

The ego, in Jung's model, must choose: "Every problem . . . brings the possibility of a widening of consciousness, but also the necessity of saying goodbye to childlike unconsciousness and trust in nature" (CW 8/751). 'Problems', Jung's term for the general dilemma of an ego faced with conflicting inner imperatives, present the ego with a choice between the status quo and the unknown possibility. According to Jung, the ego is by nature reluctant to choose the unknown:

> When we must deal with problems, we instinctively resist trying the way that leads through obscurity and darkness. We wish to hear only of unequivocal results, and completely forget that these results can only be brought about when we have ventured into and emerged again from the darkness.
>
> (CW 8/752)

Against the pressure from the psyche for individuation, the imperative from the unconscious, the ego has the choice of defense. In Jung's writings, defense is portrayed at times as a conscious action, at other times as unconscious. The following are examples of this ambiguity of Jung's stance toward defenses:

1 In a discussion about a woman who consulted him he said, "The patient could use her old defense mechanism against this new difficulty and could simply ignore the point of obscurity. That is to say, she could begin repressing again, instead of keeping things conscious . . ." (CW 7/148).
2 In a discussion of the compensatory function of dreams Jung says, "Just as the body reacts purposively to injuries or infections or any abnormal conditions, so the psychic functions react to unnatural or dangerous disturbances with purposive defense-mechanisms. Among these purposive reactions we must include the dream . . ." (CW 8/488).
3 "When I first took this path I did not know where it would lead. I did not know what lay hidden in the depths of the psyche-that region which I have since called the 'collective unconscious' and whose contents I designate as 'archetypes'. Since time immemorial, invasions of the unconscious have occurred, and ever and again they repeat themselves. For consciousness did not exist from the beginning; in every child it has to be built up anew in the first years of life. Consciousness is very weak in this formative period, and the same is true of the psychic history of mankind – the unconscious easily seizes power. These struggles have left their mark. To put it in scientific terms: instinctive defense-mechanisms have been built up which automatically intervene when the danger is greatest, and their coming into action during an emergency is represented in fantasy by helpful images which are ineradicably imprinted on the human psyche" (CW 11/532).

In addressing the question of whether ego defenses are conscious or unconscious phenomena, I would first like to relate a clinical example:

Some time ago, a woman came to see me who complained of nightmares. In the course of relating to me her story, I learned she had been called to jury duty 20 years before for a murder trial. It had been a horrific crime; a man had stabbed his girlfriend to death. She remembered the trial quite well – the lawyers, the look and smell of the courtroom, the sight of the victim's family and of the defendant himself. All the details of the crime as it had been presented and described in court stayed with her, with one important exception. She could not recall, even with willful concentration, the crime scene photos. She remembered the fact that she had seen them, but it was as if they were erased away completely from her memory. A reasonable interpretation of this would be that the images themselves were repressed.

Before I continue I would like to comment on just this aspect. There were two kinds of experiences going on in that courtroom for this woman: the first was the case and the facts and the testimony and the crime. And this she remembered. This would represent in other words the world of the visible, the world of consensual, or outer, reality. This is similar to what Plato called the world of the senses, or what the philosophers would call empirical, or objective, reality. So at this level her experience was about a particular story in a particular time and place in which to some extent she witnessed and participated.

However, there was another level of ego experience for this woman occurring simultaneous to the first, an invisible or subjective level of ego experience. What was going on at this other level was connected to the photos, the ones she could not remember, which could be said to be the part of her memory of the trial that was repressed. For the same event in her life, one level of experience was remembered and another level not remembered, indeed, lost completely even to the conscious desire and will to remember.

What brought her to analysis, however, was the return 20 years later of the gruesome images in the form of nightmares – which she could not now push out of her mind with all her best efforts. How can these reactions, the initial as well as long-term repression and then the later autonomous return of repressed mental images and emotional reaction, be understood according to Jung's theory of ego? What explanation can Jung's theory offer in terms of ego defense?

In general, what the ego does not want conscious is opposed through a defensive action. This is evident in Jung's statements cited earlier. What is less clear is the extent this is a conscious or unconscious operation. In psychoanalytic theory ego defenses are not deliberate acts of will to suppress or avoid something unpleasant, say, but rather an unconscious act on the part of the ego. They are not a conscious choice but an unconscious reaction. It seems paradoxical that something associated with consciousness like the ego would contain unconscious mechanisms, and this raises the first problematic area in Jung's theory. Since he defines the ego as the center of consciousness, it is contradictory to assign unconscious action to it.

Jung made the point that there are no purposeless psychic processes; that the psyche is essentially purposive and directed (CW 5/90). Repression, according to Jung's writings on the topic, is a way to avoid a conflict, say, between one's conscious attitude and the inner world. This is the defensive aspect. But also, Jung says there is a creative aspect; he says, "Were there not a secret purposiveness bound up with the supposed repression, it is certain that such a process could not take place so easily, so naturally, and so spontaneously" (CW 5/91).

So the fact of repression, according to Jung, means we are confronted with something of tremendous meaning for the inner world of the individual. Going back to my example, then, the question is now, why were these particular memories, images, repressed and the other aspects of the trial not? The short answer, following Jung's reasoning, is that the images in the photos had a meaning and reality for this woman that the other aspects of the trial did not. The images connected to a different ego experience than the other aspects. There was a reaction in the ego that could not integrate the reality of the photos into her consciousness. Following Jung's theory of adaptation to inner and outer reality – there arose after 20 years a pressure to adapt to these images (and attendant emotional reactions I hasten to add), which now constituted part of her inner reality.

As I said, my client had begun to recall these images. She had begun to have nightmares that included certain details specifically associated with the photos from years ago. As soon as she had the dreams, she remembered the photos, so there was a return of the repressed image. The question becomes then: what had brought these images and emotions to consciousness now? In Jung's theory, failure of adaptation to outer reality forces one to 'dream one's so-called life'. The logical interpretation would be then that she was dreaming of 'violent murder' in an interpersonal relationship in her inner life because she was defending against the conscious awareness of 'murderous rage' in the context of an interpersonal relationship in her outer life. This was indeed the case.

Ego defenses are in a sense the mirror of adaptation – just as the ego can (must!) confront and integrate inner and outer reality, it will also defend itself against just that integration. For Jung, the force toward integration can overcome the ego defense in the form of an enantiodromia. But, the opposite would also be true. The force toward integration can also be overcome by a defense against it. In other words, the ego would be capable of blocking integration, as an unconscious operation.

This leads to the issue Jung raised: if the proximate purpose of defense is to protect the ego, what is the ultimate purpose? What is the "secret purposiveness", the creative aspect to repression, to ego defense in general? Jung would differentiate 'purposive' according to purpose in outer reality as opposed to purpose in inner reality – or, in his words, according to "persona" and "soul" reality (CW 6/280).

In the persona, defined as the ego's relationship with outer reality, the critical factor is the outer object (CW 6/280), that is, the expectations and judgments and prohibitions of the world we live in and its cast of characters, familial and beyond. He states,

> Just as the persona . . . is always conditioned by the external object and is anchored as much in it as in the subject, so the soul . . . is represented by that object; hence she [the soul] is always distinct from the subject in one sense and is actually perceived as something different. . . .
>
> (CW 6/280)

The external object therefore acts as a factor of definition for the ego. The persona is constructed and defined by the outer reality and anchored in the ego. The 'otherness' of the external object, however, represents for the ego the unknown and not-understood reality of the unconscious. So the external object exists at two levels and possesses actually two dimensions for the ego: a self-defining dimension where the ego merges with the collective imperative, and an alien 'Other' dimension, where the ego is confronted by its counter-pole.

Therefore, each object, experience, and relationship in one's external world exists and is received by the ego on a persona level and on a soul level. Defenses operate purposively on two levels – a defense at the persona level would preserve collectivity and the aim is preservation of the status quo. A defense at the soul level, however, would be part of the dynamic action of confrontation of consciousness and the unconscious. This aspect of ego defense would therefore be a mechanism of individuation.

In the discussion of purpose in ego defenses, then, it is essential to separate at which level defense is acting: at the persona level or at the soul level. To return to the discussion of defenses, repression is a good place to begin, since it was the first and most, shall we say numinous defense identified by the Freuds. For Freud, all the other ego defenses were ultimately the means to bring about repression. Repression was ultimately, for Freud, the resolution of an intra-psychic conflict.

That we as human beings can repress an emotion or forget an image is potentially lifesaving. As the 1986 Nobel Laureate and Holocaust survivor Elie Wiesel said in his Oslo lecture 'Hope, Despair and Memory',

> [F]orgetting allows us to go on living. How could we go on with our daily lives, if we remained constantly aware of the dangers and ghosts surrounding us? The Talmud tells us that without the ability to forget, man would soon cease to learn. Without the ability to forget, man would live in a permanent, paralyzing fear of death. Only God and God alone can and must remember everything.

Wiesel would then pose a question that speaks to the duality of the ego's task: "How are we to reconcile our supreme duty towards memory with the need to forget that is essential to life?" (in Abrams, 1997).

	Persona	Soul
External object:	Anchored in ego	Represents 'Other'
Defensive purpose:	Maintain status quo, block suffering	Creative process
Dynamic function:	Ego preservation	Mechanism of individuation

Figure 4.3 Comparison of Two Ego Defense Characteristics

In my case example, the client was not able to continue forgetting. At the persona level, there was a repression in order to preserve the ego from any number of ego-dystonic emotions. The external object, that is, the photos, in the persona context, was anchored in the ego and therefore too disturbing to allow. This led to the original repression. At the soul level, however, the external object (the photos) was a confrontation with an unknown and not understood inner reality. To which possible inner reality could the gruesome photos correspond? Jung had this to say about the nature of individuation:

> This moral differentiation is a necessary step on the way of individuation. Without thorough knowledge of 'good and evil', ego and shadow, there is no recognition of the Self, but at most an involuntary and therefore dangerous identification with it.
>
> (letter to Kirsch, 16 February 1954)

In other words, the gruesome images correspond to a repressed ego quality associated with the shadow: murderous rage.

Figure 4.3 summarizes the characteristics ego defense for these two types of ego experience.

A Jungian theory of ego defense

Jung places the TF as a central mechanism of transformation. He wrote, for example, that the "synthetic method" (i.e. meeting the unconscious) is a process that leads to the differentiation of the personality and of which he said, "I have termed this transition to a new attitude the transcendent function" and "it is equivalent to a renewal of life" (CW 6/427). As he argues in his essay 'The Transcendent Function', there is seldom agreement between consciousness and unconsciousness and this disagreement seeks resolution through a self-regulating, natural process. This resolution is enabled by the symbol, the reconciling entity.

In order for the Transcendent Function to proceed, the conscious ego stance needs to be clear. In his essay on the subject, Jung seems to assume that the conscious stance is known and that the work is to elucidate and react to the unconscious content. In practice this may not be the case as defenses can operate against conscious awareness as well as against contents of the unconscious.

As a mechanism, the TF involves a dynamic of two opposing standpoints – an ego standpoint and a contrary unconscious standpoint – which are held by the ego in its capacity as an integrating and reconciling third position to lead to symbol formation and change in the form of increased consciousness and relatedness. Jung stated, "Were it not for the directedness of the conscious function, the counteracting influences of the unconscious could set in unhindered" (CW 8/159). Therefore a truly Jungian theory of ego defense would focus less on the traditional specific ego mechanisms such as repression or splitting or projection, and instead focus on the areas in which the ego blocks the natural function of the TF. One can view then the TF as having three legs: the conscious ego stance, the unconscious opposing stance, and the integrating ego/*individual*. The defensive mechanisms would act therefore on those three areas. Theses defenses can be summarized as defense against conscious perception, defense against feeling (unconscious standpoint), and defense against integration.

Defense against conscious perception

This defense is called defense against perception because it deals with the absence or deficiency in observing or knowing one's own conscious ego stance. This may be due to ego weakness, ego dependence, or the dominance of an autonomous complex which supplants the ego-complex. Due to the mechanisms of individuation, dreams can indicate to the dreamer his or her misperceptions or lack thereof. For example, a young medical student was dating a businessman in New York City who was very ambitious yet only moderately successful. She was not consciously aware of any discomfort in the relationship but found she inexplicably refused his request to move in with her when he asked. She dreamt that night, "I am standing on the top of the World Trade Center building with [boyfriend]. There is a tall rickety ladder on the roof and he is pressuring me to climb even further to the top of the ladder, putting me in even greater peril". Upon awakening, she saw how he was pushing his ambition onto her in large and small ways and soon after ended the relationship.

In the preceding example, the medical student was so busy with her studies, and so lonely, that she did not want to see what the true nature of the relationship was. The unconscious responded to this conscious stance with the dream but also by her inexplicable reaction not to let him move into her apartment. Her defense against perception prevented her ability to see the true conscious situation. This defense can also be seen in situations where, for example, a partner has an addiction but this behavior is minimized or excused rather than seen as the destructive behavior it is. The attachment to the other and the need for that relationship appears to override the conscious perception of reality.

Defense against feeling (the unconscious standpoint)

Perception of feeling is a conscious act yet I have chosen to call the defense against the unconscious standpoint defense against feeling because emotions are essentially products of the unconscious, not consciously chosen. Images from the unconscious are merely aesthetics if the emotional reaction is lacking. Many a client in analysis, for example, has had amazing and fantastic dreams and active imagination experiences, but could still avoid the unconscious and true transformation by defending against the emotional core of the experience. A defense against the unconscious standpoint must involve a defense against feeling.

The earlier discussion about repression illustrates one example of this. This individual had conscious awareness that disturbing images had been repressed but no recall at first. This repression would have represented a defense against perception in order to avoid this conscious awareness. When the images returned via dream images, they were filled with emotional resonance. It was only when she made the emotional connection to them, and thus had access to the unconscious emotions, that true transformation could occur.

Sometimes there is a defense against emotion itself rather than emotions associated with images. For example, a young physician working in an emergency department made an error that led to the death of a patient, and she was subsequently sued by the family. She carried on with her work and told her friends and colleagues this was part of the job and that she was fine. However, she found herself one day standing on the top floor of the hospital parking garage ready to jump off, and it finally hit her she was in fact not fine. This was a dramatic breakthrough of the emotional experience of the events in her life facilitated by the mechanisms of individuation. This kind of defense is also called denial but other defenses such as projection or splitting serve as well as defenses against feeling and prevents access to the unconscious standpoint. These can be protective when the conscious standpoint cannot bear the reality of the emotions but ultimately do not serve transformation.

Defense against integration

In the TF, elucidating conscious and unconscious standpoints is the first step of the process. As described earlier, the second step is the ego – as the reactive ego operationally and the *individual* experientially – bridging the two conflicting standpoints and experiencing the symbol formation. The experience of the *individual* at this moment of symbol formation is an experience of the *individual*–Self connection through the symbol, transforming the ego in the process toward greater consciousness and relatedness.

What would be the purpose of a defense against this integration? As the earlier discussion concerning repression showed, there is an ego level but also a soul level. At the ego level, there is a desire or need to preserve collectivity and therefore there would be a defense against integration in order to preserve the persona. Every individual has a sense of how much challenge they can bear to their personal or cultural identity or role in life at any given time. As well, the challenge does not occur in isolation, for collectivity means that one's own individuation may need to be subsumed to one's cultural or familial identity in order to preserve the group. As Jung said, individuation in such circumstances is accompanied by guilt which must be redeemed (CW 18/1095), a cost some may find too great to bear.

The mechanisms of defense versus the mechanisms of individuation

The mechanisms of defense in the traditional psychoanalytic sense involve actions by the ego to exclude from consciousness, according to Anna Freud, "painful or unendurable ideas or affects" (Freud, 1993, p. 42). The purpose or goal of the defense in this instance is to avoid conflict between id impulses or painful affects and the ego, although more recent psychology has also identified external stressors as mobilizing defenses as well (Perry, 2014). This model of ego defense remains an energic one.

The mechanisms of defense according to this proposed Jungian model does not focus on the individual defense as such but instead shifts the focus to the legs of the Transcendent Function disabled and thus blocked by defense. This places defensive mechanisms in opposition to symbol formation and subsequent transformation. This is not to discount the fact that defenses understood in the traditional sense are not useful for understanding adaptation and other means of coping with the chaos of life. There is even a role that handling life's stresses plays in creativity through defenses such as sublimation or being able to manage thoughts and feelings for a goal (see Vaillant, 1993, for example). However, supporting the psyche's natural mechanism for transformation and individuation, the Transcendent Function, requires attention to the defenses that act on the legs of the TF itself.

The mechanisms of defense in this new sense then are opposed by the mechanisms of individuation. While the mechanisms of defense operate at the ego level to manage perception, affect, and integration, the mechanisms of individuation act at the soul level to facilitate the process of individuation. As discussed previously, these mechanisms include the Transcendent Function itself, enantiodromia, and projection.

Enantiodromia is a mechanism of contrast used by the psyche to correct a one-sided ego stance. Projection as a mechanism acts in two ways. As an ego defense, it protects the ego from disturbing self-perceptions and painful affects by seeing these qualities in the other rather in oneself. Projection also prevents integration by maintaining the split between the ego stance and the unconscious standpoint. As a mechanism of individuation however, projection acts by placing the unconscious content vis- à-vis the individual, thereby allowing a confrontation with this psychical content.

Chapter 5

1945–1961

Later works

Biographical background

In February 1944, in a Europe wracked with war, Jung suffered a more personal cataclysm. The 68-year-old Jung slipped while walking in the snow and broke his foot. He was hospitalized and, 10 days later, suffered a severe heart attack. Near death and delirious for weeks, his doctors and family were not sure he would even survive (Hayman, 1999, p. 379–380; Jung, 1983a, p. 320). Jung was hospitalized or convalescing after this illness for more than a year. Later, in a letter to a terminally ill colleague, he was to refer to this experience this way: "As you know, the angel of death has struck me down too and almost succeeded in wiping me off the slate" (letter to K. Mann, 1 February 1945).

He wrote further, however, about the meaning of this experience for him:

> On the whole my illness proved to be a most valuable experience, which gave me the inestimable opportunity of a glimpse behind the veil. The only difficulty is to get rid of the body, to get quite naked and void of the world and the ego-will. When you can give up the crazy will to live and when you seemingly fall into a bottomless mist, then the truly real life begins with everything which you were meant to be and never reached. . . . I am free, completely free and whole, as I never felt before.
>
> (letter to K. Mann, 1 February 1945)

Jung would later describe the visions he had while delirious as "the most tremendous things I have ever experienced" (Jung, 1983a, p. 326).

Jung began a new phase of his work after this experience, one begun earlier with his contact with alchemical texts but intensified and given new meaning by his tremendous near-death experience. What he had experienced in his delirium was a vision of the purpose of the psyche not just in the life of the individual, but its meaning in the life of mankind. He would say that only after this illness was he able to understand the need to "affirm one's destiny" in order to build up an ego that, "endures the truth, and that is capable of coping with the world and with fate" (Jung, 1983a, p. 328–329). This period of Jung's life would be the time when the psyche's place in nature would occupy him. This is also the period when his work became increasingly spiritual and fully in a symbolic paradigm.

In his autobiography, Jung tells the story of sensing his medical doctor must die in order that he himself would return to health and live on (Jung, 1983a, p. 323). He came to believe that he had been spared for important work left to do. He wrote shortly after his return home: "It seems to me as if I am ready to die, although as it looks to me some powerful thoughts are still flickering like lightenings in a summer night. Yet they are not mine, they belong to God, as everything else which bears mentioning" (letter to Victor White, 18 December 1946). Discussing this episode later, he would say, "After the illness a fruitful period of work began for me. A good many of my principle works were written only then. The insight I had had, or the vision of the end of things, gave me the courage to undertake new formulations" (Jung, 1983a, p. 328). This period of new formulations had its roots, however, in one piece he wrote before his illness – 'A Commentary on *The Secret of the Golden Flower*'.

'A Commentary on *The Secret of the Golden Flower*' (1929)

Despite being written more than a decade earlier than the time frame I have given this period of Jung's work, I believe this essay, 'Commentary on *The Secret of the Golden Flower*', due to its theme and spirit, rightly belongs here. As I have discussed in the last chapter, Jung had begun in the 1920s and '30s to construct a new model of the psychic structure built around a mutual dynamic process between the ego and the unconscious. He had already begun to identify the unconscious as the counter-pole to the ego in the psychical dynamic process. However, in this essay, he takes a further step and begins to use the concept of the Self, alluding to it as the totality of the psyche and as its organizing principle (CW 13/67). It is here the ego truly emerges as the counter-pole to an entity called the Self.

Jung received this work on Chinese alchemy in 1928 from its translator Richard Wilhelm, a missionary and noted sinologist. Jung was so enthusiastic about it he wrote a 90-page foreword to an already slim 60-page translation. Fordham (1985, p. 12) describes Jung's encounter with this work as a synchronistic breakthrough. He had found a link between the mandalas he'd painted to calm himself in the years after his break from Freud and the mandalas of Eastern religion. Generalizing his personal experience and finding material reflecting his interest in archetypes and collective patterns, Jung began to understand the mandala as a manifestation of a "psychocosmic system" (CW 13/31) that was reflected in Chinese philosophy and alchemy.

Cleary (1991) has retranslated the original 'Chinese Secret of the Golden Flower', commenting that the Wilhelm translation is so flawed as to be "practically dysfunctional" (p. 134). Not only are there errors in grammar, terminology and conceptual structures, but also the last five chapters were not even included and to which Jung therefore had no access. Cleary, in his comments on the new translation, makes several critical points about Jung's original commentary but before I address these I would like to summarize the main concepts in *The Secret of the Golden Flower* (from the corrected translation by Cleary) and then summarize the main points Jung makes in his own commentary as they relate to the ego.

Summary of the main points of the original **Secret of the Golden Flower:**

1 *The Secret of the Golden Flower* concerns a specific meditation exercise in Taoism and Chan Buddhism for turning attention away from involvement in mental objects and to refocus on the essence or source of mind. This exercise is known as 'turning the light around' and likened to a golden flower blossoming (hence the title).
2 There is a distinction made between an 'original spirit' and a 'conscious spirit'. The original spirit is understood as a formless essence of awareness which transcends culture and history, whereas the conscious spirit is the mind set of feelings, thoughts, and attitudes conditioned by personal and cultural history and bound by habit to specific forms.
3 The essence of this exercise is to refine one's thoughts so that the 'original spirit' is the master or host of the 'conscious spirit'. In other words, one practices turning the mind away from mental objects or preoccupations and focusing instead on the essence or source of mind.

In his commentary, Jung makes the following points:

1 *The Secret of the Golden Flower* clarified his own work on the unconscious: it was "the text that put me on the right track" (CW 13, p. 4) and the "long-sought connecting link between Gnosis and the process of the collective unconscious" (CW 13, p. 4).
2 There is a need for balance between consciousness and the unconscious. In resolving the conflict between these two conflicting standpoints, Jung offers three observations from his reading of *The Secret of the Golden Flower*: (a) that with a "new level of consciousness" the conflict is simply outgrown; (b) that this new consciousness is reached by opening up to a "new thing" (CW 13/18) which takes the form of a profound inner or outer experience; (c) that having this new experience entails openness to the unconscious and to "[letting] things happen in the psyche" (CW 13/20), that is, stopping the conscious mind from judging the products of the unconscious and to let fantasy have free rein (CW 13/21) to act on the conscious attitude.

3 The union of the opposites of consciousness and the unconscious creates a symbol (which often takes the form of a mandala, or, as in this Chinese work, a golden flower). The development of the symbol produces a unifying effect on the psyche, the main thing being the experience of the symbol: "Such a symbolic unity cannot be attained by the conscious will because consciousness is always partisan. Its opponent is the collective unconscious, which does not understand the language of the conscious mind. Therefore it is necessary to have the magic of the symbol, which contains those primitive analogies that speak to the unconscious. The unconscious can be reached and expressed only by symbols, and for this reason the process of individuation can never do without the symbol" (CW 13/44).
4 The resolution of this conflict between consciousness and the unconscious through the symbol leads to a position above the two, a kind of objective cognition: "What, on a lower level, had led to the wildest conflicts and to panicky outbursts of emotion, from the higher level of personality now looked like a storm in the valley seen from the mountain top. This does not mean that the storm is robbed of its reality, but instead of being in it one is above it" (CW 13/17).
5 With this operation the "center of the personality" is no longer the ego, which is "merely the center of consciousness", but "might be called the Self", a kind of point between consciousness and the unconscious (CW 13/67).

Jung's commentary introduces a number of advances or developments in his theory – it is the first time he discusses his new concept of Self, for example – but it must be said that *The Secret of the Golden Flower* seems to function as a literary inkblot onto which Jung projects his developing ideas more than anything else. For example, one purpose of this meditative exercise is to free the mind from images and emotions and not to unite with them. A passage in *The Secret of the Golden Flower* specifically warns against getting stuck in images: "When there is an image in the mirror, there is no more mirroring" (Cleary, 1991, p. 51). Cleary comments, "[T]he mirror being occupied by an image represents the attention being occupied by the contents of consciousness and thus losing sight of the essence of consciousness" (p. 121) and that this was a good description of how Jung "became mired in images". Yet Jung emphasizes that the emotion-filled image – the symbol – is the goal and the mutative element in the process.

Jung's approach to consciousness is also different from how it is understood in this text. Jung, according to Cleary, assigns qualities to the unconscious, such as 'primal organization', which are considered part of worldly consciousness (Cleary, 1991, p. 120) in Buddhist and Taoist literature. I also have the impression that Jung associates qualities of the 'original spirit', a transcending source of total awareness in Buddhism (Cleary, 1991, p. 139), to the Self. But the 'original spirit' is not a psychical entity; its essence is more associated with emptiness or openness of mind, than a totality of the personality. I believe this reflects the background influence of materialism and energic mechanisms in Jung's overall theory in which the entity of conscious personality needs a counter-pole. In Buddhism and Taoism, the true opposite of Jung's conscious personality would be the essence of awareness itself beyond systems of perception or archetypes, a concept of Self Jung indeed introduces in his work *Mysterium Coniunctionis.*

Cleary (1991) feels it is Wilhelm's poor translation as well as his lack of experience that led Jung to equate the psychoanalytic method with the golden flower practice (p. 149). Jung describes Europeans turning toward Eastern philosophy as a compensation for Western attitudes (Jung, 1994, p. 622–3) but fails to grasp the essence of the Eastern teachings and interprets *Golden Flower* in the context of a Western model.

Despite these criticisms, it can be said Jung was not directly transforming an Eastern system of meditation into a Western psychotherapeutic method. Rather, it appears *The Secret of the Golden Flower* inspired Jung to explore new dimensions in his own psychological theory.

Developments in the role of consciousness and ego

Jung, in his more idiosyncratic reading of the text, alters his concept of consciousness and ego based on *The Secret of the Golden Flower:*

> If the unconscious can be recognized as a co-determining factor along with consciousness, and if we live in such a way that conscious and unconscious demands are taken into account as far as possible, then the center of gravity of the total personality shifts its position. It is then no longer in the ego, which is merely the center of consciousness, but in the hypothetical point between conscious and unconscious. This new center might be called the Self. If the transposition is successful, it does away with the participation mystique and results in a personality that suffers only in the lower stories, as it were, but in its upper stories is singularly detached from painful as well as from joyful happenings.
>
> (CW 13/67)

In this passage Jung is alluding to a new role for the ego. He has dropped his concept of *individual* and declared the new center of personality is the Self; a kind of transcendent center beyond ego and very much an Eastern idea similar to the 'original spirit' of Chan Buddhism ("detached from painful as well as joyful happenings"; CW 13/67). This move on his part drops a useful ego developmental concept and embraces a form of spiritualism and abandonment of ego. Rather than the ego evolving into an entity that has objective cognition, he has introduced an entity that is a defeat for the ego through its subordination.

On the other hand, Jung emphasizes the mutuality of the conscious/unconscious encounter. The ego is a dynamic factor – "co-determining" – on par with the unconscious, and in this capacity must necessarily possess psychical energy. This energy, however, has lost a development path, and Jung even implies that is a good thing because the ego is an entity caught in "painful and joyful" emotions. One can see here the influence of Eastern philosophy and religion on Jung's theorizing. He has begun to focus on a self-concept more relevant for a psychology of religion than a clinically useful psychological theory.

Alchemical studies (1938–1954) and Aion (1951)

Studies in alchemy became the central focus of Jung's later research efforts. He felt he had found in these texts the 'objective' manifestation of the psyche and its processes through alchemists' 'psychological projections' onto their chemical experiments. Von Franz (1975), herself a collaborator with Jung on alchemical research, wrote that after Jung's own encounter with the psyche,

> the most important problem which remained for Jung was assisting other people in achieving the sort of personal inner experience he had discovered [. . .] but first there had to be some objective form, or objective material, with which he could connect it. He found this when he became familiar with alchemical symbolism.
>
> (p. 121)

Jung summarized the practice of alchemy (CW 13/252–253) as an investigation into the nature of nature. By investigating nature, however, the alchemists projected their own unconscious structures and processes onto the material as explanations for what they observed.

At the same time Jung was investigating alchemy, he was deepening his already profound interest in the religious questions attached to psychology. This came about in part due to his near-death experience, but also as a natural progression of his philosophical interests. He felt a revolution in Christianity was long overdue (letter to Hans Meyer, 30 January 1946). He would have for example, beginning in 1945 at the age of seventy, a significant correspondence with the Catholic Dominican monk Victor White. Their dialogue was to be "an explicit attempt to integrate the findings of psychology into the ecclesiastical doctrine" (letter to V. White, 5 October 1945).

Jung's outlook has been called "fundamentally religious" (Tacey, 1997). Main (2003), however, rightly points out the dualistic nature of Jung's core concepts:

> [T]he religious aspect of Jung's outlook is only half the story, for his outlook is also, and no less 'fundamentally', secular, by which I mean

> concerned with natural, specifically scientific, and human-centered principles and methods of explanation rather than supernatural ones.
>
> (p. 191)

The tension between Jung's pull toward the scientist using empirical data and the man of religion looking for the key to the soul's redemption through transcendence of ego concerns becomes especially evident in his alchemical work. Alchemy was 'empirical' yet also deeply spiritual, for the alchemist's quest in the end led to a union of God and man.

In Aion (CW 9ii), Jung reformulates his ego concept in the light of his alchemical researches. The ego, now in a subordinate position to the Self (CW 9ii/1), is described as resting on two "seemingly" different bases: "the somatic and the psychic" (CW 9ii/3). Jung describes the somatic base of the ego: "[It] consists . . . of conscious and unconscious factors" (CW 9ii/4); for example, memory amenable to voluntary retrieval and other unconscious contents not retrieved voluntarily. In other words, the conscious and unconscious factors are contents rather than functions. The ego also arises "from the collision between the somatic factor and the environment, and once established as a subject, it goes on developing from further collisions with the outer world and the inner" (6). The ego, which is the center of the conscious personality, is not the totality of the personality. The totality is the Self (9). What distinguishes the ego from the Self is the ego's capacity for 'free choice' inside the field of consciousness (9).

The process of individuation is no longer a focus on developing and creating the *individuum*, but rather, "the step by step development of the Self from an unconscious state to a conscious one" (418). The Self, as the totality of the personality, is not an *individuum* equivalent, but rather "the apotheosis of individuality" (115). Jung continues,

> [T]he Self has the attributes of uniqueness and of occurring once only in time. But since the psychological Self is a transcendent concept, expressing the totality of conscious and unconscious contents, it can only be described in antinomial terms; that is the above attributes must be supplemented by their opposites if the transcendental situation is to be characterized correctly.
>
> (115)

In this definition, individuality in terms of ego has lost its meaning. The ego is reduced to a function that, albeit a necessary counter-force for the unconscious, is no longer a focus of psychical development. The ego's individuality is accounted for through its "infinitely varied . . . clarity, emotional coloring, and scope" (10). From looking at how Jung uses these phrases elsewhere, it appears he is talking about the ego's typology, discrimination ability, and breadth of consciousness. In the next work, however, he would elevate the counter-force character of the ego to a world-creating level.

Mysterium Coniunctionis (1955–1956)

Writing this volume occupied Jung for 10 years and was completed in 1954, his 80th year. Subtitled *An Inquiry Into the Separation and Synthesis of Psychic Opposites in Alchemy*, this work was a culmination of all Jung's research in classic alchemical texts, with special emphasis on the symbol of the *coniunctio*.

No one has ever accused this work of being an easy read: even with an extensive background in Jungian theory it is a dense book to absorb. It is remarkable in fact how few Jungians themselves have actually read it in its entirety. Edinger (1995) calls it "oceanic", like the psyche itself, but nevertheless believes *Mysterium Coniunctionis* "will be a major object of study for centuries" (p. 17). It has to be worked on, according to Edinger, "the way one works on a dream" (p. 18) because it is a book of images and the language of the collective unconscious, that is, impressionistic and synchronistic rather than linear and logical.

The subject is the psyche itself, specifically, the psychodynamics of the opposites. Although the book proceeds from one set of alchemical images to another, the subject of inquiry is the way these images emerge and transform. There is notably no clinical material included in this analysis, and only tantalizing brief forays into interpretation directed toward specific clinical practice. Rather, Jung offers a broad examination – his philosophy, really – of the structure and dynamics of the psyche itself, its processes, and its rules, all that directs psychical life. He identifies a logic to the psyche that can be translated into meaning and understanding by the clinician for specific circumstances or individual cases.

Up to this point in his work, Jung has gradually built up an understanding of the ego as first, the center of consciousness; second, a partner with the unconscious in the process of individuation; and third, an entity ultimately replaced at the experiential level by the individual/*individuum*. In his late phase of work, however, Jung has dropped an emphasis on the *individuum* entity, and he more and more focuses on the character and meaning of individuation for the world, and the place of the ego in that process.

Fundamental in this last evolution, then, in Jung's thought is the idea of the *Unus Mundus*, that is, One World. The world possesses an underlying unity at every level: physical and psychical. It is the philosophy behind his concept of synchronicity, for example – that physical and psychical realms communicate because they are one entity. *Unus Mundus* is but the final stage of development, however, in a process of confrontation of opposites. The stages are

1. *Unio Mentalis*: union of soul and spirit which are separated from the body.
2. Union of the *Unio Mentalis* with the body.
3. *Unus Mundus*: union of soul/spirit/body with the world.

Jung uses soul and spirit in specific ways. Soul in the first instance is the individual's relationship to the unconscious, but it is here also meant as a collective structure – a world soul *anima mundi* – that is an expression of the laws of nature itself. It is analogous to Plato's 'realm of eternal ideas', the universal form of all organic and inorganic substance. Spirit is variously described as reason and insight ('*anima rationalis*', CW 14/673), eternal ideas and moral values. Jung saw spirit as similar to Freud's 'superego' but with a more archetypal, that is, impersonal and autonomous, nature.

With a focus on world soul and *Unus Mundus*, Jung then explores the implications for the ego. He wrote in a discussion on consciousness:

> For just as we perceive nothing of the real sun but light and heat and, apart from that, can know its physical constitution only by inference, so our consciousness issues from a dark body, the ego, which is the indispensable condition for all consciousness, the latter being nothing but the association of an object or a content with the ego. The ego, ostensibly the thing we know most about, is in fact a highly complex affair full of unfathomable obscurities. Indeed, one could even define it as a relatively constant personification of the unconscious itself, or as the Schopenhauerian mirror in which the unconscious becomes aware of its own face.
>
> (CW 14/129)

Jung is here quite directly saying the ego and the unconscious are two sides of one reality: the ego is the mirror of the unconscious. The ego now is not 'merely' the center of consciousness, but rather a complex affair that makes consciousness possible. The difference between these two positions is that in the first the ego is a dynamic structure that is characterized by function, whereas in the second position, the ego as mirror, the ego is (1) the equivalent, in the outer conscious world, of the unconscious world, and (2) the 'Archimedean point', so to say, in which the *Unus Mundus* separates, is seen, and, through the act of being seen, is created.

Jung identifies the ego's perception as a creative act in this following passage:

> All the worlds that have ever existed before man were physically there. But they were a nameless happening, not a definite actuality, for there did not exist that minimal concentration of the psychic factor, which was also present, to speak the word that outweighed the whole of creation: this is the world and this is I! That was the first morning of the world, the first sunrise after the primal darkness, when that inchoately conscious complex, the ego, the son of the darkness, knowingly sundered subject and object, and thus precipitated the world and itself into definite existence, giving it and itself a voice and a name.
>
> (CW 14/129).

Jung is therefore proposing a creative function for the ego that is not only creative for the individual personality (creating wholeness or wider consciousness for example) but also a creativity that is world creating – *Cosmogonic.* The ego's act of perception splits the world into the object and the observing subject and this separation is in essence the birth of the world.

Edinger (1995) describes the Gnostic roots of Jung's world-creation schema. As in the creation myth of Basilides, a second century Gnostic, in which God has three sons, the ego has a threefold structure.

> At the initial point of birth of the ego, one part never separates from its origin – it remains unborn, in the state of complete ego-Self identity. That's the first 'son'. Part three, the third 'son' falls totally into matter, into the concrete, manifest existence. Only the second 'son' achieves an intermediate position between the opposites and is thus able to perceive the opposites. Only this portion is truly conscious.
>
> (Edinger, 1995, p. 93)

I believe this scheme of a threefold ego helps explain the different aspects of the ego that Jung is now using. Jung describes an ego that is not conscious of itself, but that through individuation processes later becomes aware of its separateness from the collective. Although differentiation is an ego characteristic, it is implied that the ego is initially undifferentiated. This would be the 'first son'. The 'second son' would be the ego that operates at an unconscious structural level, close to the autonomy of the instincts. This would be the ego that operates defensively, for example. The 'third son' would represent the ego that experiences itself and the Other, that is, is engaged in a mutual relatedness. This is the individual that Jung identified as a product of individuation in his earlier works (the *individuum*).

Although Jung has emphasized the teleological perspective for the individual previously, in *Mysterium Coniunctionis* the teleological perspective in the individuation process for the world is emphasized. Jung seldom stressed this aspect in his previous writings although it was evident as a subtext. He certainly saw teleology as a universal, as well as individual, force. In a letter, for example, he wrote,

> Thank you very much for sending me the interesting book by Paul Petit. [. . .] I'm absolutely of the same conviction as he is, that there is a *teleos* in each community. But I should add that this *teleos* is a summation of the individual *tela*. Each man has his *telos* and insomuch as he tries to fulfill it he is a real citizen. The community is nothing without the individual and if a community consists of individuals that do not fulfill their *telos*, then the community has no *telos* or a very wrong one. That is the reason why the 'confirmisme social se transforme en idolâtrie, quant il devient en soi'.
>
> (letter of 18 June 1947)

Jung also wrote in this context, for example,

> Every advance in culture is, psychologically, an extension of consciousness. [. . .] If [the individual] succeeds in giving collective validity to his widened consciousness, he creates a tension of opposites that provides the stimulation which culture needs for its further progress.
>
> (CW 8/111)

For Jung, individuation was not just in service to the individual and his personal achievement of consciousness. The teleological goal of individuation was ultimately the achievement of world consciousness. In the preceding letter, Jung tells us that he sees this process beginning with the individual and then all the individuals as a group create a movement toward consciousness of the collective.

For Jung, the ultimate goal of individuation was not simply consciousness for the sake of consciousness. The world-creating aspect of individuation was to give a voice and face to the unconscious, the Self, and here Jung came to the edge of the spiritual. Although Jung often said he did not identify the Self as God but rather the psychic equivalent of God (in a letter of 13 January 1948, for example), he nevertheless did come very close to that, calling the Self "the God within us" (CW 7/399) as far as "all our highest and ultimate purposes seem to be striving toward it". He would even write at the end of his life, "I cannot prove that the Self and God are identical, although in practice they appear so" (in a letter of 15 June 1955).

The process of individuation as a spiritual process, then, is much more than a dynamic process for broadening individual or even community consciousness, if one takes consciousness to mean awareness or perception of one's totality (knowledge and integration of shadow aspects, *anima/animus* aspects, for example). At the end of his life, Jung speculated that individuation was a manifestation of "*cosmogonic* love": that through the agency of an ultimate power we experience in the psyche as God – but that cannot ultimately be known except through psychological means – we as individuals become the vehicles of a force whose goal is relatedness and whose instrument is relatedness. As he wrote, "For we in the deepest sense are the victims and the instruments of cosmogonic love" (Jung, 1963, p. 387).

Although individuation is a process of separation and integration, the ultimate goal of individuation, but also the instrument of individuation, is Eros: mutual relatedness. This relatedness is not meant in the same sense as object relations theory or in the same way psychoanalysts speak of relational theory. In these other psychological theories, relationship with one's fellow man is motivational in itself for development and behavior in general. In other words, humans are innately social and relational, and social interaction becomes a means toward healthy psychological development as well as the goal.

For Jung, relatedness was the essential element in the process of individuation: "[W]ithout relatedness individuation is hardly possible. Relatedness begins with conversation mostly. Therefore communication is indubitably important. For 60 years I have practiced this simple truth" (letter, 11 November 1960). Jung saw relatedness as concrete – at the level of actual human interaction – but also imaginal, i.e. relatedness to the inner world. He wrote further, "[A] religious experience depends upon human relatedness to a certain extent. I don't know to what extent. There is for instance the apocryphal *logion*: 'When there are two together, they are not without God, and when there is one alone, I am with him'" (letter, 11 November 1960). He is saying here in part that relatedness is a quality that exists at the interpersonal level as well as the intrapersonal level, because ultimately the Other – as fellow man or as inner figure – is a creation of the psyche and therefore numinous.

In *Mysterium Coniunctionis*, Jung associates relatedness with Eros (CW 14/224): the tendency for connectedness and integration in the psyche. In his essay on the phenomenon of the transference, Jung describes the developmental stages of Eros. What is significant for my purpose here is not the specific stages themselves – Eros develops in four stages from a purely physical level to a spiritual level – but rather the idea that Eros has a developmental sequence at all. Rather than being a single quality of connection, Eros is a form of relatedness that becomes through development more and more conscious. Ultimately relatedness is a form of consciousness through our connection to others rather than through our separateness.

Why is this distinction important? Why does Jung see connection to others, or to the Other, as the teleological goal of individuation, rather than as merely consciousness and separation from the collective? Partly it has to do with the quality of the connection. Rather than fusion or immersion, related connection means receiving as well as perceiving the Other in consciousness.

The ego quaternity

A lecturer at the Jung Institute in Zurich once said, "If we talk about Jung, we talk about the opposites". This indeed sums up his concept of the psyche; as he wrote in the first sentence of *Mysterium Coniunctionis*, "The factors which come together in the *coniunctio* are conceived as opposites, either confronting one another in enmity or attracting each other in love" (CW 14/1).

The psyche, in other words, is organized and driven by the conflict or attraction of opposites. This basic energic concept has been a motif throughout all of Jung's work. The goal, or motivation, for the confrontation of opposites, is teleological, as I have described earlier.

Up to this point I have discussed this confrontation of opposites and a binary relationship of conscious and unconscious, or of ego and Self. In his alchemical writings, however, Jung introduces a concept beyond the binary psyche – the quaternity. This is composed of two sets of opposites (CW 14/1). Although it appears Jung had a particular attachment to the number four (and for which he has been criticized; see Gould, 1997, for example), the basis of the quaternity concept involves the definition of the ego.

The conscious ego has four functions consisting of two pairs of opposites (the 'rational' functions of thinking and feeling, and the 'irrational' functions of sensation and intuition). It also consists of a somatic and a psychical base: "[The ego] seems to arise in the first place from the collision between the somatic factor and the environment, and, once established as a subject, it goes on developing from further collisions with the outer world and the inner" (CW 9ii/6).

The ego, in order to exist and function at conscious and unconscious levels, would be rooted in the psychical and the biological. The psychical base comprises the elements of conscious awareness, will, and intention. This represents the conscious ego. The unconscious ego would then be the somatic base that perceives and reacts according to ego intention outside, however, from conscious awareness.

Such a formulation, that the ego has a psychical pole and a somatic pole, would account for the unconscious processes of the ego. An individual would perceive and react (with ego defenses, for example) outside conscious awareness according to the conscious ego stance.

Jung therefore conceives the somatic/psychical ego created through the collision with the environment as having the structure shown in Figure 5.1.

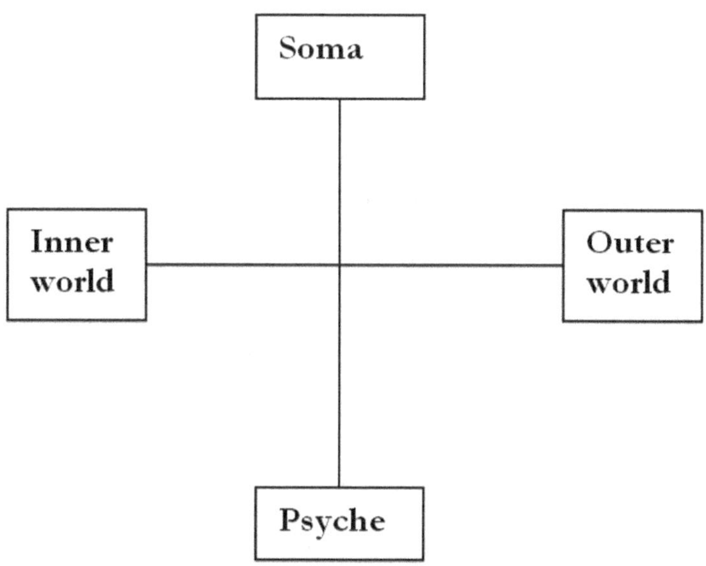

Figure 5.1 Ego Quaternity

In this model, there is a balance between consciousness and the experiential ego and the unconscious ego function at the somatic level. As Jung wrote earlier, it is assumed the ego arises as a subjective experience out of the physical sense of being and through the interaction of the subject and the environment. Only then is the ego established enough to confront inner and outer reality.

What is the difference between the environment in the first stage of this process, and the outer world encountered later? In using the word 'collision' (*Zusammenstoss*), Jung is emphasizing the conflictual nature of the individual's encounter with the limitations imposed by physical reality; the way a child may cry in frustration when he is unable to climb out of his crib, for example. This assumes, however, that the awareness of conflict and limitations shapes awareness of the personal self. It is just as likely, however, that physical limitations and environmental constraints contribute to ego formation and consolidation by giving the child a sense of being held and bounded. Winnicott (1965) stressed the difference between the kinds of experience the child feels depends on whether the child encounters the environment through his own initiative and discovers it through a "spontaneous gesture", or whether the experience is imposed on him through intrusion of the environment.

Winnicott's model is a relational one, however, and Jung's in this instance is not. For Winnicott, the environment is an object that the subject discovers, whereas in Jung's model, the environment is either an obstacle or a mirror of the individual's own inner world, seen through projection.

In Jung's binary model, there is not a true relatedness initially in the sense of *Bezogenheit*. Rather, it is an encounter that is conflictual or attractive yet defined by the subjective experience of the individual. The opposite pole in the dyad is based on and defined by the subjective experience of the first pole. The outer world feels hot to the ego, in other words, as compensation for the inner feeling of cold. The environment and the outer world are means to collect or re-collect the unknown parts of oneself. True relatedness, perceiving the reality of the other rather than as a projection of one's own unknown self, is actually an end product of development in the individuation process.

The binary structure proceeds to a quaternity structure. For Jung, the question of quaternity symbolism was not a theory but a fact, "a phenomenon" (letter, 24 August 1960). Jung has been criticized for his tendency to find quaternity structure (see, for example, Dry, 1961; Friedman and Goldman, 1964), and to view this as the natural state – he even noted regarding a mandala painted by a patient that failed to show a quaternity structure as indicative of psychical disturbance (Jung, 1976, p. 104).

Is it useful for constructing an Ego Psychology to use this quaternity structure? The basic premise from the ego quaternity diagram in Figure 5.1 is that the ego develops out of duality (psyche/soma) and then, in this continuing duality, is part of a second duality (inner/outer). The two processes are presumed consecutive; that is, the first must proceed before the other is possible. The first premise, that the ego arises out of the psyche/soma conflict, is a well-established part of ego theory. The second premise, that this ego formed out of the psyche/soma conflict proceeds then to develop through encounter (a more neutral word than conflict but in the same spirit) with the inner and outer world, has parallels in other depth psychologies. The Freudian model sees the ego encounter the inner world through the instincts, on the one hand, and through the superego on the other, as well as continuing encounter with the outer world through physical reality and interpersonal reality. Object relations theory also assumes outer objects represent inner objects for the subject. Both Jung and psychoanalytic models presuppose a level of ego development before the encounter with the inner and outer world – the superego is understood to develop after the ego for example.

Implications for clinical practice

Individuation according to the model above is dependent on ego development but is itself an ego *developing* process. In other words, individuation requires an ego capable of perceiving, reacting, differentiating, and integrating, as well as relating. All these capacities have a developmental sequence. By exercising these ego functions, the ego progresses in this development. Therefore clinically the analyst concerned with the individuation process will first need to assess the state of the client's ego. This is usually described as assessing ego strength.

An initial interview with a potential analytical client would involve a careful assessment of several ego capacities. These include capacity to differentiate one's own thoughts and motivations from others', ability to consider points of view other than one's own, the capacity for relatedness, and the capacity to resist or quickly recover from the influence of an autonomous complex. Also, what are generally considered executive functions of the brain such as impulse control, self-awareness, and capacity for reflection would be considered. Finally, the capacity for symbolization should be assessed. This latter capacity would be evident by the ability of the client to see beyond concrete representation when dealing with a dream image or emotional experience, for example.

There is a world of difference between the ego experience and the ego observing itself having an experience. This is the initial stage of ego development; the ego is able to step outside itself as an observing and reacting ego. In his essay 'The Transcendent Function' (CW 8), in which Jung outlines the mechanics of individuation, he states that the ego must approach the other unconscious point of view as if it were between equals (CW 8/186) and to bear the conflicting standpoints. Although Jung does not name this third position that observes and bears the contradictions of the ego and unconscious standpoints, based on theory discussed earlier it is proposed that this entity is operationally the ego-complex but experientially the *individual*. The formation of the *individual* and the action of the ego-complex through perceiving and reacting to the conscious and unconscious standpoints connects the ego-unconscious at the personal level to the totality of the psyche and therefore to symbol formation.

The state of the ego is key with this operation. The analyst, therefore, in order to support the individuation process, would want to focus on three areas: ego strength, access to unconscious standpoint, and the reactive ego standpoint.

Ego strength

As discussed earlier, the ego has certain capacities and functions with which the analyst can work. One of the areas to assess in this regard is the capacity of the ego to meet the contents of the unconscious or the inner world. This is an extreme example of the need for caution in approaching the contents of the unconscious without adequate ego strength:

> Many years ago as a psychiatric nurse in an acute care facility, I had as a patient a young woman with auditory hallucinations, which took the form of quiet voices commenting on her activities and surroundings. Her therapist, in the mistaken belief that these voices were therapeutic, (unbeknownst to the treatment team) encouraged her to focus on the hallucinatory contents in the therapy sessions. The character of the voices began to change and become more threatening. Eventually the young woman became violent, acting out the urges of these voices by attacking her therapist.

For psychosis and other forms of extreme ego weakness, the prudent therapist or analyst would do well to focus on building up the client's capacity to function in and adapt to the outer world. The inner world may be acknowledged if appropriate but in general should not be given additional libido through interpretation or amplification of contents of the unconscious.

The capacity to resist falling into a complex, as described earlier, is another aspect of ego strength. Beginning work in analysis may involve helping the client differentiate the ego from the autonomous complexes in order to develop this capacity. It may be that the client enters analysis precisely because of complex formulations and the work of differentiation of the complex from the ego is life altering in itself. This was the case, for example, with the young banker discussed previously. He recognized and was distressed by who he became in the world of banking and had an awareness this was not him. That he was open to other points of view facilitated the formation of the symbol – the stag – that led to a deep sense of who he truly was and what were his authentic values.

In his model of the first half of life/second half of life, Jung emphasizes that the task of the first half of life is to build up an ego that can support the individual as he or she develops life structures in the outer world such as a profession and personal relationships. As well, Jung emphasized the need for a strong ego in encounters with the unconscious. Therefore, ego strengthening becomes important for individuals with weak ego capacity. Similar to what is known from brain research and strengthening frontal lobe executive function (see, for example, Enriquez-Geppert, Huster and Hermann, 2013), use of these capacities in a variety of ways reinforces and strengthens them. For example, with adolescents, an age group in which brain executive function is at a critical developmental phase, asking them to articulate and reflect on their thinking process reinforces their capacity to think and reflect.

Observing one's thinking through reflection and in the context of a relationship strengthens these capacities and strengthens the ego in analysis as well. In the therapeutic relationship, the analyst acts as the auxiliary observing ego for the client. This function can then be internalized by the client through example but also through internalizing the analyst as an ego adjunct. In this way, through the analytical relationship, the client incorporates the analyst as a kind of ego exoskeleton which becomes over time the client's own. One client, for example, revealed to me that in the early phase of her analysis, she had typed up short reflective phrases of mine and blown them up into posters she hung around her apartment. She felt comforted and held by me outside the sessions through these posters but also over time incorporated the reflective capacity and ego strength as her own.

Access to unconscious standpoint

In his essay, 'The Transcendent Function' (CW 8), Jung emphasizes the absolute necessity of the unconscious having its say in order for the process of symbol formation and expansion of consciousness to occur. However, the unconscious and the inner world can be quite frightening to those unaccustomed or indisposed to looking inward. One client who began to dream while in analysis confessed that she could not sleep in the same room as the piece of paper upon which she'd written out her dreams. I also had the experience, while working in a community mental health clinic that some clients would very much prefer medication alone rather than consider looking at their emotional life as part of their treatment. One cannot overestimate the fear and anxiety the unconscious can arouse and a first step in approaching the unconscious would be to assess the client's experience of this dimension.

There are many ways to access the unconscious; dreams are not the coin of the realm. Many Jungians now use other representational methods to allow the unconscious a voice, such as pictures and other types of artwork or sandplay (a technique in which clients create a spontaneous picture in a small sandbox using any number of small objects). Jung also described clients using movement or dance to represent unconscious content. In addition, clients can report utterances of the inner voice, or even music that has become an *Ohrwurm*. They may find themselves obsessed with a certain subject, for example, collecting a certain object or fascination with a particular celebrity. All of these methods and others connect the individual with his or her unconscious.

Jung assures us that the unconscious is always speaking and even in the absence of any of the preceding methods, the analyst and client can still access the voice of the unconscious through looking at patterns in relationships. These patterns may manifest in the analysis itself through transference/countertransference but are also revealed in the everyday interactions in other relationships such as with family, friends, and work situations. For example, Jung describes in a number of his works the case of a young woman who had a strong father transference toward him but which was revealed by a dream to be related to her need for an experience of God. This same scenario could be repeated, for example, with a tremendous fascination or revulsion involving any individual in one's life.

The reactive ego standpoint

Jung describes the dynamic of this ego versus unconscious confrontation thusly (CW8/189):

> The shuttling to and fro of arguments and affects represents the transcendent function of opposites. The confrontation of the two positions generates a tension charged with energy and creates a living, third thing – not a logical stillbirth . . . but a movement out of the suspension of opposites, a living birth that leads to a new level of being, a new situation.

What Jung does not describe is the ego experiencing this living, third thing but rather describes ("a new level of being, a new situation") an experiencing ego that is changed. This process requires, therefore, a reacting, experiencing ego that is not the ego-consciousness of the usual ego stance. This observing and reactive ego is a third ego form, one that spans consciousness and the unconscious and is closer to the *individual* than to the ego as described in other contexts.

In Jung's late works, he had moved away from the *individual* concept. At this point in his theory he places great emphasis on the archetypes and the Self, but he also elevates the ego to equal status with the Self and a partner in the transformative processes. This formulation of the ego in his later works echoes back to the dilemma he had in his understanding of the ego in this early work, 'The Transcendent Function'. While the ego is the "exponent of the Self" (CW 11/391), that is, the representation of the Self in consciousness, it must also function as something separate in order to perceive the ego-unconscious polarity.

The ego, individuation, and a way forward

One way to avoid confusion when evaluating the role of the ego in the individuation process is to understand the ego as a multilayered concept. The ego as center of consciousness, that is, ego-consciousness, is not the experiencing ego that bridges consciousness and the unconscious in a non-collective way and is best characterized by the concept of *individual.* Ego-consciousness, however, the seat of conscious memory and experience, is transformed – becomes more conscious and related – by experiencing the *individual* state.

Having this experience also becomes part of conscious memory and facilitates its recurrence. An older woman recounted to me, for example, a numinous experience she had had as a young girl. It was an experience of oneness with the world and it gave her a sense, even as a child, of something powerful and structuring beyond the world's physical reality. This experience then became a leitmotif in her life that she found comforting and, eventually, became part of a deep personal spirituality. Having had this initial experience led her to recognize and allow the subsequent experiences to occur and develop over time despite the vicissitudes of life. In this way the fleeting experience at a young age of the *individual* eventually became a substantial part of how she experienced herself and the world in her 70s. This, I believe, illustrates the relationship between the experience of the *individual* and individuation.

Chapter 6

Ego theory in Jung's psychology

In the more than 50 years Jung worked and developed his psychological theory, his ideas about the ego evolved so that the early formulations became reworked, expanded, and differentiated. This led to confusion as terms were used throughout whose meaning evolved. For example, the 'self' concept was an aspect of the ego in the original 1923 edition of *Psychological Types* (CW 6) and this viewpoint was not revised by Jung in that work until 1960. Finding a theory of ego in Jung's works, therefore, has been part textual and content analysis and part detective work. If there is a 'golden thread' that runs through his work, it is this: the ego is first a part of a psychodynamic process, second it has a developmental pathway, and third it represents a standpoint in which what is not ego can be seen and integrated. The ego concept for Jung, therefore, has elements of structure, dynamics, experience, and the transpersonal.

Throughout Jung's work, his basic premise, the dynamism of the opposites, never wavered. This is certainly a legacy of his background in science. What evolved, however, were the deeper theoretical assumptions regarding the dynamics of the psyche beyond the energic characteristics. There was an evolution in Jung's theoretical paradigm from the materialist-based energic paradigm to a more philosophical/spiritual-based symbolic paradigm. Two factors driving this evolution that impressed me as affecting Jung at a personal level were his drive to dispute Freud and his drive to understand himself. As I have read his collected works, seminars, and letters, I see an ongoing argument – at times gentle, at times vehement – against Freud and the established psychoanalytic theory he developed. Yet it is a Freud that Jung constructed; after their break, Freud went on to further develop a theory more differentiated and more open to revision than Jung credits him. The Freud in Jung's works is a chimera Freud that Jung needed to battle: his own counter-pole who represents his own materialist roots which he simultaneously embraced by proclaiming himself an empiricist yet rejected by denigrating Freud.

In many ways, as he describes in his autobiography, he was seeking to understand himself. Regarding his first encounters with the unconscious he wrote, "From the beginning I had conceived my voluntary confrontation with the unconscious as a scientific experiment which I myself was conducting and in whose outcome I was vitally interested" (Jung, 1983a, p. 202). His life, his experiences, his visions and fantasies and relationships, led him to seek understanding that represented a universal truth. He succeeded to the extent anyone recognizes his or her own true experiences and emotions in what he writes. As I wrote in the introduction, his theory represents a dissident voice in the traditional community of depth psychology, and an almost alien voice in the modern world of psychology that embraces cognitive-behavioral science and neuropsychology over care of the soul.

Jung's theory is not an anachronism in the modern world; however, it is dismissed as Western-centric (see, for example, Friedman and Goldstein, 1964) or patriarchal or mystical. Key to understanding Jung and his theory is that his 'empirical' evidence is phenomenological rather than materialist-scientific. He approached this phenomenological data in a sense through the lens of his late 19th/early 20th century European and male viewpoint and yet it is the phenomenological spirit itself that speaks to Jung's readers today. What he offers the modern reader is a challenge to the 'received' wisdom of psychoanalytic theory and modern psychology; to remember the roots of meaning, and what is transcendent in a world devoid of transcendent experience, are in human experience and emotion.

Towards a Jungian theory of the ego

Although overshadowed by his fascination with the archetypes and the Self, Jung's psychological theory fulfills the criteria for an Ego Psychology. The seven criteria presented in the introduction (self-concept, developmental concept, integration concept, defense concept, adaptation concept, deficit concept, structural concept) are all elements that are present in Jung's writings. His ego concept is not organized according to these seven criteria, but is better understood when organized into the four different attitudes he had toward the ego: a subjective ego, a structural ego, a developmental ego, and a cosmogonic ego.

Subjective ego

The subjective ego is that part of our personality that is our sense of being ourselves, our perceptions, our personal identity, our personal story with our memories and sense of continuity: how we experience ourselves in the world and in ourselves. In Ego Psychology this is what is meant by the 'self-concept', as opposed to the uses of the term 'Self' in Jungian psychology. For Jung, as has been discussed earlier, the term 'Self' refers to the totality of the personality, the archetype, and the organizing principle in the psyche (Fordham, 1985).

When I say 'subjective ego', then, I am referring to the aspect of personal experience associated with conscious awareness, identity, continuity of self-experience and self-agency, and will. This is not the archetype or the totality of the personality – it is a concept perhaps best described as 'I'-ness. Therefore, it comprises what is conscious and is often described in Jung's writings as ego-consciousness to emphasize this relationship of the ego to consciousness. The subjective ego would include the persona, that aspect of the personality in Jung's theory associated with one's adaptive attitude toward the world and toward oneself. It is also the expression of one's typology, as these ego functions color our perception and scope of consciousness.

The subjective ego and the individual

A central aspect of the subjective ego is that it undergoes development. It is a relatively collective entity at first in so far as the ego itself is a collective structure and as far as subjective reactions and thinking are directed by instincts and collectivity. Through the process of differentiation and individuation, however, the personality develops an individual standpoint. This new psychical entity, the *individual* (sometimes referred to in Jung's writings as the *individuum*), then comprises the qualities of awareness, identity, continuity of self-experience and self-agency, and will previously associated with the ego but now free of collective associations. The ego then continues to function at the structural level but the subject's sense of self is contained in the *individual*, a third psychic entity that bridges the ego and the unconscious.

Jung describes the *individual* as "everything that is not collective" (CW 6/756) and development of which is the goal of individuation. The *individual* is created ultimately through the actions of the Transcendent Function, first because there is a need for a third psychical entity that bridges the difference between the ego and the unconscious attitudes, and second because the Transcendent Function "creates individual lines of development" (CW 6/759).

These individual lines of development include greater consciousness (CW 6/762) and greater relatedness (see CW 7/275 for example). Greater consciousness occurs because as the ego loses its collective properties, it is capable of perceptions and emotions that had previously been excluded due to ego defenses. There is greater relatedness because the 'Other' is less an object seen through collective attitudes or projections and other defenses, and more another individual whose reality is seen more clearly. All of these qualities of consciousness and relatedness can occur fleetingly in varying ways as the *individual* develops and can thus become a foundation for further development. A simple example of this development of consciousness is the common childhood experience of realizing one day that one's parents are not omniscient. From that day forward, consciousness of that fact shapes not only the relationship with the parent but every subsequent relationship.

It is my belief Jung failed to develop this concept of the *individual* further in his last phase of life, choosing instead to concentrate on the Self-as-archetype. The *individual* concept was more or less dropped and Jung instead speaks of the ego, incorporating *individual* qualities to the ego. For example, one can see this in his writings about the relationship between the ego and the Self. On the one hand he raises the ego to be a partner with the Self in creation of consciousness but on the other hand the relationship between the ego and *individual* and the Self is left unexplored. This has implications for identifying an 'integration concept' in Jung's works.

The Self as the function of integration in the psyche has been extensively reviewed in Jungian literature (Fordham, 1985, for example) and I will not repeat that topic here. I would, however, like to argue that the role of the *individual* as a function of integration has been obscured by the role of the Self. The *individual* is not only a product of individuation, but is 'created' for a purpose. That purpose, I believe Jung implies as a subtext in his writings, is to personify the mature capacity for mutual relatedness as well as act as the authentic partner vis à vis the Self. As was described in the previous chapter, the Self, according to Jung, needs this partner in order to become conscious in the world.

A characteristic of the *individual*, and central to its integration function, is the idea of 'objective cognition': the detachment from emotional valuations and ties similar to enlightenment in Buddhism. Jung wrote about this after describing the series of visions he had at the time of his 1945 illness and a dream of his wife after her death:

> The objectivity which I experienced in this dream and in the visions is part of a completed individuation. It signifies detachment from valuations and from what we call emotional ties. In general, emotional ties are very important to human beings. But they still contain projections, and it is essential to withdraw these projections in order to attain to oneself and to objectivity. Emotional relationships are relationships of desire, tainted by coercion and constraint; something is expected from the other person, and that makes him and ourselves unfree. Objective cognition lies hidden behind the attraction of the emotional relationship; it seems to be the central secret. Only through objective cognition is the real *coniunctio* possible.
>
> (Jung, 1983a, p. 328)

For the *individual* to act as an integrating function, it must have emotional ties to neither the ego position nor the Self. This, it seems to me, is the real position of the ego in the Transcendent Function. Although Jung describes the Transcendent Function as collaboration between the ego and the unconscious, there must be an aspect of the subject that stands outside and is aware of the conflict of opposites, perceives the ego attachment to one position and the power of the opposite in the polarity even if for fleeting moments. The *individual*–Self collaboration then would be a more authentic view of the action of the Transcendent Function. In this way, the ego, as the subjective ego, acts in collaboration with the Self as a function of integration in the psyche.

Subjective ego and collectivity

It may be the subjective ego, being a collective entity, is the element of the ego that is most vulnerable to cultural influences. In Western countries, for example, where a sense of individuality is valued and a dominant trait in the culture, then the subjective ego will develop as a persona that relates out of this value. In other cultures where group cohesiveness and group identity is valued and individuality is not considered desirable or a part of the culture for whatever reason, then this collectivity will define the subjective ego and sense of personal self.

As Jung described in his essay 'Adaptation, Individuation, and Collectivity' (CW 18), the relationship to the collective and outer world is through the persona, and adaptation to the inner world through individuation is at the expense of collectivity. The persona is created and defined by family, group, and cultural identity. This external arbiter of what is acceptable becomes an internal function, in some ways similar to the role of the superego in Freudian psychology.

For Jungian theory, however, this function is also of relatedness to collective attitudes and values. Each individual will have their own inner barometer of when collectivity becomes intolerable and the compensatory drive for individuation is constellated. It may be in some homogeneous cultures that value collectivity over individuality, the subjective self is not experienced as separate from the Self and therefore individuation is not experienced as such a stark contrast to collectivity. This may be due to a culture that values this ambiguity at a personal level as part of the collectivity. Yama (2013) for example summarizes the personal experience of collectivity versus individuation for the Japanese. Because the subjective ego is only one aspect of the ego concept, it cannot be said that this cultural difference embraces the totality of the ego.

The dream ego

The dream ego presents a unique example of the subjective ego as it evolves toward the *individual*. Jung had relatively little to say about the dream ego, describing it as a "very limited and curiously distorted ego" (CW 8/580) but that it interacts with the contents of the unconscious present in dreams in a way similar to waking life. Dieckmann (1980) has noted that the dream ego exhibits the same defenses and has the same or similar subjective experience as the waking ego. The dream ego reflects a continuum of consciousness and individuation depending, I believe, on the evolution of the ego from its collective roots to the more individuated entity, the *individual*.

For example, the three dreams described at the beginning of Chapter 1 illustrate three different ego/*individual* states. The first dream, in which the dreamer is approached by a stranger and flees, reflects a fight-or-flight ego response. This is characteristic of an instinctual and therefore collective response. The third dreamer responds to the stranger approaching by attacking: this is the fight aspect of the fight-or-flight response and, again, an instinctual and collective response. The second dreamer, however, demonstrates a relational approach to the stranger. This demonstrates a more individuated response and shows the evolution of the ego toward its *individual* position. The *individual* is able to bridge the ego-consciousness position and the contents of the unconscious, personified in these cases by the stranger.

Viewing the dream ego in this way has assessment as well as treatment implications. By listening carefully for the dream ego actions and attitudes in dreams, the analyst can assess the degree to which the dreamer is individuated, what defenses are employed against the unconscious, and what complexes are confronting the dreamer in waking life. Defenses are evident in the response of the dream ego to other dream elements. The fight-or-flight responses in the dreams described above are collective responses but also ways of avoiding unpleasant feelings, knowledge, or perceptions. These defenses themselves can thus become a subject of analysis rather than confronting the client with the noxious unconscious contents.

By using active imagination or guided imagery to support the client to dream the dream forward while awake, the analyst can introduce the client to more differentiated and individual responses. For example, a young woman dreamt she was walking along a path and was beckoned toward a cave by an old Crone. This older woman then directed the young woman to sit in a circle of broken bones and to smash them up even further, and thereafter abandoned her. By considering if these were directions she would obey in real life, and by examining what this destructive inner figure represented in her waking life, this young woman was able to perceive and feel the effect of the complex in her life. She was then able to imagine another version of herself who was able to differentiate the negative qualities of a complex from the loving supportive qualities of the authentic Self.

The dream ego's viewpoint will often reflect the dreamer's conscious attitude with implications for understanding the dream. The dreamer in his or her own dream will view the figures of the unconscious through the lens of the usual ego-consciousness standpoint. For example, a young man dreamt of standing very obediently in line to board a bus, and an outsider comes up to the line and begins pushing ahead of others. From the ego-consciousness and persona perspective, this pushy figure appears to be a negative figure and would be viewed as such in waking life. However, when the dreamer can look at this inner figure as an unknown and unlived aspect of his or her own inner world, a shadow figure, the person may begin to look through a different lens, to see the possibilities of letting this assertive non-conformist trait into his or her life. What matters is that the ego has a relationship to the attitude it represents and therefore it is not autonomous in the manner of a complex but rather is integrated into the ego. In this way this new attitude becomes one more color in the ego's palette of possible emotions and manner of relating to the world.

Structural ego

A structural ego concept describes the executive functions of the ego that operate beyond conscious awareness: defense mechanisms, adaptation, and in collaboration with the Self-directed mechanisms of individuation such as the Transcendent Function and enantiodromia. The structural ego is also responsible for the individual variations in the more general process of individuation. As the individual experiences or is affected by the individuation drive from the psyche, the structural components of ego defense, adaptation mechanisms, and mechanisms of individuation (in collaboration with the Self) regulate the rate and degree of movement toward consciousness.

Adaptation

Ego psychology is defined by having an adaptation concept. Adaptation indeed has a vital role in Jung's theory and is outlined especially in his essay 'Adaptation, Individuation, Collectivity' (CW 18), which was written in 1916 at the same time as his essay 'The Transcendent Function' (CW 8). These two works constitute some of Jung's clearest early writings on the energic mechanisms of the psyche. As he describes, not only is the ego the essential element in the adaptation process, it is considered to have an innate capacity to adapt. Jung places the ego at the center of the adaptation process, a process not only directed toward outer reality through the persona, but also toward an inner reality through the soul figures of anima/animus. Jung also envisions a process of development in this adaptation capacity in that the personality becomes more differentiated and individual. As well, during this process the ego's capacity for adaptation becomes more flexible and differentiated.

Unique to Jung's version of Ego Psychology is his view of adaptation as the tension between the competing demands for adaptation between the two realities of inner and outer life. Adaptation to outer reality, in order to fit into one's family or community, for example, may lead to resistance to authentic attitudes and feelings that are not accepted by the group. These authentic attitudes and feelings, part of the realm of inner reality to which the ego is also responsible, may provoke an extreme reaction in the form of an enantiodromia, for example, if the differences are very great. The pressure toward individuation versus the pressure toward collectivity may evolve over the lifespan, creating new adaptation demands.

Between the Scylla of outer reality in the form of collective adaptation and the Charybdis of inner reality in the form of individual adaptation, the ego has an additional responsibility. Jung wrote that the individual has the moral duty to bring new values gained by adaptation to inner reality through individuation back to the world of collective outer reality in order to contribute to the general consciousness of all. With this perspective, Jung implies that the ultimate responsibility of the evolution of world consciousness lies with the individual. I believe this is one of the functions of the Elder in society: to support and sustain one's community after a lifetime of experience and hard-won knowledge.

Ego defense

A concept of ego defense is integral to Ego Psychology. This concept describes the ego's role in regulating ego-dystonic emotional reaction or cognition in the subjective ego. Although less explicit than in other ego psychologies, Jung also has an ego defense concept.

I have discussed earlier the dual nature of ego defenses in Jung's psychology. The ego defense can be understood at two levels: at the persona level in which the ego defense serves to protect the integrity of the persona stance, and at the soul level in which the ego defense creates a dichotomy, setting in motion the mechanisms of individuation. I would also like to suggest that these two perspectives, the persona and the soul levels of defense, reflect an energic point of view for the former and a symbolic point of view for the latter.

Ego psychologists note that ego defense analysis has special relevance for clinical practice. Ego defense analysis addresses the reaction to intra-psychic conflict rather than addressing the conflict itself, the latter a practice associated with traditional analysis. In depth psychology in general, the assumption of causal determinism leads the therapist to explore in analysis the early childhood environment. In Jungian analysis, the analysis might additionally explore the influence of the parental archetype. In all these, however, the client is still seen as the victim of the parental figures, or the archetypal constellation. In defense analysis, however, the focus changes and the analysis looks at how the client is, instead, the victim of his own defenses. This kind of work keeps the focus continually on the subject and understands any deviation away from this stance as itself a defense. By focusing on ego defense this way, the role of ego defense at the soul level is supported.

In Chapter 4, I propose a uniquely Jungian model of defense mechanisms based on the dynamics of the Transcendent Function. How conscious or unconscious is this process? The shadow (created by collective norms and attitudes) plays a role in the defense process by defining at an unconscious level what is unacceptable to ego-consciousness. This compels the ego at the unconscious structural level to defend against these unacceptable perceptions or feelings. In this process, there can be very brief fleeting perceptions or feelings that have not reached the threshold of consciousness but to which the structural ego reacts before there is full awareness. These subconscious perceptions and feelings nevertheless register in the psyche and may, in the same manner as the shadow elements, present themselves again to the ego through the mechanisms of individuation. This process remains essentially unconscious until the ego defenses are broached by the unconscious position.

The following case example can illustrate this dynamic. There was a young woman Jung saw for analysis who must have made a great impression on him as he describes her in a number of places in his writings (for example, CW 7/189–90, 281; CW 16/ 549–51; CW 18/336) in what has become known as 'the woman in the castle tower' case. She was 'exotic' looking, wearing bright colors and flamboyant accessories, and she appeared to Jung's sensibilities dubious or unsavory (*zweifelhaft*). He recounts that there was a good beginning to the treatment but after some hours, the analysis became stale and Jung grew frustrated with the lack of progress. He then described having a dream about this client in which he saw her atop a tall tower which was on a high castle on a steep hill. He had to crane his head back so much in the dream it even left him with a 'crick' in his neck upon awakening. He concluded afterward that this dream was a compensation for his critical appraisal of her, and led him to realize he had misjudged her badly. With this dream, his attitude changed and he saw his client in a new light with a positive effect on the analysis.

One can see in this example the action of the ego defenses on Jung's perceptions. Although his stated conscious perception was that his client was unsavory, Jung saw from his dream that in fact he misjudged her. He described this as a function of compensation, which I have described as one of the mechanisms of individuation. Seen in this light, it would appear that his initial perception of her or feeling toward her, which was subject to immediate censorship, was that of deep admiration or perhaps even envy. However, these positive feelings were anathema to his persona, exemplified by his concerns about what his maids would think when they saw this woman when she entered his home and practice. It is of note that this dream came after a session in which Jung had used a pejorative toward her appearance and manner which he described as "exceedingly drastic" (CW 18/335).

According to this model of ego defenses as acting to thwart the Transcendent Function that I have presented earlier, Jung's authentic ego perception of and feeling toward this client mobilized the defense that blocked further progress in their work together. He had stopped 'seeing' her. This stasis accounts for the stale feeling Jung described in the analytical process. At this point the mechanisms of individuation facilitated the Transcendent

Function by giving Jung a dream with sufficient imagery and emotional power to break through his ego defense. The effect of the dream even broke through to his physical self. In the end, what the defense was specifically (splitting, repression, denial, etc.) is not determinative; it is the defense's action in blocking the ego perception (defense against conscious perception) and/or the emotional experience (defense against feeling) and thus thwarting the action of the Transcendent Function that is significant. For Jung, his ego defense blocking an authentic and related view of his client started a cascade of effects which led to the mechanisms of individuation acting. This action led to movement again in the relationship and in the individuation of both participants.

Adaptation and ego defense would therefore have an interrelated function. The adaptation response can be ego-expanding, integrating new attitudes or values, or it can be ego-limiting and directed toward persona preservation. Ego defenses would function to preserve the status quo persona, but at the same time stimulate the cascade of mechanisms of individuation that lead to ego-expanding adaptation. These mechanisms of individuation I have already discussed include the Transcendent Function and compensation/enantiodromia as well as any mechanism which places the ego in contact with the unknown such as projection.

Developmental ego

Ego psychology assumes there is a mind that grows and as it does there is a corresponding growth and development in its functions, in its content, and in relations between the elements of the mind. There is a developmental concept in Jung's work at a number of levels.

First, Jung is credited with originating a theory of adult and second half of life development. This is first a process of ego differentiation in the first half of life, leading to a process of conscious relatedness to the Self in the second half of life. Jung's writings emphasize that what grows and develops throughout the life of the individual through individuation is consciousness and mutual relatedness.

According to Jung, the ego, acting in concert with the unconscious, expands and deepens the field of consciousness. In Jung's later theory, the counter-pole to the ego became the Self, the totality of the psyche rather than one part. He did not elaborate a theory of the Self in childhood, however. Fordham (1955) did propose a theory of the Self in childhood in which it exists initially as a totality but deintegrates spontaneously to form an ego out of the deintegrates. The difficulty with this formulation, similar to criticism of theories of an initial 'autistic' phase or 'uroboric' phase in early childhood, is that children have been shown to be responsive and related to their environment from birth onward. In other words, there is no phase of fusion or merger in which boundaries are absent. Just as Fordham proposed the dawn of the ego development process after birth, we may here propose that the formation of an ego or ego prototype is, perhaps, already accomplished in the womb.

Jung also proposed a three-stage process of development of consciousness in the first half of life. There is the basic assumption that there is a fundamental tension between competing demands on the ego. In the initial phases of life, these demands are from external sources and are dealt with through instinctual action. It is only when there are competing inner demands that the possibility of consciousness arises. Therefore the first stage of development is ego creation. The ego is experienced as 'islands of consciousness', which begin to coalesce: this is the second stage of development of consciousness. The third stage of the development of consciousness occurs, according to Jung, with the advent of puberty.

Coincident with these stages is a growth in the capacity to respond to mental images and openness to emotional experience. As the ego progresses in the individuation process to become the *individual*, there is a corresponding growth in the integrative function. This integrative function is a result of the development process, but also a factor that supports and promotes the development process. For example, a middle-aged woman who had overcome many personal obstacles in her life was found on a routine mammogram to have a suspicious lump in her breast and was scheduled for a biopsy. Before the biopsy, she had a series of dreams. First, she dreamt she was putting up the storm windows on her house. Another night she dreamt she was deep in an Amazon rainforest and an old female shaman stood next to her. The ground began to shake and heave from earthquakes and the shaman told her to stand close and she could see that the ground beneath them both was firm and still. The next night she dreamt she would need to gather many blankets. After other such dreams over several days' time, on the night before the biopsy she dreamt that she heard a voice which said, 'It will be cancer but it will be ok'. She went into the clinic to face whatever the outcome sure she would manage. As it happened, she did have extensive cancer and subsequently underwent aggressive treatment and ultimately survived.

It would be understandable were she to react to the initial news of a breast lump with extreme anxiety and to use any number of ego defenses to avoid the fear of a devastating diagnosis. But by facing her earlier life troubles consciously, she had developed a great deal of resilience and had the capacity to perceive the reality of her current situation. Dream figures responded to her anxiety with support and reassurance and from which she could take comfort. Without falling into panic or denial, she could see, as the poet Stevens (1984) wrote, "nothing that is not there and the nothing that is" (p. 10). Because she had developed the capacity through the experience of confronting her difficult life consciously to see clearly and feel honestly, she was able to integrate this experience of cancer diagnosis and treatment with courage and clear eyes.

The journey through breast cancer treatment was not without emotional pain and physical setbacks, and she had strong support from her friends and family. However, she described that through the experience she felt accompanied, as if there was a deeper process. She used the image of the ocean, that on the surface there was a storm and safe harbors but at the deepest levels there was stillness and calm. Here was an indication that she had developed a sense of connection to something beyond her personal self, in the way tremendous illness like Jung's heart attack had for him.

This example illustrates the development of the ego that is associated with the second half of life. In the first half of life, energy is directed toward adaptation to outer reality and building a life structure such as establishing a profession and personal relationships. The second half of life is associated with turning inward and adapting to inner demands through individuation. This process is experienced as occurring multiple times at many phases of life and certainly not in such stark dichotomous terms. In any case, the dynamic movement between adaptation and individuation remains a constant throughout life.

Cosmogonic ego

A position unique to Jung, and therefore one to which I assign a discrete category, is the idea of the ego as an instrument in the incarnation of the unconscious in the world through the ego–Self mutual dynamic process. This is a philosophy really on Jung's part: that beyond the development of the *individual*, there is a larger development of the consciousness of mankind. The individuated ego contributes to the whole by bringing to the collective his own new hard-won attitudes and values.

In his work 'Answer to Job', Jung addresses the issue of God's unconsciousness and need for man to mirror Him into existence. Jung describes God's nature as animal-like: "Of the four animals of Yahweh only one has a human face" (CW 11/600), and therefore "This symbolism explains Yahweh's behavior, which, from the human point of view is so intolerable: it is the behavior of an unconscious being who cannot be judged morally. Yahweh is a phenomenon and, as Job says, 'not a man'" (CW 11/600).

This state of unconsciousness can only be overcome through the reflection of man:

> Loudly as his [the interlocutor in the Eighty-ninth Psalm] power resounds through the universe, the basis of its existence is correspondingly slender, for it needs conscious reflection in order to exist in reality. Existence is only real when it is conscious to somebody. That is why the Creator needs conscious man. . . .
>
> (CW 11/575)

Jung also makes the point in *Memories, Dreams, Reflections* about the need for mankind to bring about God's incarnation, "If the Creator were conscious of Himself, He would not need conscious creatures" (Jung, 1983a, p. 371).

By proposing that the ego plays a role in the increase in world consciousness, Jung leaves his disparaging stance toward the ego and instead elevates it to a partner within the totality of the psyche, for the individual possesses something the Self does not: ego-consciousness and physical reality. The physical roots and concrete nature of the individual – his limitations imposed by time/space physical reality – are the instruments for this incarnation. Just as Jung compared the relationship between God and man as an act of mutual creation, so too is the ego a partner in creation with the Self. In this way, the ego has a place in nature, in its participation in the ongoing creation of consciousness.

As Jung described in his 84th year, in 'Late Thoughts' in *Memories, Dreams, Reflections*, individuals in their physical reality and human consciousness are the implements used by God for His ongoing creation. He wrote, "We are in the deepest sense the victims and instruments of cosmogonic 'love'" (1983a, p. 387), indicating that the process of creation is a process through relationship. This bases creation in the principle of Eros, the uniting principle.

This notion of cosmogonic love brings Jung's work back to one of the foundations of his psychology, the place of religion in the psyche. Rather than construct a religion, Jung is more interested in understanding the experience of God as an authentic inner experience. In his concept of cosmogonic love, he is conveying, in the sense of Meister Eckhart's inner God, that what man experiences as opposites is in many ways an encounter between conscious man and the God within.

Bibliography

Abrams, I., ed., *Nobel Lectures in Peace: 1981–90*, Singapore: World Scientific Publishing, 1997.

Arlow, J. and Brenner, C., *Psycho-analytic Concepts and the Structural Theory*, New York: International Universities Press, 1964.

Atwood, G.E. and Stolorow, R.D., "Metapsychology, Reification and the Representational World of C.G. Jung", *International Review of Psycho-Analysis*, 4(2): 197–213, 1977.

Bleuler, E., "Versuch einer Natur- wissenschaftlichen Betrachtung der Psychologischen Grundbegriffe", *Allgemeine Zeitschrift für Psychiatrie und psychischgerichtliche Medicin*, 50: 133–168, 1894.

Blum, H.P., "Ego Psychology and Contemporary Structural Theory", *Newsletter of the International Psychoanalytical Association*, 7(2), 1998.

Boring, E.G., *A History of Experimental Psychology*, New York: Century, 1929.

Boring, E.G., *History, Psychology, and Science: Selected Papers*, New York: John Wiley & Sons, Inc., 1963.

Brenner, C., *The Mind in Conflict*, New York: International Universities Press, 1982.

Butz, M.R., "The Fractal Nature of the Development of the Self", *Psychological Reports*, 71(3): 1043–1063, 1992.

Cahan, D., ed., *Hermann von Helmholtz and the Foundations of Nineteenth Century Science*, Berkeley: University of California Press, 1993.

Charney, R., "Speech Roles and the Development of Personal Pronouns", *Journal of Child Language*, 7(3): 509–528, 1980.

Cleary, T., *The Secret of the Golden Flower: The Classic Chinese Book of Life*, San Francisco: Harper, 1991.

Colledge, E. and McGinn, B., "Introduction", in *Meister Eckhart: The Essential Sermons, Commentaries, Treatises, and Defense*, edited by Colledge E. and McGinn, B., p. 5–68, Mahwah, NJ: Paulist Press, 1988.

Dieckmann, H., "On the Methodology of Dream Interpretation", in *Methods of Treatment in Analytical Psychology*, edited by Baker, I., p. 48–59, Bonz: Fellbach, 1980.

Donn, L., *Freud and Jung: Years of Friendship, Years of Loss*, New York: Scribner, 1988.

Dry, A.M., *The Psychology of C.G. Jung: A Critical Interpretation*, London: Methuen & Co Ltd, 1961.

Edelson, M., "Causal Explanation in Science and Psychoanalysis", *Psychoanalytic Study of the Child*, 41: 89–127, 1986.

Edelson, M., "Psychoanalysis as Science: Its Boundary Problems, Special Status, Relations to Other Sciences, and Formalization", *Journal of Nervous and Mental Diseases*, 165(1): 1–27, 1977.

Edinger, E.F., *The Mysterium Lectures*, Toronto: Inner City Books, 1995.

Eisold, K., "Jung, Jungians, and Psychoanalysis", *Psychoanalytic Quarterly*, 19(3): 501–524, 2002.

Ellenberger, H., *The Discovery of the Unconscious*, New York: Basic Books, 1970.

Ellenberger, H., "Fechner and Freud", *Bulletin of the Menninger Clinic*, 20(4): 201–214, 1956.

Enriquez-Geppert, S., Huster, R. and Hermann, C., "Boosting Brain Functions: Improving Executive Functions with Behavioral Training, Neurostimulation, and Neurofeedback", *International Journal of Psychophysiology*, 88(1): 1–16, 2013.

Erikson, E.H., *Childhood and Society*, New York: Norton, 1950.

Fairbairn, R., *Psychoanalytic Studies of the Personality*, London and New York: Routledge & Kegan Paul, 1981.

Fordham, M., "Defenses of the Self", *Journal of Analytical Psychology*, 19(2): 192–199, 1974.

Fordham, M., *Explorations Into the Self*, London: Academic Press, Inc., 1985.

Fordham, M., *Freud, Jung, Klein: The Fenceless Fence*, London: Routledge, 1995.

Fordham, M., "Individuation and Ego Development", *Journal of Analytical Psychology*, 3(2): 115–130, 1958.

Fordham, M., "The Infant's Reach", *Psychological Perspectives*, 21: 59–76, 1989.

Fordham, M., *The Life of Childhood: A Contribution to Analytical Psychology*, London: Kegan, Paul, Trench, Truber, 1944.

Fordham, M., *The Making of an Analyst*, London: Free Association. Books, 1993.

Fordham, M., "On the Origins of the Ego in Childhood", in *Studien zur Analytischen Psychologie C.G. Jungs Band 1: Beiträge aus Theorie und Praxis*, Zürich: C.G. Jung Institute, Rascher Verlag, 1955.

Freud, A., *The Ego and the Mechanisms of Defense* (1936, in German), London: Karnac Books and The Institute of Psychoanalysis, 1993.

Freud, A., *The Writings of Anna Freud*, 8 Volumes, New York: International University Press, 1966–1980.

Freud, S., References are to the Standard Edition (SE) and by volume, except as below, edited by Strachey, J., London: Hogarth Press.

Freud, S., *Analysis Terminable and Interminable*, SE 23, London: Hogarth Press, 1937.

Freud, S., *Civilization and Its Discontents*, SE 21, London: Hogarth Press, 1930.

Freud, S., *Early Psycho-Analytic Publications*, SE, London: Hogarth Press, 1893–1899.

Freud, S., *The Ego and the Id*, SE 19, London: Hogarth Press, 1923.

Freud, S., *Five Lectures on Psycho-Analysis, Leonardo and Other Works*, SE 11, London: Hogarth, 1910.

Freud, S., *Inhibitions, Symptoms and Anxiety*, SE 20, London: Hogarth Press, 1926.

Freud, S., *Instincts and Their Vicissitudes*, SE 14, London: Hogarth Press, 1915.

Freud, S., *The Interpretation of Dreams*, SE 4, London: Hogarth Press, 1900.

Freud, S., *New Introductory Lectures on Psychoanalysis*, SE 22, London: Hogarth Press, 1933.

Freud, S., *On the History of the Psychoanalytic Movement*, SE 14, London: Hogarth Press, 1914.

Freud, S., *On Narcissism*, SE 14, London: Hogarth Press, 1914.
Freud, S. and Breuer, J., *Studies on Hysteria*, SE 2, London: Hogarth Press, 1895.
Friedman, L.J., *Identity's Architect: A Biography of Erik H. Erikson*, New York: Scribner, 1999.
Friedman, P. and Goldstein, J., "Some Comments on the Psychology of C.G. Jung", *Psychoanalytic Quarterly*, 33(2): 194–225, 1964.
Gallant, C., *Tabooed Jung: Marginality as Power*, New York: New York University Press, 1996.
Gay, P., *Freud: A Life for Our Time*, New York: Doubleday, 1988.
Glover, E., *Freud or Jung*, New York: W.W. Norton & Company, Inc., 1950.
Goodheart, W.B., "C.G. Jung's First 'Patient': On the Seminal Emergence of Jung's Thought", *Journal of Analytical Psychology*, 29(1): 1–34, 1984.
Gould, S.J., *Questioning the Millennium a Rationalist's Guide to a Precisely Arbitrary Countdown*, New York: Harmony Books, 1997.
Gould, S.J., *Rock of Ages: Science and Religion in the Fullness of Life*, London: Jonathan Cape, 2001.
Greenberg, J. and Mitchell, S., *Object Relations in Psychoanalytic Theory*, Cambridge: Harvard University Press, 1983.
Harker, L. and Solomon, M., "Changes in Goals and Values of Men and Women from Early to Mature Adulthood", *Journal of Adult Development*, 3(3): 133–143, 1996.
Hartmann, H., "The Development of the Ego Concept in Freud's Work", *International Journal of Psychophysiology*, 37(6): 425–438, 1956.
Hartmann, H., *Ego Psychology and the Problem of Adaptation*, New York: International Universities Press, 1958.
Hartmann, H., *Essays on Ego Psychology: Selected Problems in Psychoanalytic Theory*, New York: International Universities Press, 1964.
Hayman, R., *A Life of Jung*, London: Bloomsbury, 1999.
Heidelberger, M., "Helmholtz als Philosoph", *Deutsche Zeitschrift für Philosophie*, 43(5): 835–844, 1995.
Hillman, J., "Abandoning the Child", in *Loose Ends: Primary Papers in Archetypal Psychology*, p. 5–48, New York and Zürich: Spring Publications, 1975b.
Hillman, J., *Anima: An Anatomy of a Personified Notion*, Dallas: Spring Publications, 1985a.
Hillman, J., *Emotion: A Comprehensive Phenomenology of Theories and Their Meanings for Therapy*, London: Routledge & Kegan Paul, 1960.
Hillman, J., "Extending the Family: From Entrapment to Embrace", *The Texas Humanist*, 7(4): 6–11, 1985b.
Hillman, J., "First Adam, Then Eve", *Eranos Jahrbuch*, 38: 349–412, 1969.
Hillman, J., "The Great Mother, Her Son, Her Hero, and the Puer", in *Father and Mothers: Five Papers on the Archetypal Background of Family Psychology*, edited by Berry, P., p. 75–127, New York and Zürich: Spring Publications, 1973.
Hillman, J., *Healing Fictions*, Barrytown, NY: Station Hill Press, 1983.
Hillman, J., *The Myth of Analysis*, Evanston, IL: Northwestern University Press, 1972.
Hillman, J., *Re-Visioning Psychology*, New York: Harper & Row, 1975a.
Hillman, J., "Some Early Background to Jung's Ideas: Notes on G. Jung's Medium by Stephanie Zumstein-Preiswerk", *Spring*, 123–136, 1976.
Jacobi, J., *Complex/Archetype/Symbol in the Psychology of C.G. Jung*, Princeton: Princeton University Press, 1959.

Jacobi, J., *The Psychology of C.G. Jung* (6th ed., revised), London: Routledge & Kegan Paul, 1962.

James, W., *The Principles of Psychology* (1890), Cambridge: Harvard University Press, 1983.

James, W., *The Varieties of Religious Experience* (1902), New York: Penguin American Library, 1982.

Jarrett, J., "Jung's Theory of Functions: Some Questions", *Journal of Analytical Psychology*, 33(4): 355–372, 1988.

Jodock, D.H., ed., *Ritschl in Retrospect: History, Community, and Science*, Minneapolis: Fortress Press, 1995.

Jones, E., *Das Leben und Werk von Sigmund Freud, 3 Bände*, Bern: Huber, 1960–1962.

Jung, C.G., References are to the Collected Works (CW) and by volume and paragraph number, except as below, edited by Read, H., Fordham, M., Adler, G., McGuire, W., Translated in the main by Hull, R., London: Routledge and Kegan Paul.

Jung, C.G., *Analytical Psychology: Notes of the Seminar Given in 1925*, London and New York: Routledge, 1990.

Jung, C.G., *Dream Analysis: Notes of the Seminar Given in 1928–30*, London, Melbourne and Henley: Routledge & Kegan Paul, 1994.

Jung, C.G., *Letters*, Vol. 1 & 2, selected and edited by Adler, G., Translated by R.F.C. Hull, London: Routledge & Kegan Paul, 1973 and 1976.

Jung, C.G., *Memories, Dreams, and Reflections* (1963), London: Fontana Paperbacks, 1983a.

Jung, C.G., *Modern Psychology: Notes on Lectures Given at the ETH*, Zürich, privately printed, 1933–35.

Jung, C.G., *Nietzsche's Zarathustra: Notes on the Seminar Given in 1934–1939*, Vol. 1 & 2, edited by Jarrett, J.L., Princeton: Bollingen Series XCIX, 1984.

Jung, C.G., *The Visions Seminars: From the Complete Notes of Mary Foote*, Vol. 1 & 2, Zürich: Spring Publications, 1976.

Jung, C.G., *The Zofingia Lectures*, CW Suppl. Vol. A, edited by McGuire, W., Translated by J. Van Heurck, London: Routledge & Kegan Paul, 1983b.

Kennedy, R., "Response to Blum", *Newsletter of the International Psychoanalytical Association*, 8(1), 1999.

Kernberg, O., "Self, Ego, Affects, and Drives", *Journal of the American Psychoanalytical Association*, 30(4): 893–918, 1982.

Klein, M., *The Writings*, Under the General Editorship of Roger Money-Kyrle, 4 Volumes, London: The Hogarth Press, 1975.

Kohut, H., *The Analysis of the Self*, New York: International Universities Press, 1971.

Kuhn, T., *The Structure of Scientific Revolutions*, Chicago: The University of Chicago Press, 1962.

Levinson, D.J., *The Seasons of a Man's Life*, New York: Knopf, 1978.

Levinson, D.J., *The Seasons of a Woman's Life*, New York: Knopf, 1996.

Lifton, R.J., *The Broken Connection: On Death and the Continuity of Life*, Washington, DC: American Psychiatric Press, 1979.

MacMillan, M., *Freud Evaluated: The Completed Arc*, Amsterdam: North Holland, 1991.

Main, R., "Analytical Psychology, Religion and the Academy", in *Controversies in Analytical Psychology*, edited by Withers, R., p. 190–202, Hove and New York: Brunner-Routledge, 2003.

Marcus, E., "Modern Ego Psychology", *Journal of the American Psychoanalytic Association*, 47(3): 843–872, 1999.
Marshall, I.N., "The Four Functions: A Conceptual Analysis", *Journal of Analytical Psychology*, 13(1): 1–32, 1968.
McGuire, W. and Hull, R.F.C., eds., *The Freud/Jung Letters*, Princeton: Princeton University Press, 1974.
Meier, C.A., *Consciousness (Psychology of C.G. Jung, Vol. 3)*, Boston: SIGO Press, 1989.
Meier, C.A., *The Unconscious in Its Empirical Manifestations (Psychology of C.G. Jung, Vol. 1)*, Boston: SIGO Press, 1984.
Meissner, W.W., *Freud and Psychoanalysis*, Notre Dame: University of Notre Dame Press, 2000.
Meissner, W.W., "Psychoanalysis: The Dilemma of Science and Humanism", *Psychoanalytic Inquiry*, 5(3): 471–498, 1985.
Milner, M., "Aspects of Symbolism in Comprehension of the Not-Self", *International Journal of Psychoanalysis*, 33(2): 181–95, 1952.
Mitchell, S.A., *Relational Concepts in Psychoanalysis: An Integration*, Cambridge: Harvard University Press, 1988.
Mitchell, S.A. and Black, M.J., *Freud and Beyond: A History of Modern Psychoanalytic Thought*, New York: Basic Books, 1995.
Moore, N., "The Transcendent Function and the Forming Ego", *Journal of Analytical Psychology*, 20(2): 164–182, 1975.
Nagy, M., *Philosophical Issues in the Psychology of C.G. Jung*, Albany: SUNY Press, 1991.
Nagy, M., "Self and Freedom in Jung's Lecture on Ritschl", *Journal of Analytical Psychology*, 35(4): 443–457, 1990.
Noll, R., "Multiple Personality, Dissociation, and C.G. Jung's Complex Theory", *Journal of Analytical Psychology*, 34(4): 353–370, 1989.
Oeri, A., "Some Youthful Memories of C.G. Jung", *Spring*, 182–189, 1970.
Ornstein, P., "Response to Blum", *Newsletter of the International Psychoanalytical Association*, 8(1), 1999.
Padel, J., "Ego in Current Thinking", *International Review of Psycho-Analysis*, 12: 273–284, 1985.
Papadopoulos, R., ed., *Carl Gustav Jung: Critical Assessments*, 4 Volumes, London: Routledge, 1992.
Perry, J.C., "Anomalies and Specific Functions in the Clinical Identification of Defense Mechanisms", *Journal of Clinical Psychology*, 70(5): 406–418, 2014.
Rangell, L., "Choice-Conflict and Decision-Making Function of Ego", *International Journal of Psychoanal*, 50: 599–602, 1969.
Rangell, L., "The Executive Functions of the Ego: An Extension of the Concept of Ego Autonomy", *The Psychoanalytic Study of the Child*, 41: 1–40, 1986.
Rapaport, D., *Emotions and Memory*, NewYork: International University Press, 1950.
Rapaport, D., "The Theory of Ego Autonomy: A Generalization", *Bulletin of the Menninger Clinic*, 22(1): 13–35, 1958.
Redfearn, J.W.T., "Ego and Self: Terminology", *Journal of Analytical Psychology*, 28(2): 91–106, 1983.
Samuels, A., "Dethroning the Self", *Spring*, 43–58, 1983.

Samuels, A., *Jung and the Post-Jungians*, London: Routledge, 1985.
Samuels, A., ed., *Psychopathology: Contemporary Jungian Perspectives*, New York: Guilford Press, 1991.
Schelling, F.W., *Ideas for a Philosophy of Nature* (1797, rev. 1803), Cambridge: Cambridge University Press, 1988.
Scruton, R., *A Short History of Modern Philosophy* (2nd ed.), London: Routledge, 1995.
Segal, H., "Some Aspects of the Analysis of a Schizophrenic", *International Journal of Psychoanalysis*, 31(1): 268–279, 1950.
Shorter, E., *A History of Psychiatry: From the Era of the Asylum to the Age of Prozac*, New York: John Wiley & Sons, Inc., 1997.
Spitz, R., *The First Year of Life*, New York: International University Press, 1965.
Spitz, R. (R. Emde, ed.), *Rene Spitz: Dialogues From Infancy: Selected Papers*, New York: International University Press, 1983.
Stepansky, P.E., "The Empiricist as Rebel: Jung, Freud, and the Burdens of Discipleship", *Journal of the History of the Behavioral Sciences*, 12(3): 216–239, 1976.
Stern, Daniel., *The Interpersonal World of the Infant*, New York: Basic Books, 1985.
Stevens, W., "The Snow Man", in *The Collected Poems of Wallace Stevens*, p. 9–10, London and Boston: Faber & Faber, 1984.
Sugarman, L., *Life-Span Development: Frameworks, Accounts and Strategies*, New York: Taylor & Francis Inc., 1986.
Sullivan, H., *The Interpersonal Theory of Psychiatry*, New York: Norton, 1953.
Sulloway, F.J., *Freud: Biologist of the Mind*, London: Burett Books, 1979.
Tacey, D., "Reply to Responses", *Journal of Analytical Psychology*, 42(2): 315–316, 1997.
Vacek, J., "Irrationality in Analytical Psychology", *Cesk Psychiatr.*, 87(1): 12–16, 1991.
Vaillant, G.E., *The Wisdom of the Ego*, Cambridge: Harvard University Press, 1993.
Von Franz, M.-L., *C.G. Jung: His Myth in Our Time*, New York: Putnam's Sons for the C.G. Jung Foundation for Analytical Psychology, 1975.
Von Franz, M.-L., "Introduction", in *The Zofingia Lectures,* CW Suppl. Vol. A, edited by McGuire, W., p. xiii–xxv, London: Routledge & Kegan Paul, 1983.
Von Franz, M.-L., *An Introduction to the Interpretation of Fairy Tales*, Dallas: Spring Publications, 1970.
Von Schelling, F.W.J., *Ideas for a Philosophy of Nature* (1797, rev. 1803), (2nd ed.), Cambridge: Cambridge University Press, 1988.
Waelder, R., *Basic Theory of Psychoanalysis*, New York: International University Press, 1960.
Waelder, R., "The Principle of Multiple Function: Observations on Over-Determination", *Psychoanalytic Quarterly*, 5: 45–62, 1936.
Whitmont, E.C., *The Symbolic Quest*, Princeton, NJ: Princeton University Press, 1991.
Winnicott, D., *The Maturational Processes and the Facilitating Environment*, London: The Hogarth Press and the Institute of Psycho-Analysis, 1965.
Wottreng, W., *Hirnriss: Wie die Irrenärzte August Forel und Eugen Bleuler das Menschengeschlecht Retten Wollten*, Basel: Weltwoche-ABC-Verlag, 1999.
Wozniak, R.H., (1999). *Classics in Psychology, 1855–1914: Historical Essays.* Retrieved December 7, 2015, from York University's Classics in the History of Psychology Web site: http://psychclassics.yorku.ca/Wundt/Physio/wozniak.htm

Wundt, W., *Grundriss der Psychologie*, 12. Aufl., Leipzig: Kröner, 1914.
Wundt, W., *Grundzüge der Physiologischen Psychologie, Erste Band*, Leipzig: Verlag von Wilhelm Engelmann, 1902.
Wundt, W., *Outlines of Psychology*, Translated by C.H. Judd., Leipzig: Wilhelm Engelmann, 1896 (reprinted: Williams & Norgate G.E Stechert & Co 1907).
Wundt, W., *Principles of Physiological Psychology* (1902), Translated by E.B. Titchener, London: Swan Sonnenschein, 1904.
Yama, M., "Ego Consciousness in the Japanese Psyche: Culture, Myth, and Disaster", *Journal of Analytical Psychology*, 58(1): 52–72, 2013.
Young-Eisendrath, P. and Hall, J.A., *Jung's Self Psychology: A Constructivist Perspective*, New York: The Guilford Press, 1991.
Zumstein-Preiswerk, S., *C.G. Jungs Medium: Die Geschichte der Hélène Preiswerk*, Munchen: Kindler Verlag, 1975.

Index

Note: Italicized page numbers indicate a figure on the corresponding page.

FSC
www.fsc.org
MIX
Papier | Fördert gute Waldnutzung
FSC® C083411

Kolibri 360 GmbH
Ferdinand-Jühlke-Straße 7
99095 Erfurt, Deutschland
produktsicherheit@kolibri360.de